Janez Juhant, Bojan Žalec (Eds.)

From Culture of Fear to Society of Trust

Theologie Ost – West

Europäische Perspektiven

herausgegeben von

Prof. Dr. Janez Juhant
(Universität Ljubljana)
und Prof. Dr. Albert Franz
(Universität Dresden)

Band 17

LIT

From Culture of Fear to Society of Trust

edited by

Janez Juhant and Bojan Žalec

LIT

Cover Picture: Anka Doblekar, Photomontage

This book is printed on acid-free paper.

Bibliographic information published by the Deutsche Nationalbibliothek
The Deutsche Nationalbibliothek lists this publication in the Deutsche Nationalbibliografie; detailed bibliographic data are available in the Internet at http://dnb.d-nb.de.

ISBN 978-3-643-90414-0

A catalogue record for this book is available from the British Library

Zweigniederlassung Zürich 2013
Klosbachstr. 107
CH-8032 Zürich
Tel. +41 (0) 44-251 75 05
Fax +41 (0) 44-251 75 06
E-Mail: zuerich@lit-verlag.ch
http://www.lit-verlag.ch

LIT VERLAG Dr. W. Hopf
Berlin 2013
Fresnostr. 2
D-48159 Münster
Tel. +49 (0) 2 51-62 03 20
Fax +49 (0) 2 51-23 19 72
E-Mail: lit@lit-verlag.de
http://www.lit-verlag.de

Distribution:
In Germany: LIT Verlag Fresnostr. 2, D-48159 Münster
Tel. +49 (0) 2 51-620 32 22, Fax +49 (0) 2 51-922 60 99, E-mail: vertrieb@lit-verlag.de
In Austria: Medienlogistik Pichler-ÖBZ, e-mail: mlo@medien-logistik.at
In the UK: Global Book Marketing, e-mail: mo@centralbooks.com
In North America: International Specialized Book Services, e-mail: orders@isbs.com
e-books are available at www.litwebshop.de

Acknowledgments

We thank to all persons who have contributed to the appearing of the book. Our special thanks go to: the reviewers - Professor Ciril Sorč from Faculty of Theology and Associate Professor Borut Ošlaj from Faculty of Arts, both University of Ljubljana; to Samo Grčman for the layout; to Valerija Japelj, who helped by the final corrections of the book; last, but not least, to all the authors of the book.

Our special thanks go to Slovenian Research Agency which financially supported the publishing of the book.

Janez Juhant and Bojan Žalec, the editors
Ljubljana, December 2013

CONTENTS

INTRODUCTION

The general characteristics of the book, the motivation for it and its aims

Fear is a topic that is of great relevance regarding the whole history of humanity and especially our present situation. It is an emotion that is strongly connected with violence and with the darkest periods of our history including terrorism, genocides and totalitarianism. It is especially important for theology where it can be considered also from very positive aspects. After all, fear is a normal animal and human affection necessary for survival. However it seems to us that our culture and our way of life are too much burdened with unnecessary fear originating in our organization of economic life, political relationships, education, influence of media, lack of faith and hope not to mention our pollution of the environment with possibly catastrophic consequences.

In this book fear and its cognates or opposites are considered from several scientific points of view. Proper understanding, defining and evaluation of fear, its kinds, factors and conditions, scientific deepening and cultural-comparative researches are crucial for dealing with the most severe difficulties of the contemporary world that are originating from fear, or that are influenced by fear: violence, conflicts, vengeance, (non)solidarity, (non)cultivation of dialogue etc. Those societies in which an adequate culture of fear dominates, are more successful, more free and less divided or antagonistic, this is an undeniable fact. This holds true also for the Slovenian society, which it has been less successful in dealing with fear, as it could have been. There are different factors involved in the cultivation of adequate culture of fear, and one of them is certainly that we know how to cultivate it. Therefore we need knowledge about fear. The purpose of this book is to increase and widen this knowledge.

The book contains twenty seven essays divided in five chapters. Let us now briefly survey the main topics and theses of them.

Varieties of fear, humanity and ethics

Halik deals with fear in relation to two important topics: (mature) faith and doubt. He claims that a mature faith can live with doubts. Moreover, faith and doubt must walk together if we don't want to end in fanaticism or hopelessness. In this context he stresses the importance of distinction between fear, anxiety and awe. He reveals the connection of awe with the ambivalent nature of the sacred and the understandings of God (pictures of God). He stresses the importance of awe which has in the processes of secularization gradually disappeared from the Western culture. Halik wonders whether this disappearance has not in fact contributed to the increase of fear and anxiety and concludes that only a mature faith can overcome fear. **Trontelj** finds out that there are some important differences between the contemporary situation and the past ages from the point of view of fear. Today have many dangers from the past - and corresponding fears - almost completely disappeared but the new forms of fear have appeared or have become most important. He concludes that many of contemporary fears are unnecessary and that we should get rid of them. This would be an important contribution to the diminishing of human suffering. **Juhant** deals with fear in the context of totalitarian regimes. He finds out that totalitarian regimes didn't use fear to cultivate healthy relationships in society but rather to enslave the citizens. The effects of such a use of fear are still present today. The pro-democratic political decision and education are especially important factors in the way of their overcoming. He pays special attention to the relevant aspects of the Slovenian case (the role of the Church, possibility of dialogue etc.). **Gerjolj`s** starting point is that one of the main (damaging) characteristics of totalitarian systems is that they prevent open communication and deliberately cultivate fear of autonomous thinking and of expressing people's own opinions. They produce a communicative "vacuum" between people that is difficult to fill with the naturalness and sincerity. Such incapability for communication remains a burning and fundamental problem even after the fall of totalitarian systems and it of course seriously hinders the possibility of a quality education. He points to the sensible understanding and cultivation of forgiveness as important factors in (re)discovering and (re)establishing of honest communication. **Žalec** argues for the thesis that a basis of ethical life is not only love, but also fear. The reason is that there can be no love without fear. In order to understand better this claim he distinguishes several different kinds of fear. He analyzes also some other relevant concepts (and their kinds), as anxiety, love, respect, reverence for life, sacrifice etc. **Jamnik** deals with the question of overcoming of fear and becoming a brave man. In this respect he stresses the importance of appropriate relationships - originating in a free decision for life for the others - and of the overcoming of individualism. This brings a (new) joy of life. He claims that one can never be really courageous unless he faces his fragility and mortality. This is stressed also by Erzar & Kompan Erzar. Jamnik concludes with the reflexion about the experience of suffering (cross) and God's unconditional creational goodness. The key topics of **Petkovšek's** essay are fear, anxiety, courage, existence, life, being and non-being. He deals with them in the horizon of Heidegger's thought and Michel Henry's radical phenomenology. However, the ground intention of his essay is to face the question of the meaning(less) of human life and of fear and anxiety connected to it. Maybe the best illustration of his final point is provided with the following quotation from his present essay: "In newborn life, something impossible happens within the possible, i.e. within the world. This is the only reasonable reason, a groundless reason, to say 'yes' to the future. A newborn life is a total novelty worth living for. There is no deeper reason of courage and hope as it is." **Klun** deals with fear in the age of technology with a special reference to the work of Martin Heidegger and Hans Jonas. He claims that technology determines man's relationship to the world and distinguishes two forms of fear: the fear from the external dangers brought by the development of technology, and the fear of changing of our understanding of ourselves and humanity caused by technology. He argues for the priority of the second over the first. The subject of **Strahovnik's** essay is a society dominated by the fear perspective. Such society is called culture of fear. As one of the main signs of this culture he identifies diminished responsibility. At the end he outlines the culture capable of overcoming the culture of fear. It should be founded on trust and hope.

Cognitive science and bioethics

Pirtošek establishes that people in modern times are less able to counteract fear as they were in the past. The mental disorders are increasing and they mostly originate in the most recent parts of the brain. He suggests that the key to mental health lies in the cultivation of proper values and overbalance between emotions and reason, between "the ancient and the new brain". Szánto and Strehovec both consider the ways how bioethics can help us to face properly the fears related to bioethical problems. The subject of **Szánto's** essay is the fear induced by biotechnology. She distinguishes between three ways in which bioethics can deal with fear: alleviation, acknowledgement and utilization of fear. We deal with alleviation when the unjustified fear is dispelled by bioethics. When acknowledging fear, one realizes that the dangers are real, that concerns are justified and one also takes precautionary measures. In the case of utilization, fear is regarded as an argument, as an evidence for the truth. Szánto recognizes the first two ways as legitimate but refuses the third as a way of domination of fear over us. **Strehovec`** main stress is on bioethics as a meta-scientific discipline which creates a multicultural space of non-violent dialogue characterized by an awareness of our limitations in searching for solutions. In such space we can most adequately explain fears and resolve ethical problems in a non-conflict way.

Intellectual history, politics, tradition and authority

Šimić establishes that "although the comic genres were popular, Croatian Renaissance literary culture has retained many images of fear". He searches for the explanation of this fact what leads him to the broader and fundamental consideration of fear and its role. The frame of reference of his essay constitute works of many authors, most important among them are - beside some Croatian writers - Aristotle, Thomas Aquinas, Thomas Hobbes, Mihail Bakhtin, Jean Delumeau and Umberto Eco. Šimić concludes: "If we now return to the images of fear in Renaissance literature, we can say that the role of fear is not only social discipline but a release, perhaps more radical then liberation by laughter." **Mester** investigates the theological background of early modern opinions about the fearfulness and pridefulness of human nature with special regard to human faculties for forming of political communities. Most of his attention is devoted to Hobbes's anthropological and political views but he deals also with Calvin's political theology and concludes with some observations about the features of contemporary public people originating in early modernity. **Kovács** analyses the relation between fear, politics and civilization mostly by presenting the relevant ideas and accounts of Guglielmo Ferrero (1871-1942) and István Bibó (1911-1979). **Chan, Fitzgerald and Smoczynski** begin their essay with the description of the issues caused by the growth of cross-border migration in Europe concentrating on the case of Polish workers in UK. Thereafter they introduce the concept of moral panics and use it to conceptualize and understand the anti-migrant societal reactions. The last part of their essay deals with the Polish migrant workers in UK and the crucial role of UK trade unions and a growing number of Polish migrant organizations in favour of them. **Pevec Rozman** stresses the importance of tradition and authority for helping us to fear properly.

(Post) communist societies: the Slovenian case

Griesser-Pečar analyses the similarities and differences between Udba, the Slovene secret police, and Stasi, the official state security of German Democratic Republic. Both agencies used fear to subject people to the regime. **Bahovec** presents the data of the empirical sociological researches about the fear relevant attitudes of Slovenian population, more specifically about the attitudes of Slovenes to their past and to the post-war slaughters. He establishes "that in Slovenia, with regard to certain aspects of the past, there is a certain duality, ambivalence and difference of opinion". Some themes of the past are still a taboo for wider public and many people are still affraid to speak about the post-war mass killings. Bahovec adds that this is in a certain regard not a surprise "because it seems many people think 'that people who speak up in favour of open discussion of such subjects [discussion of these murders] risk attracting negative consequences or difficulties'". **Erzar & Kompan Erzar** research fear from the psycho-therapeutic aspect. Regarding the overcoming of fear they stress the importance of giving oneself up to the feelings of fear, powerlessness and shame, of finding and stopping the source of fear and of the experience that fear can't touch us in our personal core. They deal also with the Slovenian culture of fear. They point out to the fatal lack of the proper verbalization and expression of our fears and establish that "we still, after decades of postwar time, in Slovenia have no true words for the innermost feelings of our grandfathers and fathers." The consequence is that our world is still a very threatening world just like the world of our fathers. **Letnar Černič's** starting point is that Slovene people were in the past strongly subjected to various political crimes, including totalitarian violence. This is the reason for the flourishing of the culture of fear in Slovenia. In the second part of his essay he deals with Slovenia from the point of view of transitional justice. He concludes with a reflection on the necessary measures for rooting out of the culture of fear in Slovenia. **Slatinek's** conclusion is that Church's fear of damage claims is warranted because quite often the aim of damage claims against Church is not to improve the perpetrator but just to get the money.

The meaning of religion

Constantineanu argues for the thesis that in the contemporary society - which is dominated by fear - a suspicion must be substituted by love. Such love is however not a naive love but rather a courageous love which seeks to understand and respect the other. The basis for such love - and for a hermeneutics of love that is adequate for the (contemporary) culture pervaded by fear and despair - is provided by the Biblical texts. Hence - according to Constantineanu - the thesis that religion generates the fear rather than eliminating it is false. **Opreanu** distinguishes between three types of fear that are importantly present also in the contemporary society: the fear of death, the fear of the other, and the fear of tomorrow. All three types are considered in the Scripture. He argues that by means of exploring the message of Bible we can find a cure for the (mentioned) contemporary fears. **Osredkar** points out that Christian doctrine teaches us to accept inconvenience, defeats, falls, pain and suffering. But exactly this acceptance is in fact a proper way to overcome the fear of failure. **Prijatelj** claims that religions encourage us to be open to the others, to support them and to cultivate a solidary attitude. Religions also contribute to the overcoming of fear by giving hope to people. For these reasons religion will play the crucial role in the future (globalized) society in the cultivation of humanity and development of life of quality for all. This however implies a necessity of interreligious dialogue. In this context Prijatelj deals also with the social teaching of the Catholic Church and the Catholic movements in various parts of the world.

Janez Juhant and Bojan Žalec, the editors

VARIETIES OF FEAR, HUMANITY AND ETHICS

FEAR AND FAITH

Tomáš Halík, Prague

During the Communist regime when I served clandestinely as a secretly ordained priest in the "underground church" (even my mother was not to know I was a priest), I was visited one evening by a close friend. He brought some bad news: one of our priests had been found dead in a pool of blood. Since the victim had had links with the underground church in Russia it was likely that he had been murdered by agents of the KGB. To date the case has never been cleared up. On that occasion my friend asked me: Are you afraid? I replied: I am, but I couldn't give a damn.

Not caring about my fear doesn't mean I don't feel it. Fear like pain has an important function as a signal that there is something wrong. Not feeling fear is not heroism; it is more of a handicap. It's not a matter of not being aware of fear but of not allowing fear to control us and determine our behaviour. We must not allow fear to take over the helm on our life's voyage.

I often find that people confuse three concepts, which in my opinion denote three very different phenomena: fear, anxiety and awe.

Fear is specific dread of something or someone.

Anxiety is an inner tension without obvious cause.

Awe is profound respect for the sacred, for something that is beyond our understanding, something that cannot be manipulated.

The thinkers of the Enlightenment linked religion, in terms both of its origins and its essence, with fear. Of course there exist pathological forms of religion that derive from fear and also disseminate fear. The most typical religious phenomenon, however, is awe – a state of wonderment at the enormity and unfathomability of the sacred, often accompanied by a sense of human smallness, vulnerability, finiteness, mortality (and sometimes sinfulness).

In the course of secularisation since the beginning of the Enlightenment, when the emphasis has been on human greatness, freedom and sovereignty (including emancipation from religion), awe has gradually disappeared from Western culture. However, I wonder whether this disappearance of awe has not provided greater scope for fear and anxiety – both in the secular sphere and in religion. "Anxiety is the dizziness of freedom, when... freedom looks down into its own possibility", wrote Kierkegaard.

Awe is a reaction to the ambivalent nature of the sacred. The sacred is a mystery "tremendum et fascinans". The Biblical concept of God as an incomprehensible mystery was replaced during the Enlightenment by a banal picture of God, which contained no darker aspects (which was criticised by both Nietzsche and Jung, for instance). However, that one-dimensional God continued to be counterbalanced by the horror element in religion – the threat of hell had not gone away.

It was experience of the tragedies and horrors of the 20th century that finally put the traditional images of hell into the shade. The regimes that promised paradise on earth created such a hell for people in their concentration camps that the traditional religious descriptions of hell became laughable. Likewise, the banal image of God as simply good (as a guarantor that what people regard as good will proove victorious in the world) became implausible in the face of those tragedies.

Our world is still a very dangerous place.

When tension in our world is too great and when frustrations and fear attain high levels among people and entire groups of people, ordinary everyday language and the language of secular politics is not powerful enough to express those emotions, then people spontaneously reach for the language of religion. Political leaders use the power of religious rhetoric and religious symbols. Religions would become a weapon in political conflicts. Nuclear weapons turn human settlements into dust and ruins. Religion, when used as a weapon, transforms the landscape of political conflicts into a battle scene in an apocalyptic cosmic war between Good and Evil. Political enemies are no longer perceived simply as people with different opinions and interests but as the army of the "Great Satan". This kind of "bedevilment" of the world leads to the strategy of destruction.

The world these days is full of monsters, chiefly because religion gets dragged into political, social and ethnic conflicts. The philosopher Richard Kearney recalls the advice of a psychoanalyst that when people are pursued in their dreams by monsters they should dare to look the monsters in the face while they are still dreaming. They will be surprised to discover that the monsters are not unlike themselves very much.

Those who are different from us can be a useful mirror for us, in which we may recognize what we are generally unable or unwilling to see. When we start to be capable of seeing in those who provoke us on account of their difference our *own shadows,* the things that we deny and displace and yet are part of us, we can say to ourselves: that is me too. It is necessary to be aware of our own imperfections and negative aspects, not to project them onto others, but draw them back. In this way we can contribute towards peace with others and a better understanding of ourselves. In place of naïve, immature, narcissistic notions about ourselves we can come to a better understanding of our own identity. In religious language this courage of the truth is called humility and this healing process is called repentance.

It is one important way how faith could overcome and heal the fear.

"Perfect love drives out fear" we read in scripture. How does it do it? Chiefly by giving us the courage to overcome our egocentricity, and put ourselves in the second place.

Most of our fears are not fears of something but instead various expressions of our fear about ourselves. Even in our fear of another there often tends to be a greater admixture of fear about ourselves than we are ready to admit (I am afraid of losing the other).

I have frequently come across cases of believers whose fear of evil (particularly when encountering suffering) is in fact fear of loss of faith. It was fear of doubt about God, about His goodness and power. Therefore in several of my books I have demonstrated that a mature faith is one that is capable of living with doubts.

There are many ways to close one's eyes to suffering and evil. Religion and theology also provide dozens of ways of "explaining away" evil and jettisoning this cross of our faith. Ever since Job's friends in that profoundest of books of the Old Testament, pious people down the centuries have thought up all sorts of theories about how to escape the burdensome and scandalous mystery of evil and pain. Many books have tried to sweeten painful wounds with pious phrases, or have advanced virtuous arguments to find a too simple way to cross the gulf between the fact of suffering and professing a good and just Father of all people. I can't help feeling that in his theodicy – possibly the weakest link in his extensive and multilayered work – even the great St. Augustine loads so much guilt on man – in a cockeyed attempt to preserve God's "good reputation" – that his pessimistic anthropology drove many believers into error and unimaginable mental distress. Isn't it more honest and in fact even "healthier" to simply acknowledge that the paradoxical existence of two scarcely reconcilable facts – evil and suffering on the one hand and a good, all-powerful God on the other – needs to be accepted as a "koan", which cannot be solved through the logical procedures of our intellect?

It was only confrontation with the tragedies of the twentieth century that evoked within theology – "post-Auschwitz" and "post-Gulag" theology – a sense of shame at the attempts to trivialise evil through pious fabrications. Many people were deflected from the path to faith and trust in God by the all too evident and undeniable presence of evil in our age. It is necessary to concede that we live in a world that sows religious doubt, a world that admits or even suggests an atheistic interpretation. Whereas Nietzsche placed the words "God is dead" into the mouth of a madman, who proclaims an event for which the people of his time had not yet opened their ears, many people these days accept the news as self-evident and nothing to get excited about. It's very easy to confuse *the silence of God* with the *non-existence of God* – the task of the theologian, however, is to remind us that we ought, nevertheless, to make a careful distinction between "God is silent" and "there is no God".

If theodicy is an attempt to "justify God" by trivialising evil or by a disquieting over-exaggeration of human sinfulness, then it strikes me – and always did – as immoral, inane and even blasphemous activity. God's goodness and justice cannot be trimmed with rationalistic shears to fit human notions of what is good and just. I suppose a dialogue with God about the mystery of evil and suffering must eventually end up like in the Book of Job: man covers his mouth and bows before the inscrutability of Reality. But that act of falling silent – the best example of which is in the Book of Job – is the outcome of a protracted and painful process of spiritual grappling and change of heart. And faith, I am profoundly convinced, is not the state reached at the end of that process but it is that entire process.

It would greatly diminish and distort the reality of faith to identify it solely with the moment of final victory over doubt. Faith is not identical with the "visio beatifica" – the direct perception of God traditionally ascribed to the saints in heaven. Faith is a worldly reality, it is part of being a pilgrim – but another part of the pilgrim's state and also of faith is all the vulnerability and difficulty of people on a journey, i.e. including the constant presence of insistent questions, temptations and doubts. Faith is not a final victory, but rather a constant struggle with doubts.

But let us go one step further: faith does not consist solely in overcoming and eliminating doubts, but in the ability to bear and endure them. Of love, the full sister of faith, it is written: love bears all things and endures all things. Doesn't the same apply to faith? *Isn't it part of the strength and authenticity of faith that it is able to endure doubts, as well as critical and thorny questions – the kind that are hard to answer?*

Jesus' words to apostle Thomas, when he touched His wounds "do not be unbelieving, but believing" are generally interpreted as: put aside your doubts and believe.

But one day – it was in Madras, near the tomb of apostel Tomas, after beeing confronted with the misery and poverty of India - another meaning of those words struck me: Take up the cross of your doubts and follow me. The place you'll always meet me – in spite of all your doubts – will not be a paradise of certainty but the wounds of the world, because they are my wounds.

When we ignore the wounds of our world – the contemporary wounds of Christ – we have no right to say: My Lord and my God!

The root of faith is the fundamental belief in meaning, in the meaningfulness of reality as a whole – and it is precisely this that tends to be wounded and threatened nowadays, more than ever before, maybe.

Doubts of certain kind can be Christians' mysterious participation in their Lord's cross and Jesus' cry "My God, why have you forsaken me?". Mystics in particular – let us recall John of the Cross and his teaching about the dark night of the soul – had respect and understanding precisely for these phases of the painful maturing of the faith in the deserts of profound existential doubts and crises.

I am deeply conviced, that faith and doubt need each other like sisters, complementing and correcting each other. If, on its journey, faith lost its sister doubt, its searching and questioning would come to an end and it could descend into soulless religious observance, ritualism and ideology. If doubt lost its sister faith it could descend into despair or corrosive cynical scepticism. Maybe our turbulent era is an "opportune moment" – kairos – for such a mutually enriching coexistence of faith and doubt. Faith and doubt must walk together and support each other if they don't want to tumble into the mire of fanaticism or hopelessness as they travel along this narrow, swaying bridge, which they cannot circumvent.

I am deeply convinced that only a mature faith can conquer fear.

FEAR AS A HUMAN COMPANION THROUHG THE AGES

Jože Trontelj, Ljubljana

We travel through our lives with fear as an inseparable companion, working in the background of our consciousness much of the time.

Fear is a part of human nature. In fact, so far as we can guess, it is rooted in the genome of all forms of life capable of sentient experience. It is a vital mechanism ensuring protective behaviour essential for survival. We cannot be sure how deep down the evolutionary scale this mechanism reaches. Similar to any other aspect of instinctive behaviour, there must be a carefully weighted balance between what is too little and what is excessive, since both will lead to misplaced, unnecessary and harmful behaviour, improperly chosen as either fight or flight. Early human races, essentially unarmed for fight, must have used fear as a strong instrument in survival strategies, as they were presumably favoured prey of large African carnivores. With the progress of civilization and the elimination of many risks of the primitive environment, one would expect the historical need for fear, originally virtually constantly present, to gradually subside. However, this has not happened. Peaceful intervals may now be longer, but spells of fear persist. In fact, fear and anxiety may be the prevailing state of mind over prolonged periods of time, for example, during war, severe crisis, political oppression and economic and social instability. Fear and anxiety may linger in the background.

Fear of the forces of nature is nowadays largely superseded by other sources of fear. These are actions or threats by our fellow human beings. The last century was marked by painful experiences of many millions who went through the horrors of wars, and by additional millions of those who suffered injustice, oppression and discrimination imposed by totalitarian regimes. Even many of those who were spared from direct impact spent decades in fear of the secret police, threats of imprisonment and severe human rights violations.

Even during times of peace and prosperity, considerable levels of fear remain widespread in society. We may be afraid of our superiors at work or our colleagues in the work place indulging in mobbing. Nobody can really tell how widespread fear is behind the walls of family homes. Parents, children and siblings may be tragic sources and targets of violence, leading to long-term misery and fear. This may become more pronounced during times of hardship, produced by the economic crisis.

Fear for our loved ones, when exposed to danger, violence and disease, or even risk of loss of life, can be a source of severe suffering. Extreme fear and panic are associated with acute suffering. Who will ever be able to forget the horrific scenes of people jumping to their death from the upper floors of the Twin Towers when they were ablaze in the 9-11 terrorist attack, minutes before their collapse?

However, in extreme injury, and with approaching death, an intricate and wonderfully powerful neurophysiological mechanism often comes into force. David Livingstone, the famous African explorer, described his remarkable experience when he was attacked by a man-eating lion (Kandel et al. 2000). He did not feel any pain when the big beast knocked him down and started to crush his shoulder between its teeth. Instead, he was overwhelmed by a serene feeling of calm relaxation. In an exceptional film on African wildlife, a gazelle was seen caught by a lioness. The beast slowly opened the belly of the poor animal, which still kept its delicate head in an upright position, and started tearing and eating its insides. Despite the increasingly horrible injuries the gazelle did not show any signs of pain or distress.

Nowadays, we know that these episodes were due to a remarkable structure we have in our brain for extreme situations. This is the neuronal network using morphine-like neurotransmitters, called endorphins, which switches off the pain and feelings of distress during extreme events. Apart from imminent injury and death, these events include situations where survival may depend on the mobilisation of extreme strength and abilities for successful fight or flight, since fear and pain would reduce both strength and mental abilities.

One might speculate that the release of endorphins in the brain may be the final relief granted by nature or a divine mercy to dying sentient beings just before the end of their conscious existence. Some stories of so-called near-death experiences seem to support this belief.

Death and dying are surrounded by mystery, and anticipation of death gives rise to much fear and anxiety. However, this is pushed out of our conscious everyday lives. Most people of our time seem to avoid thinking of their own death, at least so long as they are free from a serious, life-threatening disease. Many are thoroughly unprepared when such a disease strikes suddenly.

In about one-third of all cases, death is a sudden event. In the remaining two thirds, death is more or less accurately predicted by the family doctor or other treating physicians, often well in advance. In these cases, there is time for medical assistance.

In countries of the Western world, *end-of-life decisions are* made by medical doctors for different, but generally high and increasing percentages of patients.

Nowadays, in European countries, this proportion may exceed 50 % of all deaths. Often the decision is to forgo active, life-prolonging treatment that is considered futile. Some people call this passive euthanasia. In fact, this is a confusing term, used for different kinds of actions, ranging from the ethically unobjectionable withdrawal of ineffective or harmful therapies to plain murder, and it is best omitted.

In the Netherlands, about 3 % of all deaths are due to true euthanasia. A minority of these belong to a closely-related category, i.e. physician-assisted suicide. According to Dutch law, euthanasia should be reserved for mentally competent patients who have made a persistent request, who are close to death and whose severe suffering cannot be relieved. Unfortunately, these restrictions are often not respected, and a significant number of patients are euthanized without request, even when they are mentally competent. This is involuntary euthanasia, performed without a patient's knowledge, and perhaps even against his or her wish.

Within days of the new law's passage, the Dutch Health Minister, Els Borst, said the government should consider introducing a suicide pill for patients who are healthy, but are ready to die. Borst said that this would be carefully regulated. The Royal Dutch Medical Association argued that the criteria in place for euthanasia were unhelpful in defining the limits of medical practice (Sterling 2004). Stating that the guidelines were "an illusion", it concluded that euthanasia should be allowed for virtually anyone who did not want to live (Sheldon 2005).

In the same year, the University Medical Centre of Groningen published its procedures for euthanizing infants, which were intended not only for terminally ill newborns, but also for children born with spina bifida and other disabilities. The medical centre explained that the "approach suits our legal and social culture", although it acknowledged that it was "unclear to what extent it would be transferable to other countries" (Marker 2005).

Oregon, a state of USA, has enacted a patient's right to physician-assisted suicide. In the first 3 years after the law came into force, a total of 69 patients utilised this right. Nobody wished to end his or her life by committing suicide because of pain or other physical suffering. During that time, over 20,000 patients died of cancer, none of whom asked for help to suicide. The patients who did opt for the new right feared that they would lose their independent lifestyle, were frustrated by their inability to enjoy things that they used to enjoy, and they wished to decide themselves on the time of their demise. Recently, numbers have risen sharply (Oregon`s Death with Dignity Act, 2012). A report cites two cancer patients who were refused coverage for treatment by the Oregon Health Plan (state insurance programme), but were instead offered payment for doctor- assisted suicide.

Indeed, the prevailing culture of personal independence in everyday life seems to be an important reason for the general popularity of the idea that euthanasia, as a kind of *death with dignity,* should also be legalised in other countries. Behind this culture one can clearly see the fear of becoming dependent on assistance for such simple things as feeding, bathing and toileting.

Continuous deep sleep induced by sedatives, so-called terminal sedation, is another way to die. This is typically used for patients in severe pain or delirium that is not considered controllable by other means. During such sleep the patient is not given liquids or nutrients. When death occurs, it is not clear if it is due to the illness itself or just due to dehydration. The patient is considered to be at death's door anyhow, but this has been properly labelled as a self-fulfilling prophecy. In 2010, about 12 per cent of Dutch patients died in deep sedation (Onwuteaka-Philipsen et al. 2012).

An even more common way of dying is by the so-called *double effect.* The treating physician administers as large doses of analgesics and sedatives as deemed necessary to control the pain, fear and anxiety, disregarding the risk of possibly shortening the patient's life. According to a nationwide study, over 36 % of all deaths (about 130,000) in the Netherlands in 2010 were due to the double effect (Onwuteaka-Philipsen et al. 2012).

Rob George, a renowned specialist in palliative medicine, argues that the proper use of analgesics and sedatives does not cause a patient's death. The patient is killed by the disease, not by medication (House of Lords 2005). Exceptions should be very rare. When patients indeed die from the double effect, this means that most likely an unnecessary overdose has been administered. Hence, the above-mentioned 36 % of all Dutch deaths in 2010 contains an unknown, but presumably large number of patients who actually succumbed to covert euthanasia, rather than their disease. We have little reason to believe that the situation is radically different in the majority of European countries. Data, however, are not available.

Rob George, on the basis of personal experience with over 20,000 dying patients, suggests that *palliative* instead of *terminal* sedation should be used in cases of extreme suffering due to pain, vomiting and delirium. Sedation is shallow, nutrition and hydration are not interrupted, and the patient is woken up several hours or days later. Miraculously, the suffering has very often disappeared and the patient can attend to his last affairs, resolve any conflicts and misunderstandings, receive spiritual assistance, take leave of his family and friends and die peacefully.

It is unfair to deny the dying patient this last great life experience and kill him or her in an artificial coma (Virt 2009).

Imminent death may be a source of great anxiety. This may be more severe in people who do not believe in any kind of posthumous existence. It may also be increased by feelings of guilt because of harm and injustice committed against fellow human beings. For such people, dying can be a horrifying experience.

Medical interventions aimed at relieving the suffering of the terminally ill are a noble endeavour. However, actions to hasten death beyond the natural course are ethically highly controversial. It is virtually impossible to ensure that a request for assisted death is truly voluntary in all cases. Furthermore, errors in diagnosis and prognosis cannot be avoided. Finally, legalisation and the widespread use of euthanasia would change the public perception of human life as one of highest values. Euthanasia is not an act of health care, and it is a tragically wrong way out of the fear, pain and anguish of terminally ill patients (Council of Europe 1999).

In conclusion, fear has been a companion of humanity through the ages, although the causes have changed. Fear is also a companion of all human beings from birth to death. Again, the causes are very variable. Relief from fear can be a great act of mercy, as great as relief from pain. Apparently, both depend on related mechanisms within the brain of every human being. It is no coincidence that both are at least partly subserved by the same neuronal system. Medicine became aware of endogenous analgesia in the nineteen-sixties, but has only been making full use of it in the fight against severe pain during the last 15-20 years. Medicine has also been using the inborn system for sedation more efficiently in recent decades. However, it is disappointing to see that this is not put to sufficient use in our clumsy attempts to help dying patients. Even worse, a shortcut to death is advocated as a right for people who are not terminally ill, or who are not ill at all (Marker 2005), and euthanasia is actually used in such cases.

Indeed, our civilization needs to rethink its current assistance to the terminally ill and dying. *Opus divinum est sedare dolorem*, and we may add, *et horrorem*. Relieving pain and anxiety is a divine work of mercy, allowing the patient to die with dignity. Such a death has a much better chance of being accepted without fear and without a pointless, hopeless, stressful fight.

Literature

Kandel, ER, Schwartz, JH, Jessell, TM. 2000. *Principles of neural science*. 4th ed. Mc Graw Hill Co.

Sterling, T. 2004. Lifelong suffering can be valid reason for euthanasia, Dutch study finds. *Associated Press*, December 16, 2004. Available at LEXIS/NEXIS.

Sheldon, T. 2005. Dutch euthanasia law should apply to patients 'suffering through living,' report says. *British Medical Journal*, vol. 330, p. 61 (January 8, 2005).

Marker, RL. 2005. *Assisted suicide & death with dignity: past, present & future.* Part III. Patients Rights Council, Steubenville, Oh (USA). www.patientsrightscouncil.org.

Oregon's Death with Dignity Act. 2012.

Onwuteaka-Philipsen, BD, Brinkman-Stoppelenburg, A, Penning, C, de Jong-Krul, GJF, van Delden, JJM, van der Heide, A. 2012. *Trends in end-of-life practices before and after the enactment of the euthanasia law in the Netherlands from 1990 to 2010: a repeated cross-sectional survey.* www.thelancet.com. July 11, 2012 http://dx.doi.org/10.1016/S0140-6736(12)61034-4.

House of Lords, Select Committee. 2005. *Assisted Dying for the Terminally Ill Bill. Volume III. Evidence – individual submissions.* Ordered to be printed 3 March 2005 and published 28 April 2005, by the authority of the House of Lords. London: The Stationery Office Ltd. HL Paper 86-III.

Virt, Günther. 2009. Personal communication.

Council of Europe, Parliamentary Assembly. 1999. *Recommendation 1418: Protection of the human rights and dignity of the terminally ill and the dying.*

THE POST TOTALITARIAN FEAR

Janez Juhant, Ljubljana

Introduction

An animal will react instinctively to the dangerous challenges of life. A human, on the other hand, has to deal with them within his mind. But the mind is incorporated in the body and the emotions are regulators of these corporate relations. Fear is one of the central human emotions. All interpersonal relations reflect our emotions, because this is the way through which man communicates and the emotional aspect of communication is decisive in expressing human relations. In a special sense fear emerges from basic human relations and expresses the relationship and dependence of persons to each other. Psychologists speak about the fear connected with the separation of a child from its mother (Freud 1971, 289 ff.; Rank 2007). This fear is decomposed by the 'safety attachment' of a child to the person of its mother or other primary carer and to safety separation or succeeding relationships to other people. If an individual has the possibility of preserving the safety relationship to the mother or other primary carer while encountering the strains of the world, he will be able to manage his life and to orientate himself in this world. The further safety relationships confirm the emotional sanity of the individual and give a good foundation for his unproblematic functioning in society. Because of their inherent importance the emotions in general and fear in particular were always an important object of manipulation, particularly in authoritarian societies, where weak or degenerated human relations were preferred and fostered by nomenclatures to give them better control over disoriented and unbonded people, as the masses were then easier to manipulate. This made it very difficult if not impossible to deal with fear in a human manner. The manipulative fear was driven into the unconscious, not discussed and replaced by good human relations. Totalitarian authorities tried to implement conditions within societies which would ensure that individuals were affected and gripped by fear so as to let themselves submit and be subordinate to the totalitarian authority.

Fear as a relationship

The crucial problem is to enable, develop and promote interpersonal relationships to establish personal connectedness and to stimulate the personal exchange of emotions. If this is not done we have to cope with emotional starvation in which healthy emotions will be replaced by a culture of fear, which culminates in totalitarian systems. This situation in the family and in society fails to allow one to respond to one's own feelings and to cultivate them. Fear as an emotional state could be dealt with only by implementation of the symbolic world. Good dialogic conditions in which to implement one's own language – first of all its emotional side - are a guarantee for effective processing of fear. In this sense Jesus speaks about togetherness: "For where two or three gather in my name, there am I with them." (Mt 18, 20) There are many occasions in which the affirmation of others is very important. We can achieve this through dialogue, speaking to each other and to God. The absence of such dialogue leads to total subordination of one's life to a-personal organisers, who decide over one's individual and social fate. In this sense fear is a very important emotion, which could be easily exploited for the purposes of manipulation which culminated in the totalitarian systems.

"Fear is the ability to recognize danger leading to an urge to confront it or flee from it (also known as the fight-or-flight response) but in extreme cases of fear (terror) a freeze or paralysis response is possible. Some psychologists such as John B. Watson, Robert Plutchik, and Paul Ekman have suggested that fear belongs to a small set of basic or innate emotions. This set also includes such emotions as joy, sadness <melancholy, n. J.J.>, and anger. Fear should be distinguished from the related emotional state of anxiety, which typically occurs without any certain or immediate external threat."[1]

The biggest separation seems to be death which causes and determines the last human fear. But this is not only the question of the time of death but the question of dying, which is a life as whole; the life is a life to death. "The actual exposition starts by demonstrating that, and in what sense, the 'Being-towards-one's death' belongs genuinely and essentially to the Being of Dasein, i.e.to 'Care'" (Heidegger 1967, 56).

Dictatorship

On the previous suppositions we have two opposite states of society within which to deal with fear and all other aspects of human life. Democracy and dictator-

1 http://en-wikipedia/org/wiki/fear (accessed 24 Jan 2012)

ship are both systems to regulate the individual and societal life of man. Each developed techniques to control and to administer people. "In the parliamentary democracy the rational attitude expresses itself through both discussion and vote on questions of legislation. What is good for the public wealth is found by debate through a process of critical discussion which aims at throwing light on the various aspects of a debated matter or measure. Parliament is supposed to present the substance of political reason…" (Bramstedt 1945, 2) There is a general will and general reason, "the essence of national reason" (ibid).

"In dictatorship on the other hand, the executive is no longer subject to control by the legislature, nor is the judiciary independent. Legislature and executive are totally in the hands of a dictator and of the bodies appointed by him" (ibid). There is no general consensus but the will of one or of a few preserving and implementing the general reason; the will of the dictator(s). "The individual can only act as a tool of a privileged body, such as the Party or the Army, but seldom according to his own rights" (ibid, 3). Usually the secret police is the executive and controlling organ and its tool is to "imbue the people with fear" (ibid, 4).

The totalitarian systems were founded on the culture of fear and the consequences still persist. Alexander Solzhenitsyn (1974, 535) in *The Gulag Archipelago*, describes this scene of terror: "Sit down on the ground! On your knees! Take off your clothes! In these prescribed convoy's commands is contained an elemental force (German: *Urkraft*, Slovene: *pra-moč*), against it there is no rebellion." My uncle described to me a similar situation in the communist concentration camp in Novo mesto at the end of the second world war: "After the morning's gymnastics there was the command: 'Run!' and then a warning: The last will be shot! Every day there the dead and wounded were picked up, the last ones were shot and all together thrown on lorries and driven off." Similarly in the concentration camp in Auschwitz, where the son of the commander made friends with the boy on the other side of barbed wire. One day, when he was there, both were sent to the death cell.

In these systems and in their abnormal conditions of life there was no consideration for the basic needs of women. On the contrary: The women were constantly being driven into extreme situations, they were deprived of linguistic and emotional exchange, made helpless, vulnerable and aphasic, unable to react and to defend themselves.

A functionalistic view of man grounded on fear

Behind all totalitarian systems there is a specifically negative, in a decisive sense a functionalistic view of man. Bramstedt (1945, 137) states, that "behind the cunning devices and speedy action of Secret Police as experienced from Fouché to Himmler there is a certain basic conception of what man is and how he must be treated ... the fact remains that an autocratic regime is bound to adopt a rather negative view of man and an even more negative approach to him. Man is regarded as a partly weak, partly dangerous collective animal that can be kept in check by playing on its fears and by exploiting its lusts and desires, an animal that can be eliminated as easily as a cockroach or rabbit if only an efficient method is devised and carried out with superb indifference. This cold-blooded approach is best summed up by the utter contempt of the Devil in Goethe's *Faust*:

> Denn alles was besteht,
> Ist Wert, dass es zugrunde geht.
> (For everything that exists deserves but to perish)"

This conception of man is an instrumentalist one (Žalec 2010, 27 pp.). All societal life in totalitarian states is organised in such a way that it serves only the leading nomenclature, which means only the chosen (specific) elite citizens. They usurp to themselves all political power and in this sense there are no differences between Nazis, Fascists or Communists. All others are excluded and subverted and are only means for the first and are handed over to their mercy or unmercy. "Arendt (2003) provided enduring portrait of the modern 'superfluous man', made to feel so by the crush of mass society, then made so by totalitarian regimes capable to placing death within a story of progress and joy. It is Arendt's portrayal of the killing epoch that has endured: of people (victims and perpetrators alike) slowly losing their humanity, first in the anonymity of mass society, the in a concentration camp." Snyder asserts that this deprivation of human status was an inhumane way to deal with victims. "As one of Grossman's (1995: 204-206) characters exclaims, the key to both National Socialism and Stalinism was their ability to deprive groups of human beings of their right to be regarded as human" (Snyder 2012, 380, 386).

The state's usurpers pursue only the objectives of their usurping, leading class. Other people are treated merely as resources of the system or as objects for the benefit of this minority. The remaining majority are totally subjected to this part of the political establishment. The means used to achieve such power over the whole society are very sophisticated and rationally planned. This was possible, as Zygmunt Bauman (2002) and Günther Anders (1992) pointed out, only in the modern times with the acquisitions of modernity, especially the media and other technical devices, through them the small group could rule over and control the societal masses. According to Anders (1992), man in our modern times was antiquated through technical devices. The totalitarian systems represent the perfection of this development. The fears and hopes of women were pressed down, to make women mere ciphers, which could be eliminated every time, without difference among all totalitarian systems. Such works as *Necropolis* by Boris Pahor (1997), the *Angel of oblivion* by Maja Haderlap (2012), *This night I have seen her* by Drago Jančar (2010) or *Bloodlands. Europe between Hitler and Stalin* by Thimothy Snyder (2012) attest to this sad truth.

Secret police and the culture of fear

Our modern era has seen the development of devices to maximise the instrumentalisation of man. Man should be totally subjugated or put under control. Bramstedt (1945, 138) speaks of the triangle of this societal control, comprising: "terror, corruption and propaganda". This are not irrational but rather very rational and sophisticated methods of control, which intend preserving terror over 'all enemies of state', that is the factual or supposed opponents of the leading class. For them the leading class (nomenclature) establishes a state of terror to impose pervasive fear on them all.

According to Bramstedt (1945, 51) in Italy the Fascists exploited the fear experienced in the First World War. The Fascists were "full of fear themselves, they knew how to turn it into violence, thus causing fear in others." The fear of the downfall of the system was challenged and arranged by Fascists "in impregnating the masses with fear." (Bramstedt 1945, 55) The same was true in Nazi Germany and in all forms of communism (Snyder 2012, 59 pp.). The fear of disordered circumstances prior to the revolution in the Soviet Union was turned by the communists into total communist terror and spread fear over the whole society. The disappointment and shame of Italians and Germans after the First World War was turned into dictatorship and totalitarianism by the Fascists and Nazis and in Russia during World War I they were used by the communists, to create a state of terror and a society of fear. The same terror tactics were practised by the communists in Slovenia: They exploited the fears of the occupied nation to come to power in the country. The terror began during the occupation in the year 1942.

Modern propaganda is a powerful regulator of fear in the masses. Thanks to the modern media, the leading class has a huge instrument to enable it to totally rule society. Not only in dictatorships but also in other countries the modern media devices make it possible to inflict fear on the people and to terrorise them. (Snyder 2012, 55-58) The modern propagandist could effectively direct public opinion to an appointed gaol and direct all societal streams to it. It is decisive (crucial), who has access to and control of propaganda over the people: "Authoritarian countries and theocratic states possess criminal laws forbidding propaganda against the state, complaining about social conditions to foreigners and attempting to publish works that are not authorised by the state" (Hagan 1997, 3). This is only a part of this propaganda work. The whole society has to be ruled by intricately detailed mechanisms. Nowadays it is quite possible to manipulate society totally and to instrumentalise the people.

Bramstedt (1945, 169) speaks of three types of such mechanisms: "propaganda of fear, terror without propaganda, propaganda through terror…The permanent task of the propagandist is to anticipate events and to prepare his public for them." The Nazis and other totalitarians chose scapegoats and propagated their negative and ill characterisations to isolate them and to make it possible to implement the next step: terror without propaganda: annihilation of the people thus characterised (Snyder 2012, 58-118). Then the third step is applied: The people of the old leading class, the intellectuals and so on, were negatively presented by the media and if anybody tried to oppose this image, then pressure was applied and these people had to give in and submit to authority. Bramstedt (1945, 175) demonstrates this very well in an example of the Nazi's propaganda work against the Czech president Eduard Beneš.

The proper organ for preserving terror is the secret police maintaining the myth of itself. The secret police had - and still has in all totalitarian countries -, as Hannah Arendt (2003) pointed out, the decisive role and is always the top of the society. It has to monitor all the people and to subjugate them. So the state of terror is established. All people have to be held in fear. In the revolution during the Second World War the leading Slovene communist, Edvard Kardelj, wrote to Tito, describing how terror accompanied the establishing of the partisan (in fact: communistic) Secret Police (VOS Varnostno-obveščevalna služba=*Security Informative Service*) with the words: "…daily the denunciators, the occupiers' stable men <in fact those people were the best national leaders, whose deficiency was that they were anti-Communists; n. J.J.> have fallen …No police protection can save them once they are in the sights of the VOS…VOS is feared as a devil, this gives – beside National Safeguard and Partisans – the OF (Liberation front) the character of true power."(Ferenc 1962, 325) People of the leading class are working to combat their own fears in such a way as to provoke fear in others. This means also to exclude all other people from the state life, there are no possibilities for cooperation. All others have to submit to them under the totalitarian "order" or they will be excluded. "Fascism <like Nazism, Communism, n. J.J.> is always right and brings all its opponents to dust" (Bramstedt 1945, 54).

Besides propaganda, the second means is also very important, corruption. There are always enough people who will let themselves be corrupted, especially in difficult societal circumstances. Through the old *divide et impera* (divide and conquer!) principle, the enslaved people are ready to cooperate with the leading class to get bread-crumbs from the table of their lords. The people were bought, to make them dependent on the leading class. This causes negative selection in the society and strengthens the power of the leading people. On the other hand, the vitality and compatibility of the society were and still are diminished, and so the society is drawn towards stagnation.

Alongside those two instruments there is a third, terror. The totalitarian systems are out to cover all societal life with detailed control, which places the society thus absolutely controlled in a state of terror. The leading social class controls all areas of the public and private life of the people and holds all territories in absolute subordination. This could, according to Bramstedt (1945, 140), be achieved in the following manner: "Methods of gathering information, methods of collective detention, methods of intimidation and methods of elimination." From Fouché, Napoleon's minister, to Hitler and Stalin the methods were the same. Their purpose is to gain absolute control over society and to inflict fear on all.

The Church and the Slovene: authoritative training as prerequisite for totalitarianism

The Slovenes did not have their own state. The Austro-Hungarian monarchy was a goal of nations. The Slovene Catholic Church was like a mother for the Slovenes. It did not allow her children to grow up, but it held them as children to command them. The priest had a decisive role in the life of Slovenia's Christians. He imposed decisions about marriage, family life and economic circumstances. The Slovene Christians were trained for obedience. The national proverbs confirm it: 'Use the parish-priest only for the salt!' Obedience and subordination were inculcated: 'The switch is singing the first mass.'

The Slovene Church was very close to the Slovenes, it educated them in fear of God according to the Old Testament's Proverbs (9:10): "The fear of the Lord is the beginning of wisdom…", which they were taught was fear of the priest and other Church authorities, despite the fact that in Christianity the fear of God is understood as an appropriate way to relate to the world and to live in accordance with (God's) wisdom. This use of fear in the sense of fear of the authorities was stimulated by the dictatorial Austro-Hungarian state. Besides this, the circumstances in Slovenia during both world wars promoted authoritarianism. In the new first Yugoslavia democracy and human rights were difficult to enforce. The social tensions and differences were reinforced and the communists found fertile soil for their propaganda work. The Second World War cleared the way for communistic dictatorial experimentation. They were not interested in the war emergency of the people but only in the conquest of power. They overcame their own fear in deepening and exploiting the fear of others.

Toward Democracy – overcoming the fear of dictatorship

As said, Bramstedt (1945, 2) sees in dictatorship and democracy two different types of rational order. "Both are systems of political control, both have elaborated a technique of ruling and administration, and to act according to a technique is to follow a rational pattern". There are differences in the procedures for applying these rational methods. The democratic system is based on parliamentarianism and the judiciary. The system respects human rights and also the human person in general. The whole system works in a subsidiary manner. "Parliament on the one hand, judiciary on the other are 'safety'–valves preventing and checking unlawful, i.e. irrational, behaviours of individuals and groups" (Bramstedt 1945, 2).

Not so the dictatorships or the totalitarian systems, which work without an independent legislature and judiciary. "The dictator may found his power on the army and/or on the party which then holds a privileged position, and develops a bureaucracy of its own" (Bramstedt 1945, 2). The individual is totally subjugated and given over to the will and power of the dictators. They develop the mechanisms of control "to imbue people with fear" (Bramstedt (1945, 5) Adam Michnik (2012, 209) speaks of the "stuffy odour, in which the house of communist Poland, named the Polish People's Republic died. This was a country, in which foreign policy, army and police were subordinated to the decisions of the Soviet Union, which was governed by a communistic nomenclature, controlled by police, intrusive ideology, fear and hypocrisy … Everywhere there were present fearful low-spiritedness, opportunism, apathy and cynicism." There were no ideas, the people were beaten and they could (only silently) resist.

Above all, therefore, the month of August 1980 was "the feast of Polish democracy…The workers were fighting for justice and the interests of the whole society." (Michnik 2012, 210) According to Michnik, the miracle of change was that the people were not frightened any more. The visit of Pope John Paul II in

June 1979 and his call to the Poles 'Don't be anxious!' liberated the people from stuffy odour and enabled them to think and to behave freely. Again in the words of Adam Michnik (2102, 36): "In August 1980, – in the year after the first visit of John Paul II, we threw off our masks, we came out of our hiding-places, we have decisively said our 'No!' and it was proved that our voice is a voice of the free and sovereign Poland."

The liberal and democratic state should be built on the principles of human rights. "After World War II the victorious Allies held a trial and convicted Nazi war criminals in Nurnberg" (Hagan 1997, 4). But there were no trials over the most communist dictators apart from the Serbians at the court in The Hague. Magna Charta – *The Universal Declaration of Human Rights* - of the United Nations "is a proclamation, but not a treaty or international agreement" (Hagan 1997, 5). This makes it clear why many states of the international community were not - and still are not - ready to accept human rights as a principle of democratic procedures. The main problem is, as David Harvey (2011) states, that there is always the problem of military super powers and of competition among the capitalists for economic supremacy.

The principles of human rights and related democratic values always face difficulties in overcoming the obstacles of dictatorship, totalitarianism and acceptance of an open society (K. Popper).

Moral (common sense) versus discipline or how to grow up

It is a fact, that individuals are not ready to deal with their emotions and this is an even greater challenge for society. This means, that it is difficult to leave a man free to grow up. A man is to be kept under the mother's protection and if she is no longer there, he hands himself over to other authorities. If a young man does not mature successfully, his rebelliousness will lead him into subjection to some powerful entity.

Like many ethical and religious thinkers, Bramstedt states that discipline should be replaced by ethics. For this it is necessary that an individual feels that he/she belongs to the community. The totalitarian regimes destroyed this sense of belonging and replaced it with fear of the leading class. Only "togetherness can reduce the fear and replace it by a quiet but strong collective confidence" (Bramstedt 1945, 233/4).

How to achieve the change from discipline to morality. "There are two agencies through which a solution can be attempted: the medium of education and the medium of politics, the former aiming at the welfare of the next generation, the latter at the improvement of present political institutions by change or new creation. There will always be those ready to contend that it is better to atttempt the reform of human nature than to modify laws and political codes; there will also be others who claim that the change in political structure is an indespensable condition for any possible change in human behaviour" (Bramstedt 1945, 234). The two tasks are interdependent and they should support each other. The decisive problem "is, to find democratic ways of living for little men in big societies" (Bramstedt 1945, 235). This process begins at home and its main aim is to enable the individual to belong to a community. This 'work' at home needs societal support and implementation. Bramstedt is convinced that this could be promoted by a variety of "community centres or neighbourhood associations" (Bramstedt, ibid). Similarly, the communitarians are speaking of civil entities. The civic society develops by the principle of subsidiarity. The different centres will stimulate the 'brain trust' "for the discussion of political, cultural and educational matters on a local background" (ibid). Bramstedt pleads for cooperation between different towns (Preston and Stalingrad) but it is very important to speak about the cooperation between once hostile cities like London and Berlin or Paris and Berlin and countries like Poland and Russia or France and Germany. Unlike the first two, the latter cooperate well today because of the Historians' Commission, which contributed to a common history for schools in France and Germany. In this way nationalisms could be overcome.

Education is not an individualistic effort, so a democratic education should be provided: If morality is to take the place of discipline, then there must be an active interchange between the child and the educator as well as between the child and his fellows" (Bramstedt 1945, 237). This integration means "the spontaneous emergence of co-operation and self-government within groups" (Read, 1942, 268 quot. by Bramstedt 1945, 239). According to Read, the leader should be "*primus inter pares*... This democratic leadership should be graduated in steps, of course, with due modifications in answerability from the adult leadership to children, that of political representative to voter, and finally of responsible élites forming a government to the masses whom they represent and on the close contact with whom their legitimacy depends" (ibid). The aim of ethical and political education is "the development of valuable dispositions of the individual in a spontaneous co-operating community" (Bramstedt 1945, 239).

Today this is an increasing problem, because post-modern man is going his own way, developing his own thinking and this makes it difficult to communicate and to exchange individual views.

Ways to dialogical moral education without fear

Again, Bramstedt stressed the importance of democratic education "in the countries at present ridden by dictatorship ... Their legacies of neurotic behaviour and memories of uncanny control will make the full play of normal social activities more difficult. There "is a need to 'de-totalise' this conception and to couple it with freedom" (ibid). In respect to the Nazis' case, Bramstedt states that there were enough educational ideas and profound educators in Germany but "they were somewhere unreal, living too much in an isolated 'pedagogic province' far away from the turmoil of the social and political scene" (Bramstedt 1945, 239).

The situation in post-communist societies is very similar. We are faced with a growing individualism as a reaction to the pressure of the former totalitarian time. Now everybody is taking the opportunity in this situation to get much more for himself and there is not enough readiness to be concerned for the common wealth. The post-modern paradigm 'anything goes' suggests that everyone has to evolve his own manners, rules and ethical attitudes without testing what kind of consequences such developments have on others and on the entire community. There seems to be a new ideology of the post-modern and especially transitory post-communist world as a rejection of former totalitarian and authoritarian societal pressure. So education should be free – 'neutral' from different organisational or ideological backgrounds. As we have seen, the post-modern educational paradigm could not work either without including basic educational values. These need to be discussed and there is as yet no channel for dialogue about them in our society.

In this context Hans Küng (1990) discusses a world ethos. The world ethos includes the basic commitment to the ethos in different societies and perhaps in world society. It does not mean a new general system of ethics but a common ethical dialogical attitude. The best way for society is mutuality and cooperation. This is the very urgent problem of Slovene society (Juhant & Strahovnik 2010) and a reason why the post-totalitarian fear is still present in Slovene society.

How to approach the dialogue about the 'Slovenian case' of fear

A central problem for moral education in post-totalitarian Slovenia is how to reach agreement about the moral foundations of our society. The former totalitarian system suspended moral judgment through the Marxist approach to building a classless society without morality, law, state and all other so called 'superstructures' of society. Indeed, the Marxist approach to society suspended old (Christian) values, isolated the individual and created a mass of persons without names, whose only role was to function as a classless society. After the change in 1989 the question which arose was: which values should be implemented in the education system and in the whole societal life. But as has been shown in the last 20 years, there is still no agreement about common societal ethical standards. The consequences of Marxist anthropological change persist in the individual and societal consciousness. There is no agreement about the ethical basis of Slovene society; consequently there is no dialogue with regard to how to overcome this pattern. Without such a dialogue it is not possible to establish grounds of ethical consensus and to unite the people on common basic ethical principles. Without such a dialogue the post-totalitarian fear persists and we are not a society of trust but a society of fear of each other. This fear is increasing due to the difficult economic situation, which is an excuse for unhealthy competition, exclusion and distance among the citizens.

Rifkin speaks of the "births of humanism" (Rifkin 2009, 270), but could it be promoted by mimetic rivalry and 'scapegoat mechanisms', "the ones of really satanic relations-frameworks among men" (Uhl 2010, 318), which are the remains of the totalitarian past in Slovenia? There is no 'hyper-policy' (Zimmermann 2008, 157), the instrument of regulating this is no totalitarian system, no classless society, no world policy. Only a dialogic man could implement universal moral power (Rifkin 2009, 270; Zimmermann 2008, 159). This calls for universal rules for or means of dialogue. The ways of reparation of humanity are the ways of dialogical man, of enlargement and deepening of his morality. Human dialogue is a struggle for acknowledging the imperfections of everybody and implementation of inter-human relations. Nobody should be excluded from these processes and then nobody will fear. If the Slovenes are not ready for dialogue and cooperation in society yet (Juhant & Strahovnik 2011) how are they to overcome the totalitarian fear? Without this, Slovene society will not be well fitted out for the challenges of the world crisis and for giving trust to their members to deal with it. But despite this, this work has to be done for our common life and survival.

References

Anders, Güther. 1992. *Die Antiquiertheit des Menschen* I, II. München: Beck.

Arendt, Hannah. 2003. *Izvori totalitarizma* (engl. 1951; 2004. *The Origins of Totalitarianism*. New York: Schocken). Ljubljana: ŠZ Claritas.

Bauman, Zygmunt. 2002. *Dialektik der Ordnung*. Hamburg: Europäische Verlagsgesellschaft (Engl.: 1993. *Modernity and the Holocaust*. Oxford: Polity Press/Blackwell.)

Bramstedt, Ernst Kohn. 1945. *Dictatorship and Political Policy. The Technique of Control by Fear*. London: Routledge.

Freud, Sigmund. 1971. Hysterie und Angst. In: *Studienausgabe*. Vol. VI. Frankfurt: S. Fischer, 233-308.

Ferenc, Tone. 1962 (eds.). *Dokumenti revolucije* I. Ljubljana: Inštitut za zgodovino delavskega gibanja.

Grossman, Vasilij. 2006. *Življenje in usoda* (Eng. *Life and Fate*, trsl. by Robert Chandler, New York: Review Booksc). Ljubljana: Cankarjeva založba.

Haderlap, Maja. 2011. *Engel des Vergessens*. Göttingen: Wallstein.

Hagan, Frank E. 1997. *Political Crime: Ideology and Criminality*. Boston (ect.): Allyn and Bacon.

Harvey, David. 2011. *Kozmopolitstvo in geografija svobode* (2009: *Cosmopolitism and the Geography of Freedom*. New York: Columbia UP). Ljubljana: Sophia.

Heidegger, Martin. 1967. *Existence and Being*. (Trans. W. B. Barton and V. Deutsch). Chicago: Gateway ed.

Jančar, Drago. 2010. *To noč sem jo videl*. Ljubljana: Modrijan.

Juhant, Janez, Strahovnik, Vojko. 2010. Pristno delovanje je vzajemnost in sodelovanje. *Bogoslovni vestnik*. year 70, No. 3, pp. 351-364.

Juhant, Janez, Strahovnik, Vojko. 2011. Ali je možna empatična družba dialoga? *Bogoslovni vestnik*. year 71, No. 4, pp. 495-509.

Küng, Hans. 1990. *Projekt Weltethos*. München: Piper.

Michnik, Adam. 2012. *Iskanje izgubljenega smisla. Izbrani eseji Adama Michnika (The search after the lost meaning. The chosen Essays from Adam Michnik.)* Ljubljana: Znanstvena založba FF.

Pahor, Boris. 1997. *Nekropola*. (Fr. *Pèlerin parmi les ombres)*. Ljubljana: Mladinska knjiga.

Popper, Karl Raimund. 1963. The *Open Society and its Enemies: Volume I, The Spell of Plato*. Princeton, New Jersey: Princeton University Press.

Popper, Karl Raimund. 1963. *The Open Society and its Enemies. Vol. II: The High Tide of Prophecy: Hegel, Marx, and the Aftermath*. Princeton, New Jersey: Princeton University Press.

Rank, Otto. 2007. *Das Trauma der Geburt*. (Nachdruck d. Ausg. Leipzig, Wien, Zürich 1924). Gießen: Psychosozial-Verlag.

Read, Herbert Edvard.1943. *Education through Art*. London: Faber & Faber.

Snyder, Thimothy. 2012. *Bloodlands. Europe between Hitler and Stalin*. New York: Basic Books.

Uhl, Florian. 2010. Religion, Gewalt und Relativismus. In:Wandinger, Nikolaus & Steinmair-Pösel, Petra (eds.). *Im Drama des Lebens Gott begegnen. Einblicke in die Theologie Józef Niewiadomskis*. Wien: LIT, pp. 316-331.

Zimmermann, Rolf. 2008. *Moral als Macht*. Reinbeck b. Hamburg: Rowohlt Verlag.

Žalec, Bojan. 2010. *Človek, morala in umetnost.Uvod v filozofsko antropologijo in etiko*. Ljubljana: Teološka fakulteta.

http://en-wikipedia/org/wiki/fear (24th Jan 2012)

FEAR AND EDUCATION IN IDEOLOGICAL POST TOTALITARIAN SOCIETY

Stanko Gerjolj, Ljubljana

Educational systems are closely linked to political systems. In a way, the educational and schooling system represents a reflection or subsystem of the political system. Thus, democratic political systems enable and promote democratic education while totalitarian political systems insist on the totalitarian ideological education (Kupffer 1974, 132-133).

Political system, which is basically a one-way system, controlling, monotonous, narrow and self-contained, allows only the same one-way, controlled, narrow and self-contained education in its area. Such a system on the one hand, generates fanatical followers, and on the other hand opponents and enemies. The more socially disqualified and fallen "enemies" in the society, the narrower the horizon of the system or the people who speak and educate on its behalf. In such cases, the unwanted quickly turns into unacceptable or prohibited, while arguments of power replace the power of arguments. Arguments of power, for their existence, require the existence of enemies, since they would lose their relevance without them (Gerjolj 1997, 34).

1. Environment of fear

From history and today there are dictators who defend their position of power by brutal means. In fact, dictatorship is characterized by using all available resources to deal with all those who disagree with dictatorial rulers. However, despite that differences exist between dictatorship and totalitarianism.

Dictators usually want to manage their enemies with violence, while totalitarianism, in addition to that, also tries to change them internally, spiritually and mentally, which means that totalitarianism with its ideology surpasses dictatorship (Bacher 1980, 3066). Totalitarianism builds ideology, through which it theoretically justifies and enforces its violence and brutality (Arendt 1967, 399). Ideology thus becomes a key pillar, "constitution" and "Code of Ethics" of brutal and inhumane acts.

1.1 Institutional fear

Totalitarianism is characterized by including re-education of young generations in its ideological basis. Totalitarianism as such only ostensibly provides an important role to young people, but in fact it indoctrinates and manipulates them (Schwendter 1981, 21). The fact that a communist totalitarianism, through state institutional apparatus, includes mostly less than 10% of people, among whom many were members of the Party of convenience and fear of the consequences, it thus confidently manages the entire population, eloquently testifies that the state as a partial institution used almost exclusively repressive approaches that were based on the reinforcement of environment of fear. In addition, the entire educational and training system operated as a kind of preparation for the communist political action (Franković 1976, 19). On the one hand, the system marked important life areas for private matters while carrying out the repression over the most private decisions and actions. Thus, it characterized religion as a private matter, while on the other hand created a range of economic, cultural and especially political and pedagogical functions, where believers had no access to (Gerjolj 1997, 96). Religion has become a taboo issue, which has been discussed only by declared non-religious communist chosen ones, while we the religious ones had to hide it and live "as if there is no God".

We are undoubtedly still aware of the consequences of this "inherent" fear. Customers and ideas rooted in the past totalitarianism in the public life enjoy a privileged status and this media culture is accepted as something entirely "normal", which is interestingly also revealed by various forms of interconnection communication. The finding that the parties with the communist past, in election despite that still fail to achieve the expected results, illustrates how many people continue to hide their different beliefs and express them only in elections where they have no fear because of anonymity.

The context of institutional fear also includes solving of religious instruction in public schools, which still has not experienced a satisfactory solution. Recourse to France, which opened this question in a much different historical and social circumstances, is by many people experienced more as an evading than as a realistic argument. Enforcement of the "old normality" has a much stronger effect, where the religion can only be discussed by the non-religious ones, while believers need to continue to hide and keep their beliefs and attitudes taboo. For school environment unambiguousness in the areas of religious and moral, ethical, and political issues is still something quite "normal", and religion is even something extremely harmful and therefore prohibited. In this context, it is understandable that the Organization and Financing of Education Act speaks about the autonomy of school area and not of the autonomy of man (Organization and Financing of Education Act 1996, Article 72). Autonomy liberates a man and sets him free while the room, especially when it is trapped in the totalitarian and legitimizing ideology, limits and suppresses a man in his personality.

Personal and collective history, and religion, and moral attitudes were often tabooed subjects also in families, which is today probably perceived like the hardest root of fear. From fear of the consequences, many parents hid their past and their parents' past even to their children, which resulted in an atmosphere and dishonesty, and vague or repressed communication within the family. In families, in which one of the parents enjoyed an important position or performed the teacher's profession, and where religion was also unexpressed, that burdened the natural religious upbringing. After the democratic changes young people began to be increasingly interested in the past, while parents have continued to hide it, because they were afraid of allegations that they served totalitarian system of convenience and fear, which is known to have no perspective. They persist in blurred communication from fear of issues while serving young people with benefits and are afraid to impose requirements that are healthy for the youthful growing up.

1.2 Creating idols and fear

Similarly, as the Communist Party was demonstrated as absolutely immaculate before the public, and especially in the school environment, the same integrity also applied for some idols. Marx and Engels and Lenin and Tito have been mentioned in textbooks for primary school students 1124 times, always with a positive connotation (Gerjolj 2000, 88). In connection with the above efforts to maintain the communist tradition, it is understandable that a similar integrity is now enjoyed by the current political and opinion leaders, resulting from communist roots, both in public and in schools. In accordance with the totalitarian tradition, which changed all those "different" into enemies, they are exposed to these ruthless critics even after the formal fall of totalitarianism. Post-totalitarian public and school place diversity at the centre of educational activity, but it is worth mentioning that in these cases it is only the difference that directly or indirectly supports the remnants of totalitarian ideology. Moreover, totalitarian representatives are used to create enemies and putting them in a negative light, while real dissent and sentient still fear to stand on their own feet and defend their views publicly. In this conglomerate of "ours" and "others", only "ours" have the right to interpret and defend their positions in school, while "others" are dissuaded or prohibited from doing so even in didactic instructions (Kerševan 2005, 62).

2. The need for political catharsis

Not only because of the political context, but also on the basis of historical knowledge and psychological dimensions of a healthy life democratic education that is not based on fear requires implementation of a thorough process of cathartic purification. In accordance with the interactions and integration of biblical Christian tradition in European space the biblical view of our situation can be of great help and motivation. If we "borrow" the archetype of the people of Israel here from, which in the desert also dreamed of Egyptian pots of meat (Jančar 1995), we see that a man after being released from bondage under totalitarianism, still faces a long way of education ahead of him which includes reflection on the past and formation of a common vision and a more uniform value system and ethical standards.

In terms of continuing learning God invited Moses on Mount Sinai in order to entrust him with Decalogue, the first kind of formal "constitution" of joint living. But already during the "writing of the Constitution" the people begin being lost in the search of current pleasures and their idols, which are featured in the "golden calf". Covenant that God made with Moses is already breaking behind his back.

When leaving on the mountain Moses entrusted the leadership of the people to the elders Aron and Huru (Genesis 24, 13-14), the closest and most confidential co-workers closely linked to him, however, this does not protect these people from decay. On the contrary, Aaron, brother of Moses (Exodus 6, 29), alone unreservedly participates in the devaluation of elements for more responsible ethical and moral life, as he leads and motivationally supports the creation of "golden calf" (Exodus 32, 1-6). Temporary leadership was clearly made up of too weak personalities who have irresponsibly and revolutionary marched the past and did not want to learn from history. The role of Moses and God on the road to freedom has systematically underestimated and thus prepared a place for its "Gods" (Friedman 2001, 279-280). Insidious revolution instantly shattered the sense of shared values and faith, and thus also the sense for joint continuation of the path to freedom. Obviously they got scared of conventional and independent life in freedom, and preferred to go back to old habits. Thus, Moses, when he returned from the mountain observed an unexpectedly large discrepancy between the reality and the commandments, so he indignantly breaks "constitutional norms and values" which he brought with him as a result of communication with God. Then he attempts to re-educate people and motivate them for responsible ethical, moral and religious life (Genesis 32, 19-20) immediately after he relativizes and breaks their unrealistic expectations of happiness and satisfaction represented by the golden calf. In order not to feel cheated, he empirically substantiates his observations and provides them with some feelings of reality, where living a dissolute, irresponsible and devalued life would lead them to. By shaking the dust of golden calf in the water, which he earlier called from the rocks with the help of God (Friedman 2001, 283), clearly shows to people how God's goodness is abused in the moral and religious as well as ethical and spiritual area. The only thing he must do is "drink" the reality "cooked" by the people on false idols.

After this experience, he gives the people an opportunity to decide for or against God (Genesis 32, 20), which can be understood as a verification of their personal growth, and religious, political and moral maturity (Cohen 1998, 13). He let these mature and responsible people know that promised land, meaning of life, responsibility and sustainable community do not tolerate half-heartedness (Genesis 32, 25-29).

Moses therefore deliberately avoids the impact and effect of "mass psychology" and requires a personal decision of each individual. After a personal decision he sends them again to the "catharsis". Killing a "brother, neighbour and friend" in a slightly different context and a different psychological performance, however, is distinctly reminiscent of identification of the other, shady and sinful side and his "second face". The Bible emphasizes the integration of personality, so the other dark side needs to be first accepted and integrated, and only then it can be changed. Moses placed the decision in the ethical and moral context, where we are challenged to "killing" the old, in our case, totalitarian man, and thus to a total denunciation of a past sinful behaviour or acting in accordance with the totalitarian system. Only then we shall be able of a new start and only then a "new man" can come to life in us. Also in this case, they first have to discover, recognize and accept a "brother" as one of them, so that they can "kill" him and finally give him up as a harmful dark side. This means that the "brothers in itself" will not be defeated by revanchism or hatred, but this will only be possible upon integration processes of personal growth, where we will learn to accept each other and also to forgive each other, what is undoubtedly a complex and often troubled learning process, of which the first step to change is recognition of own sins or shadows on own face. It is only after the recognition and purification that we are able, through Moses, to contact God (and man), ask him for forgiveness and explore new future with him.

As a true educator Moses does not despair of sinners and nobody is avenged. However, he does require an honest look in the mirror and a genuine encounter with itself from each individual, promising positive moral and religious changes throughout the community. After this experience of sin and purification Moses reconnects with God. God renews its commitment with him and writes commands on the new panel, which Moses, as a basis for commands prepares himself and no longer needs to break them (Exodus 34, 1-10). In light of the New Testament, Moses and his community need "a new birth from above" (Janzen 1997, 251), which puts the common existence at the immanent and transcendent level in a new light, and opens up a new perspective. This second encounter with God took Moses even more seriously and made even greater impression on him than the first one, because it has changed him to the extent that made others afraid of stepping into his proximity when he returned from the mountain (Genesis 34, 30-31). Fear of over-changed image of a man is thus something quite understandable, as it includes a fair, responsible and sympathetic behaviour and life, which according to past habits does not suit many people. In this context, fear is certainly a positive category, as it motivates people to take their responsibilities more seriously.

Somehow parallel by accepting Decalogue Israelis also form the Ark of the Covenant, which is - according to travel - most important to them. God namely ordered Moses to save the "testimony, which I will give you" herein (Exodus 25, 16). Thus it includes basic documents and records governing the life of the community and connect it with each other and with God, and in a broader sense also all the memories and events that people communicate from one generation to generation in a form of oral tradition, customs, rituals and religious life. From a slightly different angle the Ark of the Covenant reveals content that represents the history and culture, national wealth and art, shared values and norms, and everything which constitutes identity or selfhood of specific a nation, in this case the one of Israel. Ark of the Covenant thus accompanies and deepens awareness of who we are, where we come from and where we are going and the awareness that we are not left only to ourselves and to uncontrolled circumstances through the journey of life, but have God with us.

The Bible describes the form of the Ark of the Covenant with unusual precision, behind which are hidden deep symbolic messages. Important - with our educational perspective actually decisive - place in Ark of the Covenant takes the mercy seat with the cherubs on the side, which, facing each other, expand above it (Genesis 25, 17-22). This mercy seat has a deep educational and therapeutic message that important events and experiences as an integral part of national identity belong within the Ark of the Covenant only if they are so processed to be "covered" by reconciliation. The true identity of the nation is thus formed only by conciliatory processed and purified testimonials. Only processed past becomes a place of communication between God and man, in which we fix our view into the future relaxed and with confidence, religion and Moses optimistic conscience.

In accordance with God's instructions Israelis now increasingly as people travel towards the promised land and see to it that the Ark of the Covenant is in their midst. The Bible uses an interesting dynamics and points out that when the Israelis neglect Ark of the Covenant, they lose the battles with the "enemies", but when they respect and observe it and communicate with God through it, they are strong enough and confident to overcome all that is harmful to life and community.

3. Conclusion

It is discovering the truth about the atrocities of totalitarianism that will probably force school authorities to open educational space where individuals - even at the cost of negative consequences - will disburden the pressure of totalitarianism and release the environment of fear so that educators can more freely open questions of life, which have been and still are taboo. Researchers of the recent history are in this context "Cherubs of Ark of the Covenant", which purify not only our past and symbols but prepare the space for a more democratic and relaxed and inclusive and more comprehensive education. The results of international studies that show that our students feel almost the most affected, although they do not spent most of the time in school, testify precisely of the fact that school environment needs to release (Musek Lešnik 2011). In the last White Paper even supporters of totalitarian continuity learn that students in countries with religious education in schools are better informed about many life issues than in our country (White Paper 2011, 43), but at the same time still cling to "the autonomy of school environment", and keep forgetting about the autonomy of individual. Nevertheless, it is worth mentioning that the teaching staff is changing and there are more and more teachers who know how to listen to students and also dare to say what they think, thus abolishing taboos and release habitat.

Literature:

Arendt, H. 1967. *The Origins of Totalitarism*. London: Allen & Unwin.

Bacher, K. D. 1980. Totalitarismus. In: Klose, Alfred & Mantl, Wolfgang & Zsifkovits. *Katholisches Soziallexikon*. Innsbruck-Wien-München-Graz-Köln: Tyrolia & Styria, 3066-3074.

Bela knjiga o vzgoji in izobraževanju v Republiki Sloveniji (White Paper). Ljubljana: Ministrstvo za šolstvo in šport.

Cohen, N. J. 1998. *Voices from Genesis: Guiding Us Through the Stages of Life*. Woodstock, Vermont: Jewish Lights Publishing.

Friedman, R. E. 2001. *Commentary on the Torah: With a new English Translation*. San Francisco: Harper Collins Publishers.

Franković, D. 1976. *Marksistično izobraževanje v šoli*. Ljubljana: Zavod SRS za šolstvo.

Gerjolj, S. 1997. *Ideologie und Bildung*. Giessen: Justus Liebig Universität Giessen.

Gerjolj, S. 2000. Za vzgojo brez sovražnikov. In: *Državljanski forum za humano šolo. Človek in kurikul*. Ljubljana: Družina, 83-93.

Jančar, D. 1995. *Egiptovski lonci mesa*. Ljubljana: Mihelač.

Janzen, J. G. 1997. *Exodus*. Louisville, Kentucky: Westminster John Knox Press.

Kerševan, M. 2005. Predmet verstva in etika (ve) v osnovni šoli: Pojasnila k predlogu učnega načrta. In: *Učni načrt: izbirni predmet Verstva in etika*. Ljubljana: Ministrstvo za šolstvo in šport, Zavod za šolstvo in šport, 49-64.

Kupffer, H. 1974. *Jugend und Herrschaft*. Heidelberg: Quelle & Meyer.

Musek Lešnik, K. 2011. *Siva knjiga o osnovni šoli v Republiki Sloveniji*. Brezovica pri Ljubljani: IPSOS.

Schwendter, R. 1981. *Theorie der Subkultur*. Frankfurt am Main: Syndikat.

Zakon o organizaciji in financiranju vzgoje in izobraževanja (Organization and Financing of Education Act). 1996. Ljubljana: Uradni list.

FEAR AND LOVE AS A BASIS OF ETHICAL LIFE: FROM ST. THOMAS AQUINAS TO ALBERT SCHWEITZER

Bojan Žalec, Ljubljana

1. Introduction: the aim and the main thesis of the paper

In this paper I argue for the thesis that the basis of ethical life is not only love but also fear, because love is impossible without fear. Love is a necessary condition for ethical life because love is a necessary condition for overcoming fear. Such overcoming is needed for us to be able to sacrifice ourselves, which is in turn necessary for genuine ethical life.

Yet, not any kind of love and fear provides such a basis, only special kind(s) of them. For this reason in this paper I present various kinds of fear and explain important distinctions and relations between them. I also deal with a comparative analysis of other relevant concepts, such as anxiety, love, respect, and reverence for life. I interpret some important principles and commands (for instance Biblical command "Honor everyone!").

The most important constituents of the frame of reference of this paper are the Bible and works of St. Thomas Aquinas and Albert Schweitzer.

2. Importance of fear

Why fear is important? Maybe the most important reason is quite obvious: certain fear is one of the main factors, if not the main, which hinders us to act ethically or according to our conscience. I said certain fear, because as we will see not every fear has such an effect. Quite to the contrary, certain kinds of fear have an opposite effect because they give us strength to be ethical.

3. Thomas Aquinas on fear: four kinds of fear

Thomas Aquinas in his *Summa Theologica* (hereafter Sth) distinguishes four kinds of fear (Sth II-II, q. 19, a. 2):

1. filial (i.e. fear for God),
2. initial,
3. servile,

4. worldly.

Bad and the worst kind of fear is worldly fear which is in total opposition to the spirit of gospel (Cessario 2007, 61). The best fear is filial fear.

We may say that for the totalitarian societies cultivation of servile fear is characteristic. This fear is fear from punishment.[1] On the other hand, as St. Augustine teaches us (*De diversis quaestionibus*, LXXXIII, 1. I, n. 23), fear is a son of love because it is always fear to lose what (or whom) we love. A sinner loves only things of this world (Cessario 2007, 61).

Filial fear is not servile fear because we don't act out of fear from the God's punishment (especially not in the sense of losing of terrestrial goods), but from fear not to hurt the one whom we love the most. Yet also in the case of filial fear we may say that it is true that its essence is love but we shall complement this love also with the rational reflection on that what God wants of us. Interpretations of God's will in the history - and in present days - are very different, even contradictory. Just remember crusades, Spanish inquisition, crimes, committed by "zealous" believers in the proximal or more distant past and surroundings and also in our country. In this respect the role of theology is very important as also of other humanities in general to which (modern) theology is unavoidably connected.[2]

4. Love and fear

There is no love without fear. If you are not afraid of some being being hurt then you don't really love this being. On the other hand fear is founded on love: we are always afraid for the things and beings which or who we love.[3] Hence the

1 This cultivation goes hand in hand with bigger or minor violation of reverence for life. The absence of reverence for life is contrary to the fifth commandment and to the Jesus` teaching which teaches love even towards our enemies and honoring of every individual, concrete person. As such this absence is contrary to awe from God which is marked by fear from hurting God.

2 The meaning of proper theological interpretation we can observe also in the case of (Slovene) philosophy, for instance in case of theological turn of Slavoj Žižek who argues for the interpretation of Christianity which supports his Marxist view and revolutionary directedness (see Žižek 2001; Žižek & Gunjević 2012).

3 Thomas Aquinas followed Augustine in this respect. See Sth II-II, q. 19, a. 6 (servile fear). Servile fear originates in the love towards ourselves and filial fear as the fear to insult the Father or to be separated from Him.

discussion whether the true ethical attitude or a proper faith is founded on love on one hand or rather on fear on the other hand is in a certain sense mistaken or meaningless because there is no love without fear and vice versa. I said mistaken or at least not specified enough since the discussion whether the fear from God is part of proper faith or not still makes sense.

At this point of our discussion we should stress the distinction between the fear from God and the fear for God. Most of us probably agree that the fear for God is certainly a necessary part of proper faith because such faith is impossible without love directed to God.

But is a proper faith possible without fear from God? In order to be able to properly consider this question we should distinguish between different kinds of fear, as Aquinas did. So for instance the worldly fear is not a part of proper faith, quite to the contrary, it is in contradiction with it.[4] The initial fear is imperfect filial fear so we don't need to deal extra with it at this moment. There remain the servile and the filial fear. It is clear that the filial fear is an essential part of proper faith. What about servile fear? The servile fear is a fear from punishment and therefore the servile fear from God is the servile fear from God's punishment. At this point it becomes crucial how we understand God's punishment and with what servile fear we deal. Servile fear can be worldly or filial: servile fear is worldly when we are afraid that we will lose some worldly goods (that we will be in pain, that our dearest will be hurt etc.). But servile fear, i.e. fear from punishment, is filial when we have fear from God's punishment in the sense that God will leave or abandon us, that he will renounce us, when we have fear from this renouncement itself (and not only because the consequences of this renouncement), in short, when we are afraid to lose God's love.

If we really love somebody than it is necessary present in us also the fear that we will be left without his or her love. For the person that really loves (in the sense of *caritas*) the fear, that the beloved being will be hurt, is on the first place. On the second place is fear to stay without beloved being. The acts which contribute to that that the first or the second fear becomes true, the loving person considers as his mistakes, and his characteristics that lead to this acts, as his imperfections, weaknesses or vices.

4 "Do not be afraid of those who kill the body but cannot kill the soul. Rather, be afraid of the One who can destroy both soul and body in hell" (Mt 10, 28).

5. Fear, inauthenticity and anxiety

The fear from inauthentic life is fear from that that we will not succeed in devoting our life to that what we really love or what we are really capable to love most. Fear from inauthentic life is therefore fear from unrealized or unenjoyed love. If such fear appears in an indeterminate form, as fear to which we can't ascribe a definite object, we are talking about anxiety. So much as we consider life which is realized in love as something positive, as much we can regard anxiety as something positive too because it warns us that our life is not authentic, i.e. that we don't enjoy or cultivate the love which is worth of our life. Therefore we should not – from the standpoint of ethics of love – renounce the ideal of authenticity and ethics of authenticity because striving to authentic life is actually striving to live in love and out of love. We can truly apprehend and experience our love as meaningful only if it is fulfilled with love. The consequences of life without love are very various: from restlessness to the various other serious problems and illnesses (psychical or mental and physical). The consequences of inauthentic life can be mitigated, but can't be cured without love, i.e. life in love and out of love.

Fear and anxiety are not identical. This is evident from the fact that sometimes they can be in opposition. So sometimes some people - because of fear - don't take the way which would bring them the realization of their potentials. And because of that reason they experience anxiety. But on the other hand also the too big fear from inauthentic life causes that we act immorally, contrary to our conscience which is exactly the way to miss an authentic life since nobody who doesn't live in accordance to his conscience can't live authentically.[5] It happens to us that we face a dilemma: either to act ethically, according to our conscience and hence to sacrifice our possibility to realize in greater measure some of our talents, or not. Regardless what we do in such situations, we must always care that we don't miss to hear the voice of our conscience not even to mention conscious ignorance or action contrary to it.

5 Here I can point out to Heidegger's definition of conscience from his work *Being and Time* as a call of concern (Ger. *Sorge*) for the authenticity of our being. Cf. Žalec 2010, 226-228. It is worth to mention here also that one of English words for being concerned (Slov. *zaskrbljenost*) is just anxiety.

6. Fear (from suffering), love and sacrifice

We can act contrary to our conscience also because of fear from suffering. To accept suffering or not to run away from it if that demands morality is indeed very difficult. Here we do not speak only about martyrdom (Sth II-II, q. 124) which is the highest form of fortitude and it cannot be forced (Pieper 2000), but also about smaller sacrifices. Ability to accept suffering and not to run away from it even if we have this possibility demands not only a mere intellectual recognition that running away from suffering would be immoral, but also a kind of counter-weight to fear which is on the same level as fear and it has the same driving force. The decisions which have their roots in deeper layers as the rational is cannot be ousted with a mere rational decision. Fear from suffering can be beaten only by an inspiration which is in fact love. In this sense the positions which demand sacrifice are a touchstone of every love.

Of course, every love is not good as it is not every fear. In the name of love there have been committed many crimes, sometimes on the basis of great self-sacrifice. Let me note for instance Islamic extremists who blow up themselves to successfully accomplish assassination. But in such examples there the question arises: Is that really love? Assassinators think that they will be rewarded after death. One of the tests which could show if there is really real love behind those actions is if they acted the same if they believed that there would be no award after dead. Real love is free, it is enough to love the beloved person, and it does not need any other incentive.

But we can state another example: "self-sacrifying" acting or life of atheistic extremists.[6] What does it base on? On love for what? One possible foundation is negative emotions of anger and hate. At some people these emotions pervade to such an extent that they are stronger that fear from suffering and self-destruction.

For real love, joy is typical, joy because that what we love exists; for hate there is typical a wish that hated thing did not exist. If hate refers to a person herself

6 For example members of extremist left terrorist groups like RAF namely Baader-Meinhof which devastated through West Europe especially in the late 70s of the 20th century (the so called German autumn in 1977). We put the word sacrificing in quotation marks to note the difference between them and religious self-sacrificing persons: atheistic terrorist do not sacrifice their lives intentionally, they go rarely or never to sure death, but they are prepared to risk a lot and to sacrifice quite a lot in their lives for their "thing".

and to some of her properties or acts, then hate means sadness because the hated person exists, and that can transform to a wish that that person did not exist. In this sense we must distinguish between anger and hate. Anger is of shorter duration and it is more (directly) of a reactive nature. But hate can be very long lasting and it does not have so direct reactive, but more reflective character.[7]

If we turn back to the question what can lead people to accept also suffering which they could avoid, we can see that the reason may be either love or negative emotions like hate or anger.

Love or hate can be directed towards ourselves or towards others. A person who neither loves nor hates is capable only of speculative "sacrifice" which is not real sacrifice but only a kind of patience or endurance so that later he/she will be better off. Real sacrifice is only for free.

But on the other hand the question arises: can sacrifice originate from bare hate? The answer is No! Hate as hate is capable only of destroying and not of sacrificing. For sacrificing in the real sense of the word there is always needed love towards something or somebody else than that who is sacrificing himself. There can be present both, love and hate in the person who is sacrificing himself; but the ground for his sacrifice is love, and never hate. "Sacrificing" which does not ground in love can be mostly opposing to what "the sacrificing person" hates, and not sacrificing in the true meaning of the word.

Today in ethics is more usual to speak about respect than about love. We talk about respecting of the human rights, about respecting of the human dignity, followers of the ethics of Albert Schweitzer talk about reverence for life as the basis for ethics … When we speak about values of the World Ethos we do not talk about love towards the golden rule, holiness of life and of the death or human dignity, but about respecting of them. But there the question arises: Is it respecting enough for sacrificing or do we need love? I think that the last is true. The reason is that the action potential of love is much bigger than that of respect. That is the reason why those situations where real sacrifice is needed, as we have already mentioned, are a touchstone of real love. If on the one hand we can say that we respect one person very much but we are not ready to sacrifice for her, we on the other hand cannot say that we love her and that we are not ready to sacrifice. For sacrifice respect is not enough, we need love. This is also the reason why some gratis, in

7 On the origins of hate in the modern social context cf. Juhant (2010, 16-19).

some senses even "stupid" actions are so important in love relations. Persons to whom they are dedicated know how to appreciate them since the actors prove their love with them. Let`s take an example of a boy who has a scrap with a stronger boy because of one girl and he is badly hurt, and at the same time he shows his body weakness and clumsiness at fighting. But what surprise. The girl rushes to the weak and hurt, not to the strong and smart. Why? Because the weak one has shown to her with his "stupid" action, with his capacity not to avoid suffering, that he loves her (more than anything else). The girl knows or feels that the ground of his sacrificing can only be love; and more "stupid" is the fighting of the weak with the strong rival, stronger is love. What the girl looks after is love and therefore she chooses the beaten one. If she searches for reputation and power, than she chooses the stronger one.

There are some other important differences between love and respect or their characteristics which are worth to mention: because power of love is bigger than the power of respect, self-respect cannot stop actions of love. It is also a fact that we can respect someone who we do not love. But if we follow Jesus, we must try not only to respect, but also to love everybody, including our enemies.

7. Love and Schweitzer`s reverence for life

To better enlighten the relation between love and reverence for life, let us first enumerate some important features of ethics of reverence for life[8] in Schweitzer`s sense of the word:

1. This is rational ethics since it has been developed as a result of a reflection on life. Everybody who really investigates depths of thought must get to it. With other words, Schweitzer claims that if you are really reasonable you must be ethical.[9]

   But if it is really so simple, why are there not more numerous real adherents of this ethics? Are people too stupid or irrational for it? Schweitzer answers (2010, loc. 548-553):

   "Actually, whenever love and devotion are glimpsed, reverence for love is not far off, since one grows from the other. But the truth of the matter is that

8 Compare also Globokar (2010) and Ošlaj (2010).

9 "What pleasure would feel Socrates because we said that" adds Schweitzer (2010, loc. 546-49).

thought fears such an ethic. What it wants is to impose regulations and order that can be duly systematized. This ethic is not subject to such bounding. Therefore, when modern thought considers such an ethic it fears it, and tries to discredit it, by calling it irrational. In this way its development has been long delayed."

2. This ethics is absolute therefore it cannot be put into rules.
3. This ethics is universal, it stands for all forms of life.
4. This ethics is ethics of solidarity and sympathy, today we would say empathy. According to Schweitzer, David Hume and Adam Smith were on the right path but they were stopped on their further penetration to ethical depths by an assumption (of their time) that ethics is only the relation of man to man.
5. Before that Schweitzer had shown also the difference with the ethics of the Eastern (Indian) philosophy which limited itself, in his opinion, only to passivity (that you do not destroy life), but it is not extended also to activity, as for example his ethics which tries to save, protect, develop and enlarge life.

What can we conclude from the above said about the nature of Schweitzer`s reverence for love regarding its relation to love? Schweitzer himself wrote:

"Such (thinking – n. B. Ž.) leads us to define ethics as devotion to life which tilt is reverence for life. Though the word reverence for life as very general maybe sounds somehow inanimate, we name with it something which does not let you go once it has penetrated into your thought. In it are given compassion, love and everything enthusiastic. Reverence for life tirelessly and lively works on the belief in which it has penetrated and it throws it in the restlessness of responsibility which never and nowhere ends. As a screw paving his way through water runs a ship so reverence for life promotes a man" (quoted from Ošlaj 2010).

From the above said is evident that Schweitzer (maybe partly unclear) notes a very close connection between love and reverence for life. But even more important seems to me that the active part of reverence for life is one of features which shows that his reverence for life has the love character. To positive, but passive stance of the eastern thought towards everything alive better fits the code reverence for life, while about Schweitzer`s reverence for life we can speak also as about love towards life, in German we may say not only *Ehrfurcht vor dem Leben*, but also *Ehrliebe vor dem Leben* in order to stress an important difference between both attitudes. Right because of this active part Schweitzer`s reverence for life is more similar to filial fear or to Biblical fear of the Lord which is indeed love for God, than to the eastern awe of life. To approve this claim I quote the following

Schweitzer`s words:"The ethics of reverence for life is the world-wide ethics of love. It is the ethics of Jesus" (Schweitzer 2010, loc. 386-390).

Further I alert that Schweitzer`s ethics is, just like ethics of agapic love, ethics of serving. It is not passive reverence which is important in first place, but rather serving. According to Schweitzer the way to achieve harmony with the universe is not knowing, but serving, because the universe or its creative force cannot be understood but you can only serve it. And by walking the path of serving, you may come in compliance with it. It seems that Schweitzer thought that you serve to the creative force of the universe if you act in accordance with the ethics of reverence for the universe. That is another feature which connects love and reverence for love: they both serve and so create (universal) harmony.

8. The Biblical commandment of universal respect

In the Bible we can find a direct commandment of respect:"Honor all people, love the brotherhood, fear God, honor the king" (1 Pt 2, 17.). As Miroslav Volf points out for Christians therefore universal respect is not only preferred, suggested or something like that, but it is a duty (Volf 2011, 12). But what is the content of this respect? 1 Peter speaks about respect of all as about respect of kings or rulers. In the first case we should respect people only because of their humanity, because they are people; and in the second case on the basis of their position (Volf 2011, 16). Here it is useful to mention Kant`s (1990) distinction between respect and love (Volf 2011, 16-17): we respect one person if we do not treat her only as a means for our aims, and we love her when her aims are our aims. Volf says that in the Christian sense we respect when we in the act of respecting coordinate Kant`s respect and love, but we do not equate them:" We do not treat people as a means to our own ends, and we do seek to further other people`s ability to pursue their own ends. Respect, then, is a mode of love" (Volf 2011, 17).

On what can be based respect for all? We cannot justify it with any human capacity (for instance reason or intellect) (Žalec 2010, 303, also 201; Volf 2011, 30). What is left? According to Volf God`s love towards people. This love is the base of our dignity (2011, 31). Christians can have God`s relationship to the people - whom he created - as a model. God creates because of love and therefore he loves all people whom he created. To truly love one being means to love him/her regardless his/her acts, capabilities etc. To love one being means to love him/her as such, to love this being itself. Taking into consideration the mentioned premise – the scope of God`s love determines the extension of Christian`s respect – we can conclude that we must respect all people.

9. Fear is an essential part of human and God`s life

There is no human life without fear, such life is not possible. But is it possible God`s life without fear? I think that in the case of Christian God that is not possible. If a person loves a man, that means a being who can decide for bad or evil, than this person must feel fear though this person is the Person, God. Then there is a fact that Jesus was afraid. Hans Urs von Balthasar (2011) wrote that Jesus could become a man only by recognizing also human fear.

10. Fear of the Lord as a condition for ethical life

Fear of the Lord springs out from love towards God. It is fear from non-ethical life by which we hurt a being who we love, that is God. God wants only that what is good and we can hurt him only by living non-ethically. All other things can be correctly assessed only if there is fear of the Lord in us, because fear of the Lord is fear from acting non-ethically, it is love for ethical acting. For all our relations and acting (also for such ethical things as is our love for our own children) holds true: if they are not illuminated by the light of ethics, which is love towards God (which is equivalent to the fear of the Lord), they will sooner or later stray from the ethical path. People did many non-ethical things because of their love towards their children. For man, there must be nothing before the love towards God if man wants to live ethically. That is the message of the Old testament story about Abraham and Isaac (1 Mz 22), and also of Jesus` words that fulfilling of God`s will must be above all, also above our relatives (Mr 3,31-35).

References

Aurelius Augustinus. *S. Aurelii Augustini opera omnia:* patrologiae latinae elenchus. Accessed at: http://www.augustinus.it/latino/ (20th August 2012).

Balthasar, H. U. von. 2011. *The Christian and Anxiety*. Edition Kindle.

Cessario, R. 2007. *Kreposti* (trans. by M. Fridl, orig. *The Examined Life*). Zagreb: Kršćanska sadašnjost.

Globokar, R. 2010. Reverence for life: the currency of Schweitzer's ethics. In: J. Juhant & B. Žalec (eds.), *Art of Life: Origins, Foundations and Perspectives*. Berlin: Lit, pp. 221-229.

Heidegger, M. 1997. *Bit in čas* (trans. by Tine Hribar *et al.*, orig. *Sein und Zeit*). Ljubljana: Slovenska matica.

Hribar, T. 2009. *Fenomenološki etos* (Phenomenological ethos). Ljubljana: ZRC, ZRC SAZU.

Juhant, J. 2010. Človek – ovira samemu sebi na poti dialoga (Man: an obstacle to himself on the way to dialgue). In: J. Juhant & B. Žalec (eds.), *Na poti k dialoški človeškosti: ovire človeškega komuniciranja* (On the way to dialogical humanity: the obstacles to human communication). Ljubljana: Teološka fakulteta, pp. 11-23.

Kant, I. 1990. *Die Metaphysik der Sitten*. Stuttgart: Reclam.

Küng, H. 2008. *Svetovni etos* (trans. by R. Štus, a collection of translations of the following texts: *Deklaration des Parlaments der Weltreligionen*; *Projekt Weltethos*; *Wozu Weltethos?*). Ljubljana: Društvo 2000.

Ošlaj, B. 2010. *Ethica, quo vadis? Albert Schweitzer in vprašanje renesanse etične kulture* (Ethics, quo vadis? Albert Schweitzer and the question of a renaissance of ethical culture). Ljubljana: Znanstvena založba Filozofske fakultete.

Pieper, J. 2000. *Srčnost in zmernost: štiri naravne kreposti III in IV* (orig. *Vom Sinn der Tapferkeit*; *Zucht und Mass*, trans. by J. Zupet). Ljubljana: Družina.

Sveto pismo Stare in Nove zaveze (the Bible). Slovenski standardni prevod iz izvirnih jezikov. Študijska izdaja. 2., pregledana izdaja, 2. natis. Svetopisemska družba Slovenije, Ljubljana 2001.

Schweitzer, A. 2010. *The Wisdom of Albert Schweitzer*. Edition Kindle.

S. Thomas Aquinatus. *Corpus thomisticum: S. Thomae de Aquino opera omnia*. Accessed at: http://www.corpusthomisticum.org/iopera.html (20th Decembre 2010).

St. Thomas Aquinas. 1948. *Summa Theologica*. Notre Dame: Christian Classics from Ave Maria Press, Inc.

Volf, M. 2011. "Honor everyone!": Christian faith and the culture of universal respect. In: M. Volf, C. Constantineanu, M. Macelaru in K. Šimič (eds.), *First the Kingdom of God: A* Festschrift *in Honor of Prof. Dr. Peter Kuzmič*. Osijek: Evanđeoski teološki fakultet, pp. 3-32.

Žalec, B. 2010. *Človek, morala in umetnost: uvod v filozofsko antropologijo in etiko* (Man, morality and art: introduction to philosophical anthropology and ethics). Ljubljana: Faculty of Theology.

Žižek, S. 2001. *On Belief*. London and New York, NY: Routledge.

Žižek, S. & Gunjević, B. 2012. *God in Pain: Inversions of Apocalypse*. Edition Kindle.

DO NOT BE AFRAID: COMMUNITY AS THE POWER TO ACCEPT FRAGILITY AND MORTALITY IN SEEKING THE COURAGE OF BEING

Anton Jamnik, Ljubljana

1. Postmodern responsibility, creating the new quality of relationships

Contradiction is the heart of morality. I am truly Myself in so far as I exist for the other. From the world of contrasts, conflicts and striving for his own interests, man is supposed to awake to this irrational contradiction, on which in fact the moral personality is founded. According to the postmodern point of view, the foundation of morality can only be found in our retreat from the safe comfort of rationalism, where everything is predefined, controlled, where there is no room for astonishment over the enthusiasm of existence. This point of view claims that morality is neither orderly nor logical. The only foundation of the postmodern morality is contradiction.

If we move towards the postmodern contradiction of existing for the Other, it means that at the same time we are moving away from the comfortable safety of being in the direction of the horrendous uncertainty of responsibility. It is much easier to be in the 'morality' which is determined with principles, where everything is pre-calculated, where certain criteria are set to help individuals fulfill their interests. Man feels safer, more certain, better in control of the situation. Or, according to Knud E. Løgstrup, Danish ethical philosopher, in our daily lives, we are not expected to care for another person's life; we are expected to care for things which are part of conventional complaisance. There are two consequences of an agreement: the narrowing of our trust to show care and our demand to take on the responsibility for the personal life of another human being. Agreements make our lives more comfortable. They safely lead the paths of our lives, as they predominantly follow man's selfishness and egoism. Such agreements are used as our means to keep ourselves far away (above everyone else) from each other, and for our own isolation. This is what always makes agreements attractive and absolutely charming (Løgstrup 1971, 19).

Nowadays, such agreements are particularly inviting, as they 'prescribe social norms of comparatively precise instructions on what to do and what to avoid. We are usually capable of adjusting to such instructions without considering another person, and least of all taking care of his or her life' (Løgstrup 1971, 58). From this point of view, it is easier to understand the criticism of postmodern ethics on the topic of liberalism, based on agreements, procedures and principles. It is the easier way, safer and more certain, but it leaves aside the individual, his personal initiative, it leaves aside personal relationships, our care for another as a person. The latter naturally exceeds any law. Such actions cannot be made into law; they are born in the depths of the human being, exceeding all principles, beyond any selfish agreements.

To act according to principles means that individual principles constantly explain what is right and what is wrong. Man always precisely knows where he stands, he knows his own standpoint, and whether he is right or wrong. Social norms, rules and agreements in all their explicit exteriority and pragmatism above all mean the guarantee of safety and calm of conscience. Everything works 'fantastic' in this sense. "Everybody does it" is a safe piece of criteria for me to adopt it in my personal life. One can also hear: "This is how things are done", which is great prevention and a way to calm our guilty conscience.

1.2. Closeness of another, the source of existential joy and overcoming fear

Postmodern perspective in its positive form means hope for discovering life's new wisdoms; the problem is, how a spiritually void human being, raised in passivity and indifference, can tread on a path which is demanding and calls for a strong and responsible person. This transition signifies the crisis of the modern man, difficulties, and yet, at the same time, hope for the future. Postmodern thought is well-aware of the fact that equivocation, mysteries and contrasts in life cannot simply be solved on the basis of various linguistic explanations; doubts which appear in one's life cannot be eliminated by laws; and the question of suffering cannot simply be answered by specific systems of thought. Postmodern thought no longer expects to find the all-embracing system, the perfect and the last life formula with no contrast, risk, danger or fault; it is suspicious towards anyone who makes such promises. Man has to accept his position and discover the beauty of being. He must not believe any Messianic promises of the human intellect – such is the challenging message of postmodern wisdom.

The central point of postmodernism is therefore a person, the key, the solid rock in the uncertainty of times in which we all live. For man, moral responsibility is the most personal and inalienable right and one of the most basic and obvious human rights. It cannot be deleted, shared, withdrawn, pledged or paid for in order to be kept safe. Moral responsibility is conditionless and endless, it represents itself in constant fear of not being exercised enough. Moral responsibility does not seek another justification for its existence, or another excuse for the lack thereof. Moral responsibility exists before any repeated insurance or demonstration or later apology or absolution. In the end, this is the exact opposite of the most typical modern endeavours which wanted to prove that before morality was even mentioned. In such rational, contractual approach, morality is of minor importance, the consequence of a positive, autonomous agreement. Postmodernism focuses on a person, or rather on its moral responsibility for the Other. Rationally, it acquires a new role and new contents from the postmodern point of view. The role of the reason is not negated. Rather, its different role is demonstrated, along with the limitations which need to be considered when we search for the ethical foundations of our existence.

2. To Be with the Other and for the Others as New Joy of Existence, Overcoming Fear

2.1. To be responsible for the Other instead of the fear-bearing liberalistic selfishness and individualism

Responsibility does not depend on various conditions or rational argumentation. It is not the effect of man's will or decision; it is not something which could (or could not) be accepted. In postmodern ethics, responsibility is incapability of not being responsible for the Other here and now. It is the key element of my moral ability. There are no univeral standards. I cannot observe common criteria and then make excuses for myself for having acted like everybody else, who 'go to bed peacefully' every night, for they have played by the rules and even benefited from their actions. Rules can be universal and legalised according to our obligations, but in terms of moral responsibility, it only exists when it is applied to an individual and this particular individual is its true executor. Obligations are supposed to make all humanity similar, and responsibility preserves human individuality. Morality of the moral subject cannot act as a rule, even though some people observe morality as a list of formal rules, norms, a certain form of socialisation or universalisation.

In the so called liberal morality, the common characteristic of accomplishing a certain goal in the most perfect possible way, of reciprocity and contractuality, is the selfishness of one's actions. The rational element which determines criteria for each of these forms is explicitly impersonal, thus making the actions explicitly impersonal as well. Selfishness based on a specific rational interest is their key criteria. On the other hand, postmodern perspective stresses the element of unselfishness in morality. Morality cannot be a list of impersonal rules, set as universal. Moral call should be entirely personal; it should appeal to my responsibility, within which I cannot refer to others and their actions. Their actions are completely irrelevant. Moral call is explicitly personal, directed at me and my personal responsibility. Rules could account for many things and explain what decisions need to be made, but as a moral personality I am always on my own, even though I am a social being. On the one hand, the way to be with others can be defined by exact rules, but on the other hand, the way 'to be for the Other' cannot. To be moral means to be dedicated to one's own freedom. I am moral before I think. We cannot think without ideas, criteria, or rules. But once the ideas, criteria and rules prevail the moral impetus steps out. When talking about the relationship between society and individual, we must be well aware that the heart of society always implies the solitude of the moral person. Society, its legislators and philosophers, who explain ethical principles, are faced with people who are moral without external moral requirements.

2.2. Ethics of closeness and love, the alternative to atomized individual

Postmodern ethics wishes to consider and strongly stress that 'the Other' is our neighbour. "Intersubjective relation is an asymmetrical relation. I am responsible for the Other without expecting a favour in return. Reciprocity is his own concern… I am responsible for full responsibility which is interested in everybody else and everything about them, even their responsibility. Therefore I am always responsible for one more thing than everybody else" (Levinas 1985, 98–99). For Levinas, the face of the Other (the neighbour) means perfect responsibility. It comes before any free consensus, any relation, any agreement. Modernist emancipation included a socialized human being as its ideal (individuals as lonely monads must interact for the purpose of their own interests), and it was determined by rationally defined rules in the form of laws.

By Levinas, the fact of moral responsibility is referred to as immediate closeness. It is not about the fusion of identities. Immediate closeness means the unique quality of an ethical situation which tends to forget about reciprocity, as love does not really expect reciprocity. Immediate closeness does not mean an extremely short distance, it does not mean exceeding or negating the distance, it means complete control of the distance. Such attentiveness, waiting for the Other, does not want to expropriate the Other from his own will or identity. This closeness is neither the distance overcome, nor it is required that it should be. Closeness is simply content with what it is, i.e. immediate closeness. This is exactly what it wishes to remain: the state of everlasting attentiveness, regardless of what happens. Responsibility is never perfect, never fulfilled, it never passes.

My task is to be aware of fulfilling the commandment of the Other, of being his voice. If I found a book of rules, which defined this relationship towards the Other, then my 'being for' would develop into something indirect, the distance between I and You would assume another role. There is no longer room for the innocence of immediate closeness, which cannot be condensed as a set of rules, possessed or put into frames. As soon as someone tries to do this, it no longer exists. The idea of command (commandment) is the only form where I can recognise a command; it is the only commandment on the basis of which I can function.

In terms of postmodern perspective, the Other can in a way become my own creation; to act according to the best possible tendencies means to steal the Other's identity. I have become his plenipotentiary. The Other, for whom I exist, is my own interpretation of silence, the provocative presence. This makes me aware of the fact that whatever I would like to see is not the same as what I want or what I need. My relationship towards the Other creates completely Other dimensions. It is about listening to the inaudible language of the other. If I am responsible, I will act in the best interest of the other. It is not about desiring to possess the other, to impose one's own interests, defining his own good or anything similar. In postmodernism, the responsibility for the Other, interpretation of his own good, still means functioning on His behalf. I am still a moral personality, unaffected by my own interests, who never considers his own price, who is willing to make a sacrifice (Wyschogorod 1992, 11–27). This is the original apory of moral closeness. If I do not act according to my own explanation, what is good for the Other, does that not make me guilty of sinless indetermination? If I act accordingly, how far can I go in trying to break his resistance, how much of his autonomy can I take (possess with a certain degree of awareness)? There is a thin line between care and possession, responsibility and appropriation of the Other.

2.3. From liberalistic anthropocentrism (fear) to the postmodern responsibility and love

Hans Jonas, ethical philosopher, who dedicated most of his work to the problem of the contrast between what morality should do and what it actually can do, given the conditions of the modern era, recognised the roots of the problem in the frightening and enormous powers of present-day technology (Jonas 1947, 7–8). He particularly stresses the fact that it is urgent to answer the question of responsibility, which has lost its place in modern morality. This will have a decisive effect on man's future actions.

Is there any real hope that we are close to discovering a proper solution? "The same movement which gave us powers to be regulated by norms destroyed the foundations on which these norms could be based. We are now shaking in the nakedness of nihilism, where approaching the omnipotence is connected with approaching our emptiness, which is bigger than our awareness for what should be done in the end" (Jonas 1974, 19). By announcing self-sufficiency of the human mind, liberalism threw away God's legitimacy to shape man's destiny, and at the same time the possibility for proper foundations of morality. The roots of the present-day moral powerlessness go even deeper. The modern movement crumbled into dust any foundations on which we could persuasively build moral commandments; it crumbled the morality itself: responsibility which reaches beyond contractual obligations; 'to be in favour of', which cannot be limited to 'to be in favour of anyone', can no longer be found; the stress on efficiency has reduced the importance of values. In modernism, there is less room for the irrational, non-utilitarian, unprofitable moral endeavours.

"The first obligation of any future ethics," according to Hans Jonas, "is to expose the long list of the consequences of the technological development" (Jonas 1984, 26). Ethics differs from today's practice, the usual marketing and short-term prospects. Ethics should work on the future, it should be faced with uncertainty. Jonas stresses that we need to present facts, which is a legitimate claim, but it is not sufficient. Postmodern ethics does not see solutions in important scientists who offer different analyses, scientific views, which try to be as certain as possible with a number of various theories. Facing the future does not mean to lean on a very strong theory; it means to act despite our uncertainty, or rather on the basis of our only certainty and objectivity, revealed in the Other. Moral standpoint means that man accepts this uncertainty and tries to build his life on it. From this point of view, Jonas' standpoint is not very strong, as he builds on the 'heuristic of fear' and complete uncertainty.

Postmodern ethics does not mean to oppose modern ethics and create a safe and secure system which would serve as the basis for man's actions. On the contrary, it is extremely critical of such attempts and tries to indicate the weakness and tragedy of the consequences such theories have led to. In postmodern ethics, the certainty of uncertainty should be the constant and never founded starting point of the moral action.

Postmodernism has very apparently attacked the attempts of modernism to constitute the ethical legislation on universal and solid foundations. Should therefore modernism be perceived as a step forward or a retreat? There is no single-minded answer to this question. The basic guidance of modern thought was man's emancipation. Modernism did not declare war against suffering and pain; the new thing was, and that was the fundamental difference, the instrumentalisation of suffering and pain. This presents a certain level, a step in the development, acquiring a certain role, as everything has been justified and instrumentalised. Such actions are based on rationalisation. Postmodernism tries to oppose such endeavours.

2.4. Closeness of the Other, the source of existential joy, overcoming fear

When discussing postmodern space and survival of the present-day society, it is important to place moral responsibility in the basic social structures. Postmodern ethics does not provide instructions for the future. It warns against the fact that 'neither morality can be founded on nor people's moral life can be ensured by intellectual calculations and legislation. Morality being in the hands of reason does not mean that the situation is resolved. Reason cannot help the moral self without robbing it of what constitutes his moral personality: the unfounded, the unprovable, not giving excuses, the uncalculated in the relationship to the Other; the fact that it exists for the Other, lives for the Other regardless of anything. Reason makes calculated decisions, and moral responsibility is beyond any consideration, beyond any logic which would prove the action sensible. Morality can be completely rationalised, but only for the price of self-negation and negation of others. Due to absolutisation of reason, the impoverished individual is no longer capable of following the challenges of the moral world. The final consequence of such prevalence of reason is called nihilism: we are talking about the moral nihilism which in its deepest foundations does not mean the negation of the mandatory laws and introduction of relativistic theories; it means the loss of ability to be moral' (Bauman 1994, 248).

When the liberalistic moral project is shaken and thus becomes questionable – when there is no general moral certainty based on the legislative morality, when man's striving for morality is no longer under the authority of ethical codes - man finds himself all alone, left to himself, faced with various moral dilemmas, without any clear criteria for the right choice. He is faced with unsolvable moral conflicts and with the burden of what it means to be moral. Modern man has the ability to be moral. From the postmodern perspective, this ability has not been 'amputated but only anaesthetised' throughout the long period of modernism, so it can be awakened and exercised. This ability is not very apparent, it is not demonstrated by laws, it does not need any external authority; this moral consciousness is very weak and powerless. The return of morality to the moral subject from various authorities, systems and legislations presents great hope for the present-day man.

Illusion of modernism (liberalism) was most of all in its belief that the entire disorder, dirt and hypocricy of the world would sooner or later be defeated by certain systematic rational regulations. Human spontaneity, man's intentions, goals, feelings, ideals, everything was replaced by the frequently insensible and selfish (pragmatic) mind. It is therefore not unusual that many people interpret the period of postmodernism as the renewed interest in spiritual and transcendental sphere (Jamnik 1998, 257-269), in order to return to the world other dimensions, which were disregarded and hidden during the period of modernism. Postmodernism wants to teach man about respect of the vagueness and equivocation, respect of human emotions; man is not supposed to premeditate and categorise his own actions.

Postmodern criticism with its stress on personal responsibility to be for the Other, on love, common good, the decentralised and expropriated subject, presents serious challenge for the liberal pragmatism and rational selfishness. Man is a creature of relations, not a lonely and selfish monad whose morality is in submitting to universal laws and rules of the herd. Morality needs to be repersonalised, as the source of the moral action is man as a rational and independent creature. Love and care of the Other overcome the distance which originates in monadological individualism, pragmatism and self-interest. The distance is replaced by closeness, personal relations and decentralism of the subject, born out of his free decision to exist for the Other and which leads to new joys of existence (Jamnik 1998, 289 – 336).

3. Accepting one's own fragility of existence and mortality as a way towards the courage of existence

3.1. Man is an immortal diamond

There are things in our lives which transcend the human mind, inexplicable pain, trials which are extremely difficult to face. In moments like these we are often left speechless, praying and asking God to be able to accept what has happened, so that our pain would lead to salvation, through prayer, through Christ's suffering and his complete sacrifice on the cross, according to Blessed John Paul II, the Pope who personally experienced the trials of Good Friday leading to the hope of Easter morning.

Hope impels us to what is beyond our sight. It is in a sense blind, our reaching out for more than we can imagine. Courage is clear-sighted. Bravely we dare to open our eyes and see how vulnerable we are and how much we are likely to get hurt on the way to happiness. Unless one dares to face one's fragility and mortality, then one will not be brave. But Christ shares with this poor, bare, forked animal his victory over death and all his glory, so that, as Hopkins wrote: 'This Jack, joke, poor potsherd, patch, matchwood, immortal diamond, is immortal diamond'. If we live with this courage then we shall not be silent and afraid, and the freedom and the joy of the infinite existence will break through in our lives from time to time (Radcliffe 2005, 88); we will feel in the core of our existence that despite our fragility and powerlessness we are immortal diamonds, born for the eternity, freedom and love.

3.2. Between experiencing the cross and the suffering and astonishment over our existence as a sign of God's unconditional creational goodness

At the crux of our faith is the resurrection and the cross, the image of an utterly vulnerable person, hurt unto death. But when Jesus is risen from the dead, the wounds are still there. In Luke's Gospel he says, "See my hands and feet, that it is I myself" (24.39). And in John's account of the resurrection, "Jesus came and stood among them and said to them 'Peace be with you.' When he had said this, he showed them his hands and his side" (20.19). When Thomas returns, all he demands is to see and touch the wounds of Jesus. The risen Christ is still wounded. His passion and death are not just left behind, as earlier stages in his story, as is our childhood when we become adult.

The third Preface to Easter tells us that Jesus is 'still our priest, our advocate who always pleads our cause. Christ is the victim who dies no more, the Lamb once slain who lives forever.' If the risen Lord did not still bear his wounds, then he would not have much to do with us now. The resurrection might promise us some future healing and eternal life, but it would leave us now alone in our present hurting. But because of Easter Day we already share in the victory. He still shares our wounds and we already share his victory of death. We too are now wounded and healed.

When a pilgrim first went to Peruvian Andes, he was surprised by the ubiquitous images of the crucified Christ, covered with blood. It seemed as if the faith of these indigenous people stopped prior to the resurrection and they were left only with images of defeat. But he learned that he was wrong. The cross is not meant to scare us, it is not a product of our imagination saying that 'we live in the valley of tears'. In the end, the pilgrim learns the opposite: "These crosses are signs of how the risen Christ is now sharing their crucifixion" (Radcliffe 2005, 74). The risen Christ with his wounds is now close to us in our pain, he is with us and for us, when we are torn between our suffering and mortality (our crucifixion) and longing for eternity (the risen Christ is hope for our eternity). He himself entered the darkest place of suffering and death of human existence, and thus in the power of the Easter mystery, our suffering and death are shone upon by the dawn of Easter morning.

Bibliography

Bauman, Zygmunt. 1994. *Postmodern Ethics*. London: Oxford University Press.

Jamnik, Anton. 1998. *Liberalizem in vprašanje etike*. Ljubljana: Nova revija.

Jonas, Hans. 1974. *Philosophical Essays: From Ancient Creed to Tehnological Man*. Englewood Cliffs: Prentice Hall.

Jonas, Hans. 1984. *The Imperative of Responsibility: In Search of Ethics for Tehnological Age*. Chicago: University of Chicago Press.

Levinas, Emmanuel. 1985. *Ethics and Infinity*. Pitsburg: Duquesne Universty Press.

Løgstrup, Knud Ejler. 1971. *The Ethical Demand*. Philadelphia: Fortress Press.

Radcliffe, Timothy. 2005. *What is the Point of Being a Christian*. London: Burns & Oates.

Wyschogrod, Edith. 1992. *Saints and Postmodernism*. Chicago and London: The University of Chicago Press.

FEAR AND COURAGE IN EXISTENTAL ANALYTIC AND IN RADICAL PHENOMENOLOGY

Robert Petkovšek, Ljubljana

"And there, ahead of them, went the star that they had seen at its rising, until it stopped over the place where the child was."

(Matthew 2:9)

Being and Life

Fear and courage express fundamental impetus of living beings to survive. In human life, fear and courage depend on man's capacity to use symbols, which raises him to the level of a spiritual being, aware of the uniqueness of his existence and its limits, of its freedom and its determinisms. In the context of human existence, fear is basically not only fear of a particular danger, but fear of nothingness, of the possibility not to be. Anxiety, as this fundamental disposition toward one's own non-being is called, opens human beings to the fundamental dilemma of existence, which is, according to Sartre (1952: 37), pure freedom.

In the paper, we will discuss the concepts of "fear" and "courage" (resoluteness in existential terms) in the context of two larger concepts "being" and "life" as developed in the Heidegger's existential analytic and Michel Henry's radical phenomenology. Contrary to the existential analytic, in which being and time are taken as the horizons of philosophical thought, Michel Henry prioritizes the concept of life as a fundamental one, because it enables us to understand the question of truth more radically than the concept of being. Henry insists on the real difference between being and life: each belongs to its own regime of truth. Truths of being do not reveal themselves immediately but in the world as an object to a subject. On the contrary, truths of life, which is pre-worldly phenomenon, reveal themselves immediately in the life to the life itself. Henry argues that being and life consist of different substances. Life cannot be described as being. "Life 'is' not," Henry affirms (1996: 74). So, how do the affirmations "I am" and "I live" differ from each other?

"I am" in existential analytic

Judgment "I am," "I exist," is the prime object of existential analytic. It reveals the specificity of the human being. "The substance of man is existence." (SZ: 212) And existence, as man's being is categorized in existential analytic, consists of freedom. On one hand, existence is limited and determined by facticity. On the other hand, it is free as far as it is projected toward the future. The human being is described as existence – *Dasein* in Heidegger's terms – because it essentially belongs to the future. In him, "Existence precedes essence" (Sartre, 1952: 24); or as stated by Heidegger, "*Dasein*'s 'essence' lies in *existence*" (SZ: 318). Accordingly, the human being constantly creates its own essence, its own identity; because of many possibilities, among which he can be choosing, in him potentiality prevails over actuality. "'Existence' means a potentiality-for-Being ‹Seinkönnen›." (SZ: 233) "… the Being of Dasein is essentially potentiality-for-Being, … it is Being-free for its ownmost possibilities, … it exists only in freedom for these possibilities …" (SZ: 312) Freedom and future – i.e. "potentiality-for-Being" – are then concepts to be explained from the concept of being, which, according to Heidegger, means "to be." "Higher than actuality stands *possibility*," affirms Heidegger (SZ: 38). Though determined by the past and the present, man is in himself free to choose among many possibilities offered by the future and to shape his own future.

The capacity to choose among possibilities is linked to human ability to use symbols, which represents specificity of the human being. Thanks to symbols, man rises over natural determinisms and creates his own culture and spirituality. Symbols enable him to grant meanings to natural phenomena, to interpret them and to deepen understanding of them. The capacity to interpret manifests human freedom. In the light of the perspectives opened by ever new interpretations, natural phenomena reveal themselves in ever new perspectives. In response, man develops corresponding attitudes that we call "Culture" or "Spirituality". This capacity enables man to rise into a cultural, personal being, who is no longer part of nature, though he lives within natural frames.

Transcending natural determinisms allows man to create idea of the whole. It is from the idea of the whole that the idea of the world derives. "World" is not a natural givenness; it is an intellectual schema, a symbol, which enables man to encompass at symbolic level all what is or could be naturally given. "World" means the horizon by which the totality of being is encompassed. On the borders of the world, man encounters non-being, nothingness, "Nothing of being," "Nothing of existence". For man, the experience of nothingness is the possibility that he may not be, i.e. that finitude is inherent to him. This is his profoundest, most inalienable experience.

This twofold existential experience – the experience of totality of being along with the experience of "nothing of being" (nothingness) – is as old as humankind. Greek mythology expressed it in dyadic terms "*chaos–kosmos*", Plato in terms "*chōra–idea*". Function of myths in archaic cultures was to structure human experience in a unite, harmonic world experience, which protected man from threatening annihilating power of *chaos* as experienced in the depths of the human existence. The mythological idea of *chaos* refers to the same question as the idea of "anxiety" in existential analytic. (Berger, 1967: 51; *Dictionnaire de spiritualité*: s.v. Mythe) In the medieval 'Rhineland mystics', which had a profound impact on Heidegger's thought, the question of non-being reappears under the concepts of *Abgrund* and *Ungrund,* which mean "absence of fundaments", "nonground" or "abyss". The experiences of nothingness and of anxiety are thus eternal themes that humanity faces.

Experience of non-being is mystical, and therefore uncategorizable. It is given on the borders of the world experience where the possibility of non-being occurs. Anxiety provoked by the experience of the possibility of non-being is not only a deeper degree of fear, but a fundamental ontological disposition, which confronts one to the possibility of one's proper non-being as this appears in the phenomena of death, nonsense, or damnation.

On the borders of his existence, man faces the possibility of non-being. This experience is given to him as affectedness (Ger. *Befindlichkeit*), i.e. through feelings and dispositions, over which he has no control. He simply feels affected by experience of non-being. Among affections, anxiety is the original one because it opens man to the fundamental existential question: "To be or not to be." As symbolic, spiritual, cultural being, man disposes of his own being; he decides about himself. Each moment of human existence results from man's decisions to continue to live, this is from his resoluteness. Namely, man is freedom, *solus ipse* (SZ: 188), and nobody decides but him. He is free because he himself chooses his *raison d'être*. Put differently, existence is groundless, a being without ground, *Abgrund, Ungrund.* There is no ground outside of him, to which man could transfer responsibility for his decisions. Consequently, the affirmation "I am" is expression of the drama played out in the depths of human existence between being and non-being.

There are two answers to this drama. The first is existential reduction, which leads one to authentic being, i.e. to totally embrace one's own being in its finitude and limitedness. (SZ: chap. 3) The other answer consists in fleeing from authentic being, i.e. in transferring one's responsibility to others. This results in inauthentic being, in anonymity, in hiding oneself behind others. For Heidegger, "world" is synonym for such inauthentic being in the culture of everydayness and its mediocrity, namely in collectivistic, anonymous culture. The world destroys authentic being. Its impact is negative because roles played by *Dasein* in the world alienate it from his authenticity. Looking for a shelter, peace or a home in the world, man indeed flees from his responsibility, from his authentic being, which originates in embracing his finitude, his groundlessness and his non-being.

Confrontation with possibility of non-being is experienced as anxiety. Experience of non-being is possible because, "Man infinitely transcends man." (Pascal, 2004: 36) Perspective opened by such a radical transcending enables man to be aware of his own finitude and death, of uncertainty and uncontrollability of being. "Existential reduction" is the awareness of one's own finitude as defined by Heidegger, which reveals the human being in its authenticity at the bottom of his existence. This was experience described by Sophocles, "There is much that is strange, but nothing that surpasses man in strangeness." (*Antigona*: 332–333; Heidegger, 1959: 86)

Existence, whose future is not predetermined, is free in itself; and the only certainty that it has about itself and its future is "That it is and has to be" (Ger. *Daß es ist und zu sein hat*) (SZ: 134). Existence is originally determined by "to be," by pure positivity of being, which is in itself menaced by non-being. Existence is the projection of being toward its own being and its own future, but this positivity can only be properly displayed while radically exposed to nothingness, to non-being. The "to be" of being is therefore without any "therefore," without any external, worldly reasons. It is in itself without a ground; it is groundless. Accordingly, existence is essentially affected by non-being, as experienced in anxiety and strangeness.

Freedom and existence coincide. Transcendence is their true nature; by constantly transcending themselves, they are indeed groundless and utopic yet this is the only way to discover pure future. Their "essence" consists in "to be", in the future, which is pure possibility. The future is not a result of logical necessity, but of decisions that one makes in freedom about one's future, with resoluteness (Ger. *Entschlossenheit*). Existence projects itself toward the future, thanks to the pure positivity of its own "to be." But this is not all; the future is to be chosen from among many possibilities, not all of which guarantee authentic being. Anxiety is thus the expression of one's responsibility for one's own future. In order for one to really embrace one's own being, one must face one's own finitude and death, i.e. the possibility of non-being. This is the only way for existence to preserve its authenticity and to avoid the inauthenticity of the world.

Anxiety paves the way for resoluteness, for courage. In as far as it originates in anxiety resoluteness lays foundation of an authentic future. Anxiety taken as a challenge displays the positivity of being, the "to be," which projects existence into its own, authentic future. Non-being, to which existence is basically exposed, is constantly transcended by new being. As opposed to non-being, to nothingness and to anxiety, the "to be" of existence manifests itself as projection toward the future, toward new being. The "to be" reveals the fundamental fact that existence is transcendence, which can be properly lived only as resoluteness, i.e. as courage. This interplay between the transcendence of being and the resoluteness/courage displays the true nature of both of them. Paul Tillich (1980: 2) states, "Courage can show us what being is, and being can show us what courage is." The ultimate answer to the question, "Why am I?" is, "I am because I am; simply, I am – without any reason, without any 'therefore.'" This is the meaning of the idea of groundlessness of being. Groundlessness is the "ground" of the existence. Existence *is* on itself, *by* itself, *from* itself. Existence itself *projects* its ever new being and its own future while embracing its own non-being, that is, its finitude. It is based in the groundlessness. New being jumps out of finitude, of non-being – groundlessly – as a pure positivity.

The connectedness of existence with freedom reveals its origin in the future. Freedom proceeds from the future, and so does existence. We only can freely decide on future, never on the past. Accordingly, existence is being renewed from the future and the possibilities that the future brings.

"I Live" in Michel Henry's Radical Phenomenology

At this stage, it is necessary to radicalize the question of what "to be" means. "To be" means to be called by the future. In this respect, we must discuss the nature of possibilities conveyed by the future. Future possibilities, which depend on the present situation, are relative to the present. The future, based on them, is but a "future present." On the contrary, the genuine future cannot depend on the present, the true future is not only "future present." The future as properly conceived is absolute, irreductible to the present. Only the absolute future assures true freedom and guarantees free choice.

From the present perspective, the absolute future cannot be conceived of as what is possible but as what is impossible; it cannot be anticipated. For only what is apprehended as impossible from the present perspective truly belongs to the future. Consequently, the question is, "What is the genuine future?" This is, according to John Caputo, the absolute future, which "is the future that is unforeseeable, that will take us by surprise, that will come like a thief in the night (I Thess. 5:2) and shatter the comfortable horizons of expectation that surround the present ... With the 'absolute' future we are pushed to the limits of the possible, fully extended, ... beyond our powers of disposition, pushed to the point where only the great passions of faith and love and hope will see us through." (2001: 7–8)

What is then the "absolute future," which brings something that has never entered into the mind of human beings? (10) To be precise, everything that *is* or *has been*, originates in the future. "The character of 'having been' arises, in a certain way, from the future." (SZ: 326) The future generates what is new. Even more, it generates the novelty itself. The impossible, which characterizes the absolute future, has nothing to do with what is possible in the perspective of the present. From the perspective of the present, the absolute future is impossible. It is not something new, but it is novelty itself, hitherto unpredictable. The absolute future, the impossible, and the novelty are incommensurable with what is possible and expectable from the present perspective. The absolute future breaks present representations. The future is genuine because it makes the impossible possible. Hence, it is worth being engaged, for because it reveals and brings true novelty. The suggestion made by Derrida and embraced by Caputo is to conceive of God as "Becoming possible of the impossible" (Caputo, 2001: 10). As pure transcendence, God must be defined as "*the* impossible." This is the message that Saint Irenaeus of Lyon gave, as he wrote that Jesus Christ "brought all novelty by bringing Himself ..." (*Against Heresies* IV, 34, 1) These words must certainly be understood in the light of Judeo-Christian messianic expectation of all novelty, which comes to meet human history as, "A new heaven and a new earth" (Revelation 21:1; Isaiah 65:17).

How does *the* impossible become possible? How does it enter into the world? In the world, everything can be explained by reasons. To the contrary, the impossible is impossible only in as far as it comes into being in the form, in which the impossible is not reduced to what is possible from the present perspective. The impossible, which comes into the world, cannot be reduced to any of the reasons given by the world. According to Christian belief, God did not enter into the world as a concept or as an idea, but in the person of Jesus Christ. God, who incarnated himself as a man, as pure novelty. Genuine, absolute future has its full meaning only if it opens itself as pure novelty, as what is impossible from the perspective of the present. Such is the form of the newborn life. Birth is an event, the impossible made possible, within the world, a pure novelty, something that cannot be reduced to any of reasons given by the world. For existence, the future is "to be," a reservoir of possibilities. But the possibility, which makes the future genuine, is the possibility of *the* impossible. This possibility of the impossible comes to meet us in the form of a newborn life, which is without any "therefore." It is not the repetition of previous life; it is absolute novelty. Natality is, "The miracle that saves the world, the realm of human affairs, from its normal, 'natural' ruin" (Arendt, 1958: 247). These words resume Henry's conception of the relationship between being and life. Newborn life comes to meet the world as a new story, as an aim in itself, which is groundless and impossible from the perspective of the present. The newborn is neither a simple continuation nor a repetition of the parents. He or she is a pure novelty. The genuine sense of the future, of the world, of the being lies in a newborn life.

With regard to their meanings, the affirmations "I am" and "I live" radically differ from each other. They differ because being and life originate in different matters.

What is characteristic of being? By coming into being, something enters into the world. By entering into the world, it appears. By appearing, it alienates from itself, and is given to be perceived and disposed of by others. Finally, in the world, everything is given up to nothingness. Being is indifferent to what comes into being. Being means appearing, and appearing betrays by letting things disappear. Things are appearing while disappearing. In other words, being abandons things, which come into being. Being is oriented toward the "to be," toward the future, which is, as stressed by Heidegger, finite. Sooner or later, every future slides into non-being. Being flows irreversibly in non-being, the future into the past. At the bottom of the power of being lies powerlessness.

And what is characteristic of life? Life, on the contrary, does not consist of the worldly substance that we call "being." "Life 'is' not," insists Henry (1996: 74). Life as it appears in the world is not the true life. Such as it is observed by biology are molecules and chemico-physical processes. But, this is not what the Christianity calls "life." In the Gospel perspective, life is not a worldly phenomenon. True life is experienced in the depths of human existence. There, one experiences one's own life, which reveals itself to itself by itself and through itself. Life does not need to enter into the world to reveal itself; it is pure interiority, a pure "in itself", which does not need to enter into the world and to be mediated by the light of being, in order to become visible to itself. Life reveals and gives itself to itself immediately. This is what Henry calls auto-revelation and auto-generation. Auto-revelation and auto-generation consist of the pre-worldly "phenomenological matter," which is "life". As such, life embraces itself absolutely; it does not abandon itself to nothingness. It is indestructible. It is reborn always again. It is not only "to be," but it is an absolute auto-affirmation. (73–77) In this respect, it absolutely differs from being and from world.

Conclusion

As compared to being, life contains the power to survive. It does not let itself sink into nothingness. It has an inexhaustible power to regenerate. It never dies in itself. If being is only to survive, "to be," which ultimately disappears into non-being, then life reveals itself in itself as an absolute, indestructible, pre-worldly power, which erupts into the world as impossible, in the form of a newborn life. In newborn life, something impossible happens within the possible, i.e. within the world. This is the only reasonable reason, a groundless reason, to say "yes" to the future. A newborn life is a total novelty worth being lived for. There is no deeper reason of courage and hope as it is. If non-being as manifested in anxiety and fears in the midst of our being, which hinders us to live life fully engaged, then newborn life brings courage and helps us embrace the absolute future, the impossible, which gives us hope that true novelty, which is beyond our past and present, is possible. To conclude with Hannah Arendt, "It is this faith and hope for the world that found perhaps its most glorious and most succinct expression in the few words with which the Gospels announced their 'glad tidings': 'A child has been born unto us.'" (1958: 247)

References

Arendt, H. 1958. *The Human Condition*. Chicago: University of Chicago Press.

Berger, P. L. 1967. *The Sacred Canopy*. Garden City, N.Y.: Doubleday.

Caputo, J. D. 2001. *On Religion*. London, New York: Routledge.

Dictionnaire de spiritualité: ascétique et mystique; doctrine et histoire. 1937–1995. Paris: Beauchesne.

Heidegger, M. 1959. *An Introduction to Metaphysics*. New Haven: Yale University Press.

– – – 1986. *Sein und Zeit*, 16th ed. Tübingen: Max Niemeyer. English translation by J. Macquarrie and E. Robinson, *Being and time*, Oxford: Blackwell, 1967.

Henry, M. 1996. *C'est moi la vérité : Pour une philosophie du christianisme*. Paris: Editions du Seuil. English translation by S. Emanuel, *I Am the Truth: Toward a Philosophy of Christianity*, Stanford: Stanford University Press, 2003.

Pascal, B. 2004. *Pensées*. Edited and translated by R. Ariew. Indianapolis: Hackett Pub. Co.
Sartre, J.-P. 1952. *L'existentialisme est un humanism.* Pariz: Nagel.
Tillich, P. 1980. *The courage to be.* New Haven: Yale University Press.

THE AGE OF TECHNOLOGY AND THE QUESTION OF FEAR

Branko Klun, Ljubljana

The modern age, which is closely linked to the new, modern conception of the scientific method, has been characterised by a positive attitude towards science and its technological achievements. However, the advent of atomic technology in the middle of 20th century, and its capability of destroying the whole planet, led to a reconsideration of technology's role. In fact, Hans Jonas writes that "the promises of technology turned into threats" (1984, 7). Today, the role of technology is perceived in a much more ambivalent way. A positive attitude towards technology still prevails, but at the same time there is also a growing awareness of man's need to (im)pose ethical limits on its development. Now, fear has begun to arise from the question of whether man still has control over technology, or if technology has started to dominate our lives.

Discussions about the role of technology usually oscillate between two extremes. The first is represented by a blind faith in technology which allows for no substantial doubts: technology ensures man's emancipation and expands his horizon of freedom and power. It has the means to improve itself and solve its own problems, if and when those problems represent a threat to man. The response to such threats is nothing other than more technology. The other extreme consists in the somewhat romantic belief that technology profoundly changes human life, and deprives it of its natural order, and that we should possibly avoid technology altogether. This belief is motivated by the illusion that we can step back from the technological world we live in and shape our life independently from it.

A philosophical consideration of technology should include an attempt to understand what technology essentially *is*; what its essence is. A reflection on the essence of this complex phenomenon will enable us to address both the question of what technology is and why we should have concerns with regard to technology. Perhaps the greatest danger of technology does not lie in its external threat of irreversibly damaging the conditions for life on Earth, but in its challenge to man's understanding of himself and his "inner" relationship with technology. While Hans Jonas emphasises the external threats of technology and the need of a new (form of) ethics, Martin Heidegger analyses how a technological *way of thinking*, which represents the true essence of technology, poses a much more profound threat and challenge to man.

1. The Heuristics of Fear

Hans Jonas was one of the first philosophers who recognised the growing importance of technology and the ethical challenges which stem from its overwhelming development. His work (1984a), *Das Prinzip Verantwortung* ("the principle of responsibility", translated in English as "The Imperative of Responsibility") with the subtitle "In Search of an Ethics for the Technological Age" (1984b) has become a classic reference in the field of philosophical reflection on technology. The title of the work alludes to "The Principle of Hope" (*Das Prinzip Hoffnung*) by Ernst Bloch (1959), who was at that time an influential philosopher with a strong affinity to Neomarxism. Bloch shares the Marxist utopian vision of the future and of the positive role technology plays in the process of man's liberation and emancipation. Jonas, who previously worked on a philosophical understanding of Gnosticism (Jonas 1954), and considers modern utopian thought to be a distant echo of that phenomenon, does not accept the paradigm of a utopian future ideal which induces an existential attitude of hope. The future is not an ideal state beyond the horizon of the present, and in a certain sense independent from it, but rather something which depends entirely on our present actions. For that reason hope cannot be a fundamental attitude toward the future, but a "principle" or "an imperative" of responsibility which takes into account the future implications of our present activities. It is precisely this that Jonas considers to be an epochal transformation of human activity – the range and impact of this activity has been radically changed by the development of technology. The actions of man in our technological civilisation reach far beyond the horizon of the present.

Traditionally, the consequences of human actions were limited in both the spatial and temporal sense. However, with modern technology man is capable of actions which are not locally limited, but affect the entire planet. These actions can damage nature to such an extent that it would be no longer possible to restore it to its initial state. The irreversible consequences of such actions force us to rethink the connection between ethics and temporality. Traditional concepts of ethics focus on the present, as the future is not considered to be something which can differ essentially from the present. However, with the power of technology the future of our planet can be changed irreversibly, and future generations will not have the same present as we do. Similarly, the status of nature has also undergone considerable changes. In the past nature was considered independent from man, and there was a clear separation between natural being (what is "born" – lat. "natus" as the etymological basis of "nature") and what came about as the result of human activity (that which is "artificial"). To a great extent the development of technology has served to blur this difference (Jonas (1984a, 52) already mentions genetic manipulation) and nature is now dominated by man. Jonas observes that for the first time in human history nature is experienced as fragile and vulnerable (1984a, 26). The combination of nature's vulnerability and our human capacity to inflict irreversible damage to it requires a new (form of) ethics and an extension of ethical reflection which goes beyond the horizon of traditional ethical issues.

Jonas suggests widening the ethical imperative by including two mutually dependent elements: the protection of nature and the future of mankind (1984a, 245). These two elements represent two pillars of the new ethics of responsibility (both towards nature and future generations). Jonas shows how the notion of responsibility receives a new signification in modern technological times. Traditionally, responsibility related to actions done in the past, but today it takes into account the future consequences of our actions. For this reason, the anticipation and prediction of consequences both take on a crucial importance within the new ethics of responsibility.

A reflection on the consequences which become possible by means of technological progress is, according to Jonas, closely connected with the notion of fear. For him, fear – similar to doubt in Cartesian philosophy – plays a methodological role. It is not fear in itself that has value, but rather its function in aiding us to search for the right decisions. Jonas speaks about the "heuristics of fear" (1984a, 392), where heuristics signifies a loose methodological framework for seeking a solution in situations where we cannot rely on a fixed and methodologically precise procedure. The future is far too complex to allow for its exact prediction, and we can only achieve an approximate anticipation of the consequences of our actions. The moment of fear accompanies our ethical reflections, contributing to their seriousness and thoroughness. Jonas further states that he does not have in mind that fear which dissuades us from action, but the fear which stimulates us to action, and essentially belongs to responsibility (1984a, 391). For this reason, in opposition to Bloch's principle of hope Jonas does not place the principle of fear, but rather the principle of responsibility.

But, does an ethically motivated fear sufficiently guarantee that man will restrain his egoism and limit the power he has been granted by means of technology (Juhant 2008, 27)? Especially in the field of genetics, does not our technological development of today actually reveal the fact that man knows no fear, in the sense of awe and reverence, and that there is no moral norm which will not be transgressed? In contrast to Jonas, Heidegger does not see the central problem of our technological civilisation in the (in)efficiency of ethical norms and imperatives, but in a connection between man and technology that is much deeper than we are prepared to recognise.

2. The essence of modern science and technology according to Heidegger

For Heidegger, the interpretation of technology as an external instrument in the hands of man hides rather than discloses its true essence. In order to better understand Heidegger's analysis of science and technology it is necessary to highlight some basic phenomenological presuppositions. One of them is the fact that it is impossible to speak about things in themselves. Everything that is, in some way or another, must be "given" ("presented") to human consciousness. As such, every thing is always bestowed with meaning; it is "meant" in one way or another. Even the presumed objectivity of the external world, which science swears by, cannot ignore the fact that man is the one who speaks of this objectivity and ascribes to it such a meaning. It is precisely because of the fact that everything is given to man through meaning that he is not only encircled by environment, but has a *world.* This world represents a nexus of significance; it is a world understood by man. This understanding is not purely subjective, but socially and historically constituted. Man's way of understanding the world is closely related to the way he understands himself, and how he lives his life.

This fundamental phenomenological situation, which is characterised by the correlation between the intentional openness of man and the world, can be explained through the difference between the intentional meaning of a thing in the world, and the shape of our intentional approach to it, which allows a thing to appear with a given meaning. In ancient Egypt the sun was long held to be the highest deity. The content sense of every phenomenon depends on a specific intentional relation which we take towards it. From the perspective of modern science, which interprets the sun as an astrophysical object made of hydrogen and helium, the mythical understanding of the ancient Egyptians is overthrown by scientific truth. But, modern science does not question its own intentionality, its own form of openness towards the world. This openness preconditions the constitution of meaning of every phenomenon; or of reality as such. The question concerning the essence of modern science thus becomes an inquiry into the specific nature of "scientific" intentionality.

In this light it is easier to understand why Heidegger rejects the prevalent opinion concerning modern science which states that it is more advanced and closer to truth than ancient science. The latter is characterised by an entirely different approach to nature and asks different questions. To assert that modern science is more progressive than its ancient counterpart would be like claiming that the literature of Shakespeare is more advanced than that of Aeschylus (Heidegger 1994b, 77). One of the main differences between modern and ancient science is the role played by mathematics. The mathematical treatment of natural phenomena relies on the specific "metaphysical" assumption that mathematics – as a pure formal science – represents the true fundamentals of our empirical reality. This is therefore a specific way of regarding nature as a mathematical "project". Heidegger writes about science as a "theory of reality" (1994a, 42), where the theory precisely signifies a way of regarding things/reality – a way which determines both what and in what way something can even appear to us. This specific "intentionality" determines in advance the horizon of meaning of any possible phenomenon. Contrary to the usual assumption, the scientific approach is in no way neutral. Heidegger writes that this way of looking at things ("theoria"), which is performed by science, is an "incredibly intrusive manipulation of reality (*eine unheimlich eingreifende Bearbeitung des Wirklichen*)" (1994a, 52).

In our usual understanding of science, we consider it to be the foundation of technology, since technological devices are designed on the basis of scientific discoveries. Heidegger, however, reverses this relationship and speaks about technology as a foundation for science. He interprets technology as a specific way of looking at things, and it is precisely this technical approach which lies at the core of modern science. "The basic position (*Grundstellung*) of the modern age is 'technical'. It is not technical because we had the existence of steam engines [...], but rather these things exist because this age is 'technical'" (1981, 17). An instrumental understanding of technology, which sees it only as an external aid, does not grasp the true dimension of this phenomenon. Technology determines the way modern science "discovers" nature in the first place. Heidegger uses the expression "disclosing" (*Entbergen*) of nature: the technological approach "discloses" nature in its own specific way and determines what the (scientific) truth is. However, this disclosure, which is considered self-evident and taken for granted, is only one possible way of approaching nature, and conceals other possibilities. The ancient Egyptians disclosed the world in their own way, and even the Greek concept of science (*episteme*) has its own manner of disclosing the world, and consequently its own "truth" (*aletheia* etymologically means "non-concealment"). Similarly, we cannot equate the Greek notion of *techne* (Latin *ars*, art, skill) with technique or technology in today's meaning. For Heidegger, there is not only a difference in degree (of advancement) between old craftsmanship and modern technology, but a difference in principle. He tries to illustrate this difference with two technological accomplishments: a bridge, and a hydroelectric dam on the river Rhine. At first glance we could speak about two different technical instruments in the service of man. But they typify two entirely different approaches to nature. The bridge connects the two river-sides and does not invade nature while, on the contrary, the hydro station "bricks in the Rhine in the electric power station" (1994a, 19). The bridge respects the river, while the hydro station transforms it into a stock, or supply (*Bestand*) of energy – energy which is to be removed from the river, stored, and disposed of.

This technical way of looking at things, which dominates modern science and the modern way of thinking, determines in advance how everything is understood. The basic meaning of everything becomes precisely that of stock (*Bestand*) which is at our disposal. Nature has been reduced to an object for man's domination and an aid in the widening of his power. The main problem of technology therefore does not lie in the technical products which pose threat to man (e.g. nuclear technology), but in the human attitude; in man's approach to disclosing nature. Heidegger asks if there is a common denominator which could summarise the essence of this approach, and he identifies it as "enframing" (*Gestell* – 1994a, 23). In this approach man manipulates (poses, composes, disposes, assembles, constructs etc – similar to German verbs connected with the verb "stellen") nature and dictates how a natural being is basically understood. "Enframing" represents the essence of man's attitude (way of disclosing) towards nature and it carries within itself an air of disrespect and even violence. It is not an attitude which would listen and respond to nature, but rather one that seeks to conquer and dominate it. Within this attitude nature is forced to answer the questions which are posed by man and which already "enframe" the extent of what the answers could possibly be. Herein lies the essence of scientific experiments. Through this form of disclosing, nature must become subordinated to man's power; to be at his disposal. But, in this disposing of nature, man does not ask himself if the world, which is disclosed in such a way, is still a world in which his life could achieve fulfilment. A question from the gospel comes to mind: "For what does it profit a man to gain the whole world and forfeit his soul [*psyche*, life]?" (Mark 8:36)

3. Fear and serenity

In today's world, Heidegger's analysis seems to be confirming its relevance, since the threat of technology does not lie primarily in the possibility of the physical destruction of human life, but rather in a specific spiritual "loss" within man, with regard to his self-understanding. The discovery of the human genome has brought about new possibilities for the technological domination of man's physical nature.

There is new hope of mastering those realms of our bodily existence (especially in the area of diseases) which, until now, have been beyond the reach of our knowledge and out of our control. But, these technological achievements also increase man's desire to influence his own life and the lives of others – especially those of his descendants – and with this aspiration of domination and control we risk losing the understanding of who and what man essentially is. Similarly to how modern science has brought about a "disenchantment" of the world (Max Weber), we now face "disenchantment" with respect to man: man has lost his "enchantment" and transcendent position with regard to the world, which had been part of the Enlightenment project for so long (e.g. in Kantian philosophy). This transcendent status granted man an inalienable dignity and had important ethical consequences. Contemporary biotechnology has reduced man to merely his physical reality, and now subjects him to the same manipulation as the rest of nature. How, in the light of today's stem cell research, is it possible not to think of the Heideggerian notion of "stock" (*Bestand*)? Namely that human beings are themselves becoming "stock" for other, more privileged humans.

Modern neuroscience would like to "disenchant" the remains of what is referred to as the spiritual dimension of man. Free will is being unmasked in its hidden determinism of brain processes, and human consciousness is becoming nothing but the emergence of complex physical activities in the brain. In this ambition to debunk the allegedly transcendent status of man, modern science, which is carried out by man and is supposed to serve him, is doing away with the humanity of human beings. Paradoxically, man is losing himself precisely by believing in an ultimate scientific explanation of and technological domination over his own being. The essence of man, however, lies in his openness and ability to question his own being; it lies in the impenetrable mystery of his questioning, which is at the same time the foundation of his freedom.

How can we face the threat of man of losing himself – a threat which in the obviousness of technological progress is not even perceived as such? The motive of fear, which plays such an important role in the ethics of Jonas, is losing its power and influence. Which attitude should we adopt towards the prevalence of technology, which dominates our world and does not allow us to naïvely step out of it? Heidegger suggests neither passive resignation nor utopian activism, because change cannot be brought about by the logic of power, especially since this logic represents the very core of the technological mentality. The first step we can take is to become aware of the situation we are in. This knowledge itself does not entail a solution, but it nevertheless lays the groundwork for a possible change in man's attitude (of understanding) towards the world and himself. According to Heidegger, the basic mood which should accompany man in our technological times is not fear, but a specific kind of "serenity" or "composure" (1959, 25). Heidegger takes this notion (*Gelassenheit*) from Meister Eckhart, and it implies an inversion of the will to power and domination: in serenity we do not want to dominate things, but we let them be (*seinlassen*). In a serene and calm (*gelassen*) attitude toward ourselves and nature we make it possible for us and nature to "be" in a more authentic way. With this new attitude we would not be refusing to acknowledge the threats of technology, but we also would not believe in naively overcoming it since, and this is inevitable, the world of technology influences our own way of thinking and living. An attitude of serene composure would enable us to take a few steps back from the technological world we live in – to be *in* the world of technology, but not to be *of* it.

References:

Bloch, Ernst. 1959. *Das Prinzip Hoffnung*. Frankfurt am Main: Suhrkamp.

Heidegger, Martin. 1959. *Gelassenheit*. Pfullingen: Neske.

Heidegger, Martin. 1981. *Grundbegriffe*. GA 51. Frankfurt am Main: Klostermann.

Heidegger, Martin. 1994a. *Vorträge und Aufsätze*. 7th edition. Stuttgart: Neske.

Heidegger, Martin. 1994b. *Holzwege*. 7th edition. Frankfurt am Main: Klostermann.

Jonas, Hans. 1954. *Gnosis und spätantiker Geist*. Göttingen: Vandenhoeck & Ruprecht.

Jonas, Hans. 1984a. *Das Prinzip Verantwortung. Versuch einer Ethik für die technologische Zivilisation*. Frankfurt am Main: Suhrkamp (Taschenbuch).

Jonas, Hans. 1984b. *The Imperative of Responsibility. In Search of an Ethics for the Technological Age*. Chicago: University of Chicago Press.

Juhant, Janez. 2008. Is a globalized ethics possible? In: J. Juhant & B. Žalec (eds). *Surviving Globalization. The Uneasy Gift of Interdependence*, 21-32. Münster: Lit.

BEYOND THE CULTURE OF FEAR: FEAR AND RESPONSIBILITY

Vojko Strahovnik, Ljubljana

A culture of fear can be defined as a state, within which it appears that fear pervades and encompasses all aspects of our lives and where the "fear perspective" is the dominant perspective through which we perceive the world around us. In the first part the paper focuses on some dimensions of such a culture of fear. In the second part it discusses the diminished responsibility as one of manifestations or symptoms of it. In the concluding part the discussion centres on causes for a culture of fear and suggests a possible way out of it towards the culture of trust and hope.

Culture of fear

The expression culture of fear itself can be met in many fields, from sociology, philosophy, and anthropology to theology, economics and political theory (Linke and Smith 2009; Moïsi 2007). What is central to most conceptions of culture of fear is that they place fear (at least in one of its forms or modifications) as the central perspective that we have on ourselves and the world around us. Our modern society is substantially determined with this perspective. Fear is not just an emotion or a response to dangers that we face, instead it became a cultural idiom, through which we regulate and express our felling of increasing uneasiness about our situation in the world (Furedi 2006, vii). In such a culture fear penetrates and regulates many important aspects of human lives.

In the culture of fear we never ran out of dangers; possibilities for fear are numerous in evermore emerging, from epidemics, pandemics, food additives, dangerous radiations, terrorist attacks, hidden serial killers among us, dangers that prey on us within the walls of our own homes, computer bugs and viruses, etc. We fear the future, we fear others, we fear loos, we fear loneliness and ageing, we fear taking risk and being at risk. Many of these dangers are framed in such a way that we cannot possibly avoid them; we can only passively anticipate them and fear them (cf. Furedi 2006, ix-x; Svendsen 2008, 26–27). The culture of fear emerges out of our feelings of endangerment and vulnerability, fear roots itself in our motives and intentions, gets reflected in our actions and provides pace for our daily routines (Bauman 2006, 3). It can become a powerful mean for manipulation and control. "Our culture of fear overestimates the dangers, that we are facing, and at the same time diminishes our ability to cope with these worries. When we find ourselves in trouble, we remain there as helpless individuals that cannot cope with it alone. This is one of the most characteristic features of our culture" (Furedi 2006, 20).

When we are speaking about the culture of fear biological dimension of fear is not crucial, it is the social dimension that is dominating. (Animals have fear but presumably no such thing as the culture of fear.) Within the culture of fear a central point is a belief that we and our community are faced with strong and devastating forces that endanger our very existence (Svendsen 2008, 19). Zygmunt Bauman labels such fear with terms like "second degree fear", "socially and culturally recycled fear" and "derivative fear" (Bauman 2006, 3).

Pervasiveness and experience of fear

Fear in the culture of fear is so pervasive that nobody is exempt from it; anybody could be affected disregarding her status (Svendsen 2008, 50). This atmosphere is additionally strengthen by the media dominated society that reaches towards its audiences by "selling them" stories presented in a way as that they can be related to their lives and relevant for everybody. "Catastrophic scenarios" range from ones that threaten whole humanity (asteroids collisions, global pandemics, climate change) to ones that are more individualized and target individuals with the relevant set of characteristics (terrorist attacks, rare fatal diseases, plane crashes).

An illustration of such a state and the mechanism involved is offered by the TV shows, book guides and internet articles on what must we fear in our own homes, and when we look at them more closely we can see that things such as a rug, laser printer, baby feeding bottles, hair shampoos and – paradoxically – even fire-safe coatings in electrical appliances made it on such list of most dangerous things (Conger 2012; rarely things such as guns, alcohol or unhealthy food make it on such list). What this illustrates is a completely skewed and distorted view on danger and the world around us. The main message of such media consumer society is that we should be afraid for our safety, wellbeing and even existence since dangers prey on us on each step that we take; dangers that might have not even be known to us till now (Furedi 2006, 23–50). Nobody is safe. Particular dangers and risks are so numerous that they must almost compete for our attention. That is why Bauman points out that the consumerist economy is dependent on the creation of new and new consumers, and that the best consumers for health ailments and security equipments are scared consumers. In such a climate fear always recycles itself with profit (Bauman 2006, 7; 53).

In a world of widespread and ever-present dangers that we represent as almost wicked and unworthy of trust, the fear is contagious (Bar-Tal 2001, 608); it can become a socially conditioned habit, which in turn increases the grip of the culture of fear. In such culture fear represent an integrative (and maybe even identification) factor that connects us together (Svendsen 2008, 19), being the basis of the frame through which we make sense of our experience; we perceive that we live in a particularly dangerous era, that challenges humanity with numerous dangers and possible catastrophes (Furedi 2006, 19–20).

All this get supplemented by the fact that our feeling of fear is less and less related with our own experiences of e.g. dangerous situations or their consequences (Svendsen 2008, 20). "The growing divergence of our sensibility of fear from our direct daily routine indicates that we are not talking about simply an emotional response to our experience. What is at issue is a more general cultural perspective on how we make sense of our lives" (Furedi 2006, x). There is a clear gap between the probability of dangers and our representation of those dangers. "The most technologically equipped generation in human history is the generation most haunted by feelings of insecurity and helplessness. [...] We – at least in the developed countries – 'live undoubtedly in some of the most secure societies that ever existed, and yet contrary to the 'objective evidence' we – the most cosseted and pampered people of all – fell more threatened, insecure and frightened, more inclined to panic, and more passionate about everything related to security and safety than the people of most other societies on record ..." (Bauman 2006, 101).

Fear migrates from one area to the other, from one danger to the other, regardless of the fact that there is no logical explanation behind that. It seems that fear somehow floats in the space among us, representing a foundation for hesitation, uncertainty and anxiety, since its indeterminateness and persistence end in expectation of the most horrible outcome. Furedi (2006, 4–9) therefore claims that dealing with uncertainty through the prism of fears points to a kind of "crisis of causality", that arises out of our disbelief in humanity. The culture of fear (especially our responses and policies) therefore does not bind us into a community, but breaks us apart on individuals; responses to such culturally conditioned fear are becoming more and more private and personal in character.

Liquid fear

Bauman (2006, 8) speaks about "liquid fear", which is perpetual and continuous, a constant companion of our lives that we cannot dismiss. This feature of fear can be illustrated by our understanding of disease, which transformed from a time-limited condition that occurs and also ends to a never ending companion of health and a constant threat that calls for our attention. Caring for our health is becoming a never-ending battle against the disease (Svendsen 2008, 61). Thus death itself is transformed into something liquid and continuous, and fear of death into something that accompanies our lives and greatly determines our choices (Bauman 2006, 41). A liquid fear is therefore a kind of permanent anxiety and tension, which raises our perception of the world as full of dangers that may afflict us every moment. "Fear is at its most fearsome when it is diffuse, scattered, unclear, unattached, unanchored, free floating, with no clear address or cause; when it haunts us with no visible rhyme or reason, when the menace we should be afraid of can be glimpsed everywhere but is nowhere to be seen" (Bauman 2006, 2). The world is unpredictable and uncertain, and liquid fear comes from our sense of helplessness and uncertainty and our being unable to control it. The liquid fear is very much like a gas, since it penetrates all aspects of our lives, which in turn also means that there is no place where you can escape from it.

Fear and risk

It seems that what contributes to the emergence and continuation of a culture of fear is that merely potential (and often very distant) threats or dangers become perceived by us as real and omnipresent (Svendsen 2008, 17). In part, this tendency can be explained through the transformation of dangers into risks. That there is something dangerous means that it presents a threat to us or to something that we value. (Already Aristotle identified fear and danger in a way that "the things we fear are terrible things, and these are, to speak without qualification, evils" (1115a).) Risks, on the other hand, require no such imminent endangerment. Risk is not something that would be only possible occasionally, but is very real at all times. In the culture of fear risks are in fact all around us, forcing us to be conservative and taking a precautionary stance. At the same time we often cannot put a limit to what represent "a still acceptable risk", because we want it to be completely eliminated. Fighting against such risks becomes an endless task (Svendsen 2008, 72). The assumptions of risk are no longer connected with real dangers, "with the real problems facing humanity. It is sustained by a worldview that is deeply pessimistic about the prospects for the future" (Furedi 2006, xi).

From a different perspective we can observe that within the culture of fear taking risk is received almost exclusively as a negative phenomenon and is not something that someone (can) choose; instead we are always only subjects of risks against our will. Risk perspective pushes us into a sort of passive state. Risks are associated with the victims of these risks, that are part of the so-called risk groups, and are with such mechanisms seemingly relieved of a large part of the responsibility (Svendsen 2008: 51–52). Risks are often inflated. An event, which is by itself extremely rare and uncharacteristic, becomes within such logic something "common" that could happen daily, so we must take all measure to avoid it. To risk from the perspective of a culture of fear means to act extremely irresponsibly. To avoid any risk represent the most sensible and responsible behaviour, which is why in some cases expressions of fear and anxiety are often evaluated quite positively, instead of being critically assessed as irrational panic. At times such culture of fear is used as a perfectly legitimate medium of raising public awareness about truly significant threats, but can also be seen as a sign of decline of the importance of authority and reason, exacerbating uncertainty (Furedi 2006, xvii; 9–10; 53–57). Since risks that are extremely rare are often the most interesting for the media, those risks become inflated and only tenuously connected with real threats. Risks are no longer necessarily linked to what we do or to what dangers we are exposed to. They are more and more becoming about whom we are (Furedi 2006, 5).

Fear and diminished responsibility

How is the culture of fear connected with responsibility? The thesis of this paper is that it can significantly decrease our sense of responsibility, our awareness of it. *Prima facie* this sounds pretty strange. Why would a state of fear, which should raise our alertness and attentiveness, preparing us for a response to a certain danger, on the other hand diminish our sense of responsibility? The answer lies in some of the above sketched characteristics of a culture of fear.

We can take responsibility to encompass the following three basic elements:

1) *normative significance*: the agent is faced with a normatively significant choice;
2) *judgmental capacity*: the agent has an adequate understanding and access to evidence required for making the judgments about his options;
3) *relevant control*: the agent has the relevant control required for choosing between options (List and Pettit 2011, 155).

One can understand responsibility objectively and evaluate those three aspects from a third-person perspective. But since our thesis is that the culture of fear somehow diminishes our sense for responsibility we will thus understand the three elements from the subjective perspective of an agent deeply submerged in the culture of fear. Does the culture of fear affect our perception of the normative significance of our choices (and we must add, significantly beyond what is still acceptable since we do not want to end up with too loose conditions for responsibility)? As a consequence of distorted view on the world around us we see some choices as important and others as not important. Perspective of fear also results in an inadequate understanding of options open to us. As we saw the media society does not direct us to the relevant evidence. Even worse, we can form a completely distorted image of what is happening. The control condition is most affected by the culture of fear. When we transform dangers into risks we remain linked to those fears, somehow frozen in the preset. Fear limits the choices that we see as open (Svendsen 2008, 43). That is why many see hope as an antipode of fear, since hope is essentially related to the future. The perspective of risks also pushes us into a passive stance. Risks are linked to their "victims" as members of risk groups. We can observe the "creation of the diminished subject" and "separation of responsibility and accountability from action" (Furedi 2006, 72). We do not even see something as a proper choice to make.

This then combined with growing individualisation and social exclusion, extended sense of vulnerability (together with the identity of the victim) and diminishing trust in institutions, leads to diminishing of autonomy and sense of responsibility in the culture of fear.[1]

One of such areas of diminished responsibility is the field of intimate relationships. In relation to them the culture of fear warns us against "too much love" and "toxic partners" (as popular titles of books and shows suggest). An individual therefore faces a distorted range of options, where first of all not entering into any close relationship is seen as the best option, and second to that entering the relationship only shallowly. His or her judgemental capacity is thus consequently seriously affected, since no proper understanding of the choice can be formed. And lastly, the control is represented as nearly impossible, since no matter how well you know your partner, he or she can at any time surprise you with a completely unexpected characteristics or response that will deeply hurt you (Svendsen 2008, 95). Therefore an objectively responsible behaviour of forming stable intimate

1 Bauman (2006, 87) locates among the causes of such diminishing of responsibility the modern bureaucratic rationality, which has replaced "responsibility for" with "responsibility to (e.g. our superiors)" and thus paved a way towards diminishing of our moral sensitivity and skills of moral judgment.

relationships, within which a person can grow and develop, overcoming fears and healing wounds from the past, becomes subjectively the most irresponsible thing to do.

Fear thus precludes trust and hope. We give up the idea to take our destiny into our own hands and we prefer to be subjects to risks and risk factors. Fukuyama (1995, 26) defines trust as the expectation that establishes in the community on the basis of predictable, fair and cooperative behaviour of other members of the community, based on shared norms. Culture of fear prevents the creation of such trust and this empty gap is filled by cynicism, apathy and mistrust (Furedi 2006, 136; Žalec 2011; Thomas 1979). Trust is a choice and not something that is given to us. Strategic trust assumes a certain risk, but this risk may not be negative or passive but a step to dare to trust someone. In addition to strategic trust an extremely important factor is moral trust that arises out of our duty to treat other people as worthy of our trust (Žalec 2011).

Conclusion

Fear implies hope and valuation of something, that we fear for and is important to us. This might be one of the key points for exiting the culture of fear. The culture of fear can also be seen as the result of utopian thinking, which sees society and the world as completely manageable and predictable, and out of which every danger can be eliminated. Future in such a culture is no longer a promise but a threat. Bauman (2006) thus argues that in culture of fear progress is not possible anymore; all we can do is perhaps to avoid making things even worse. A shift towards a culture of hope thus does not mean the abolition of the very fear that is connected to what is close and important to us (Svendsen 2008, 128–131).

The way out of the culture of fear is for us to begin finding out what is our common in our fears, their origins and their logic; but at the same time that we are poorly equipped with tools and skills for that (Bauman 2006, 21; 68). A particularly large obstacle is "individualistic nature" of our struggle against dangers and risks, since such an individualized society precludes solidarity and community responses that would have been more effective (Juhant 2011, 66). Culture of fear knows only occasional episodes of "oriented solidarity", which quickly decomposes itself into anonymous individuals, who pursue their own interests and cannot create solidarity, security and trust. Bauman also illustrates this situation with the transition from partnership to networks; while the first still stands for strong social ties, which can reduce anxiety, modern social networks of acquaintances follow the logic that we have to minimize our risks in a way to disperse and weaken links as much as possible. We need to replace fear and uncertainty with self-esteem and confidence, which we must cultivate in spite of vivid presence of culture of fear on the basis of "duty of hope", and only then we could find the right balance between security and freedom (Bauman 2006, 174–6). The detrimental effects of culture of fear must be replaced by culture of trust and hope. A culture of fear is not about the survival of mankind, "but the survival of our faith in humanity" (Furedi 2006, xii). We must do all that we can to strengthen this faith.

References

Aristotle. 1999. *Nicomachean Ethics* (trans. W. D. Ross). Kitchener: Batoche Books.

Bar-Tal, D. 2001. Why Does Fear Override Hope in Societies Engulfed by Intractable Conflict, as It Does in the Israeli Society? *Political Psychology*, 22(3): 601–627.

Bauman, Z. 2006. *Liquid Fear.* Cambridge: Polity Press.

Conger, C. 2012. Dangerous Everyday Things in Your Home. Available at: http://home.howstuffworks.com/home-improvement/household-safety/tips/dangerous-home-products.htm (accessed 10th March 2012).

Fukuyama, F. 1995. *Trust: The Social Virtues and the Creation of Prosperity*. New York: Free Press.

Furedi, F. 2006. *Culture of Fear Revisited.* London: Continuum.

Juhant, J. 2011. *Za človeka gre* [*A Human at the Centre*]. Ljubljana: Teološka fakulteta.

Linke, U. and Smith, D. T. 2009. *Cultures of Fear. A Critical Reader*. New York: Pluto Press.

List, C. and Pettit, P. 2011. *Group Agency. The Possibility, Design, and Status of Corporate Agents*. Oxford: Oxford University Press.

Moïsi, D. 2007. The Clash of Emotions: Fear, Humiliation, Hope, and the New World Order. *Foreign Affairs*, 86 (1): 8–12.

Sprengelmeyer, R. et al. 1999. Knowing No Fear. *Biological Sciences*, 226 (1437): 2451–2456.

Svendsen, L. 2008. *A Philosophy of Fear.* London: Reaction Books.

Thomas, D. O. 1979: The Duty to Trust. *Proceedings of the Aristotelian Society*, 79: 89–101.

Žalec, Bojan. 2011. Nezaupanje kot ključni dejavnik slabega delovanja skupnosti, organizacij in družbe [The Lack of Trust as a Key Factor of Poor Functioning of Communities, Organizations and Society]. *Dignitas*, 51/52: 351–373.

COGNITIVE SCIENCE AND BIOETHICS

THE ENEMY WITHIN: BRAIN CIRCUITS OF FEAR

Zvezdan Pirtošek, Ljubljana

Fear & brain

Fear can be defined as a negative emotional state triggered by the presence of a potentially harmful stimulus. Some scientists and clinicians distinguish fear from anxiety that can be defined as a negative emotional state in which the threat is not present but anticipated. Fear is a full-body experience. While the brain initiates, controls and coordinates the process, the entire body gets activated to create the fear response.

The central brain structure related to fear is amygdala (Feinstein et al., 2011), an almond-shaped structure in the depth of the brain; its name comes from the Greek word for "almond". Amygdala is essential for the ability to feel certain emotions and to perceive them in other people – particularly those that are very important for our survival, like fear. Direct stimulation of the amygdala in patients undergoing brain surgery, triggers a strong feeling of imminent danger and fear. Patients who have had their amygdala destroyed as the result of a stroke or tumor recognized the facial expressions of every emotion except fear.

The amygdala has rich connections with other brain structures:

1. Thalamus and sensory cortex: these structures, important in the analysis of the incoming stimuli, send to amygdala many sensory inputs to inform it of potential threats.
2. Hypothalamus: when informed by the amygdala that the stimulus is dangerous, hypothalamus triggers the fight or flight response of the whole body.
3. Hippocampus: explicit memories are stored and retrieved in this old part of the brain close to the amygdala which gives to some memories an intensive emotional flavour.
4. Medial prefrontal cortex is – after the initial rapid, emotional and automatic reaction to fear - involved in the final rational act of finding solutions to the threat. It also enables the stimulus that triggered a conditioned fear to

gradually become extinct. Connections between the amygdala and the medial prefrontal cortex allow a certain conscious control over our anxiety, but on the other hand, create anxiety by anticipation and imagining the future.

The process that will eventually result in the feeling of fear starts with a stressful, dangerous, fearful stimulus. In the brain, all stimuli enter the central brain sensory structure, the thalamus, which cannot categorize a stimulus as dangerous or not dangerous. However, since a threat is not excluded on thalamic level, thalamus activates (at least) two circuits for further stimulus processing: (1) a short lower circuit to the amygdala and (2) a long higher circuit to sensory cortices.

(1) The lower circuit is switched on in a 'quick and dirty' way before we even know exactly what it is all about, prepared for a threat, taking no chance and initiating the fear response 'just in case'. In a fraction of a second, amygdala decodes emotions and determines possible threat, stores fear memories and activates the hypothalamus. The hypothalamus will initiate the fight or flight response via two systems: (a) the sympathetic nervous system and the (b) adrenal-cortical bloodstream system. The sympathetic nervous system regulates glands and smooth muscles and tells the adrenal medulla to release adrenaline and noradrenalin ('stress hormones') from the adrenal medulla into the bloodstream. Simultaneously, the hypothalamus activates the pituitary-adrenal-cortical hormonal axis.

These systems trigger a chain of adaptive bodily responses, many of which have been noted and described already at the beginning of the last century (Cannon, 1929): epinephrine will act on platelets to enhance clotting and on the liver to release glucose, increased heart rate will speed blood circulation, changes in circulation will deliver less blood to the skin and gut, and more to the muscles, pupils will dilate to take in as much light as possible, hyperventilation will raise oxygen import and carbon dioxide export, sweating will cool the body and make it slippery.

(2) The higher circuit is slower but more precise and cautious in interpretation of events. It leads from the thalamus to the sensory cortices, which interpret sensory data for meaning. If meaning is ambiguous sensory cortex activates hippocampus to establish the context and to compare it with the past memories. If hippocampus concludes that there is no danger, it will send a message to the amygdala to shut off the fight-or-flight response in the hypothalamus.

The thalamus activates lower and higher circuits simultaneously. Therefore, both circuits eventually reach the hypothalamus, the ancient survival centre that triggers the fight-or-flight response. This is why, on a lonely forest path, we feel a moment or two of terror, a moment that can mean the difference between life and death – before, hopefully, calming down realizing that the brown patch on our left is not a bear but a shadow of a rocky stone.

Mechanisms of fear

There are two ways of establishing circuitries of fear in the brain: one is innate, created by evolution, the other by conditioning.

Fear through evolution

Fear – as one of the basic emotions - plays a central part in our lives. This was recognized already by Darwin (1872) who in his book on emotions emphasized the communicational aspects of fear. Fear is largely viewed as a response pattern shaped by natural selection to increase our ability to cope with threats (Plutchik and Kellerman 1980). Those who feared the right things survived and passed on their genes thus selecting the trait of fear and the response to it as beneficial.

If fear is defined in a very broad operational term as the ability to detect and respond to certain kinds of danger, and to learn about things associated with threat, then fear is pretty universal among animals from the times of early animal forms. Fear as an emotion and as an amygdala related trait occurred much later and has been constantly shaped by evolution. All mammals, birds and even reptiles have amygdalae, or similar fear related brain structures. Most of these structures – the limbic circuits – developed in 'Age of Reptiles' (Mesozoic time, 250 million years ago to about 65 million years ago) when early mammals appeared (Ohman et al., 2001). Fears emerging in this time are common to all mammals (e.g. fear of heights). Later, in the Age of Mammals (Cenozoic time, 65 million years to present), when the extinction of many groups allowed mammals to greatly diversify, fears common to all simians emerged (e.g. fear of snakes). In Stone Age (3.4 million years, and ended between 4500 BC and 2000 BC) fears unique to humans developed such as fear of mice and insects, possibly because of their association with infectious diseases ((Bracha, 2006). Fear stimuli are pre-wired in the brain because they have been perennially dangerous to our ancestors. While fear has been long thought to be hereditary, excellent experiments in behavioral research conducted by Professor Susan Mineka in the eighties showed that in monkey the "snakes fear" wiring was always there, but until it was externally triggered it never manifested (Mineka et al., 1980).

If fear is heavily related to the automatic, instinctive and emotional limbic systems, in particular to the amygdala, anxiety reflects to a large extent activities of the prefrontal structures, e.g. an ability to anticipate, to worry, to plan and to experience uncertainty. While this capacity may also be present in some animals, it is especially well developed in humans. We are beings who regret the past and who anxiously await, imagine and ruminate future and our place in it, be it the future of the next Sunday or the future of millennia to come. But in humans, too, the distinction between fear and anxiety remains unclear. Fear can be defined as a negative emotional state triggered by the presence of a potentially harmful stimulus and anxiety as a negative emotional state in which the threat is not present but anticipated.

An interesting phenomenon in humans is that fear or general anxiety are not always aversive and can even be pleasurable (a well known thrill of horror movies). This may be a form of play behavior, an enjoyable game that will teach young mammals the game of real life when time comes (Smith 1982).

Both general and more specific responses emerged in evolution. General threats arouse general anxiety-inducing vigilance, physiological arousal, and planning for defense. Specific threats elicit specific patterns of behavioral defense (Edmunds 1974; Janzen 1981). Extreme life danger may evoke freezing; threats from dominant male arouse submission; a predator suddenly occurring behind the bush provokes flight or fight. Interestingly, there exists another defense system which emerged much earlier in evolution - the immune response, which also have a capacity for both a general response (lymphocyte activation, inflammation, fever, pain, malaise) and for specific responses (immunoglobulins to bacterial infection, interferon to viral invasion, eosinophils to parasites, and natural killer cells to cancer).

However, defenses – be it emotions as fear or immune responses - are helpful only when appropriate to the degree and to the type of threat. If a defense is deficient, excessive, or inappropriate in form, it may cause harm and disable the organism. Fear and anxiety can be excessive (as in general anxiety or panic disorder), deficient (hypophobia), or in response to a stimulus that is not dangerous (simple/specific phobias).

Fear through conditioning

Conditioning is another way of establishing circuitries of fear in the brain: this mechanism was demonstrated in 1920 by a famous American psychologist John Watson in what was probably not the finest moment of psychology. Using Pavlovian (classical) conditioning Watson and Rayner (1920) paired a neutral (conditioned) stimulus (white rat) with an aversive (unconditioned - terrifyingly loud noise) stimulus and taught little boy Albert (who initially had no fear of rats) to cry and to move away in frenzy whenever he saw not only a rat but also other furry animals or a Santa Claus mask with a white beard.

Several studies demonstrated amygdala as the location of fear memories formed by conditioning. The amygdala connects the two events, forming an unconscious memory of the association (white mouse and terrifying noise, sound of airplane and New York Twin Towers tragedy). When the neutral stimulus (view of a white mouse, the sound of an airplane above Manhattan) later occurs, amygdala automatically elicits fear as it did during conditioning. Another brain region, the ventromedial prefrontal cortex (vmPFC), has been shown to have an ability to overcome fears by inhibiting conditioned fear after extinction training (the conditioned stimulus is repeatedly presented without the unconditioned stimulus). Some individuals are quick to learn to fear a stimulus but have a difficult time getting rid of that fear. The ability to deal with fears depends on individual differences and balance between the amygdala and the vmPFC function. Environmental factors may trigger fear more easily in people who have a genetic predisposition to the illness. In research focused on genes that influence human behaviour, some of the studied genes show a statistical association with specific anxiety disorders (Howatta and Barlow 2008).

Once fear mechanisms and circuitries have been established they can trigger protection in four behavioural ways (Marks 1987): (1) escape (flight) or avoidance, (2) aggressive defense, (3) freezing/immobility and (4) submission/appeasement.

21St century – the age of anxiety?

Humans in the 21st century experience fear/anxiety as they did centuries and millennia ago but fear inducing stimuli and the phenomenology of the experience have dramatically changed.

Eliminating almost all of the immediate threats (there are no snakes or freezing cold in modern cities) from our environment, we are safer and more comfortable than human beings or any other species have been any time throughout our evolutionary journey. Life expectancy in Slovenia and in Europe has doubled during the twentieth century. We are better able to cure and control diseases than any other civilization in history. But, the emergence of the prefrontal cortex has dramatically shaped the nature of our fears. Today, many fear states are conditioned and brought on by things, signposts or signals that symbolize harm rather than things that are truly harmful. On the other hand, again with the emergence of the prefrontal lobe, we now tend constantly to anticipate disasters that are never – or unlikely - going to happen (the rapist lurking behind the wall, a pandemic of a previously unknown virus), or events that will or may happen in a distant future (death of a family member, heart disease, global warming, asteroid destroying the planet).

Such anxieties shape our culture and our everyday life. Headlines besiege our minds with sad and dramatic news. The 9/11 attacks still shape the US attitudes to politics and philosophy. Films, books, songs besiege our minds with fearsome predictions. While so many fears are in the air, many of them unfounded, old fears do persist, although sometimes reshaped and changed (e.g. the fear of death, which, although present throughout the history, may have been different in the 15th and in the 21st century) and new ones are emerging (fears of losing one's uniquely human essence e.g. with genetic manipulations).

Fears of losing the uniquely human core have also deep moral connotations. Many of them are related to the power of mind and brain. The more we learn about the human brain, the more we will have the ability to change it with new drugs and new technologies that can already eliminate pain and disease and repair damaged brains thus benefiting millions of patients. But these same drugs and technologies may be used also to improve brain functions in healthy young people, reducing the need for sleep, increasing memory capacity, controlling emotional and autonomic impulses, improving attention span, increasing creativity, manipulating needs and preventing aging. Many of new drugs are just around the corner and many of powerful technologies are already being developed. Stem cell treatments are reality. Brain implants are used to monitor brain activity during epileptic seizures but also to observe volunteers' brains as they talk, think and, when connected to a computer, to move limbs, or decode words of our silent thinking. Electronic devices are being connected to people's brains that allow blind people to see and deaf people to hear. While these devices are used to replace lost senses, any sounds and images could be sent into the brain of a healthy person. With a surgical procedure known as deep brain stimulation (DBS) we can send pulses of electricity to a tiny, carefully targeted area to treat Parkinson's disease or obsessive-compulsive disorder - but this method can also change how a healthy person feels, thinks, and moves. The same can be achieved without touching neurons directly, merely by creating a rapidly pulsing magnetic field outside the brain (transcranial magnetic stimulation).

Fear of death is probably universal. Man has the ability to foresee the end of the life, the inevitability of his own death (so beautifully described in the oldest of the epic texts, the Gilgamesh) as well as an ability to quieten these existential fears. While the first ability is related to the emergent prefrontal cortex, the second may be, according to Persinger (1987), related to the activity of the brain circuits converging on the temporal lobe. This activity may be documented as micro seizures or temporal lobe transients and, according to Persinger should not be considered a disease or an abnormality. It is largely associated with the spiritual (mystical, God) experience. Spiritual experiences include also near-death experiences, out-of-body experiences, deep experiences of death and re-birth in some forms of deep-feeling psychotherapies, entheogen (LSD, ibogaine, etc.) therapy, participation in shamanic rituals and past-lives experiences and conditions of extreme physiological stress. Persinger hypothesizes that after such experiences the person is often convinced that their spiritual self is separate from their body and it will survive the death of their body; religious activity and belief in God reinforce this belief. With advanced age we may become more fearful of death, but neuronal and vascular changes in the temporal lobe may allow us to have spiritual experiences more readily. However, particularly prone to having mystical experiences are patients with temporal lobe epilepsy (among others Julius Caesar, Saint Paul, Mohammed, Pascal, Newton, Dostoevsky, van Gogh, Handel). Persinger lists three physiological properties of the temporal lobe as predisposing factors to temporal lobe transients as the source of fear alleviating and spiritual experiences: (i) post-stimulation electrical instability, an intrinsic feature of deep structures, allowing the creation of transient neuronal firing patterns that do not necessarily represent concurrent sensory input; (ii) temporal lobes are prone to vascular anomalies such as transient vasospasms; (iii) exceptional plasticity of temporal lobe neuronal and glial populations. However, microseizures could also be learned as responses to existential trauma and to fear of death potently modifying human behavior.

Persinger's work has met with much skepticism and criticism. One of his major weaknesses is that it has focused on the temporal lobe and ignored data supporting a more complete model of brain activity. Also, there are no convincing imaging studies to support the hypotheses regarding specific brain areas. In the only published attempt to independently replicate Persinger's results authors were unable to reproduce Persinger's effects. They criticized Persinger for improper blinding and idiosyncratic methodology with no physiologically plausible mechanism by which weak magnetic fields generated by his device could penetrate the cranium and influence neurons within. Gendle & McGrath (2012) found no significant difference in emotional state whether the device was on or off. Some argued that suggestibility of the participants could explain his results [Granquist et al., 2005] and criticized his theory as being based on flawed and outdated literature on religiosity in patients with temporal lobe epilepsy (Aaen-Stockdale, 2012).

Conclusion

Human beings seem to be less able to counteract ancient as well as new fears. Mental disorders are increasing. As majority of these exaggerated new anxieties emerge from the most recent part of the brain, the prefrontal cortex, the most reasonable way of counteracting them would be to modulate prefrontal activities: to set up new (or old) values, to cultivate a balance between emotions and reason, the ancient and the new brain.

References

Aaen-Stockdale, C. 2012. Neuroscience for the Soul, *The Psychologist* 25 (7), 520-523.

Bracha, H. S. 2006. Human brain evolution and the "Neuroevolutionary Time-depth Principle": Implications for the Reclassification of fear-circuitry-related traits in DSM-V and for studying resilience to warzone-related posttraumatic stress disorder, *Progress in Neuro-Psychopharmacology and Biological Psychiatry* 30 (5), 827–853.

Cannon, W.B. 1929. *Bodily Changes in Pain. Hunger, Fear, and Rage: Researches into the Function of Emotional Excitement.* New York: Harper and Row.

Darwin, C. R. 1872. *The expression of the emotions in man and animals.* London: John Murray.

Edmunds, M. 1974. *Defense in Animals.* Harlow, Essex, England.

Feinstein, J. S., Adolphs, R., Damasio, A., Tranel, D. 2011. The human amygdala and the induction and experience of fear, *Curr Biol.* 21(1), 34-8.

Gendle, M. H. and McGrath, M.G. 2012. Can the 8-coil shakti alter subjective emotional experience? A randomized, placebo-controlled study, *Perceptual and Motor Skills* 114 (1), 217–235.

Granqvist, P., Fredrikson, M., Unge, P., Hagenfeldt, A., Valind, S., Larhammar, D., Larsson, M. 2005. Sensed presence and mystical experiences are predicted by suggestibility, not by the application of transcranial weak complex magnetic fields, *Neuroscience Letters* 379 (1), 1–6.

Hovatta I., Barlow C. 2008. Molecular genetics of anxiety in mice and men, *Ann Med* 40(2), 92-109.

Janzen, D. H. 1981. Evolutionary physiology of personal defense. In *Physiological Ecology: An Evolutionary Approach to Resource Use*, C.R. Townsend and P. Calow (Eds). Oxford: Blackwell, 145-164.

Marks, I. M. 1987. *Fears, Phobias, and Rituals.* New York: Oxford University Press.

Mineka, S., Keir, R., Price, V. 1980. Fear of snakes in wild- and laboratory-reared rhesus monkeys (Macaca mulatta), *Animal Learning and Behavior* 8, 653-663.

Öhman, A., Flykt, A., Esteves, F. 2001. Emotion drives attention: Detecting the snake in the grass, *Journal of Experimental Psychology: General* 131, 466-478.

Persinger, M. 1987. *Neuropsychological bases of God beliefs.* Westport: Praeger.

Plutchik, R. and Kellerman, H. 1980. *Theories of Emotion.* Orlando: Academic Press, Inc.

Smith, P. K. 1982. Does play matter? The functional and evolutionary aspects of animal and human play, *Behavioral & Brain Sciences* 5: 139-184.

Watson, J. B. and Rayner, R. 1920. Conditioned emotional reactions, *Journal of Experimental Psychology* 3(1), 1–14.

PRECAUTION AND FEAR-MONGERING IN BIOETHICS

Veronika Szánto, Budapest

Modern bioethics is critical reflection on the technological developments achieved in the life sciences and applied in a range of fields from medicine through cybernetics to food industry. As such, bioethics is a discipline that called to existence by a certain kind of fear, a fear induced by biotechnology. In what follows I investigate the ways in which bioethics responds and treats this fear. I will not dwell much on the *nature* of the fear induced by biotechnology, because that would demand a separate enquiry in itself. I only remark briefly that this fear in a large part arises from a sense of transgression of nature's laws conceived to be sacrosanct and fixed once and for all, whether inherent in nature or established by God. In this regard, fears enticed by biotechnology are by no means novel; this idea of transgression has been an issue throughout human history. Manipulation of genes, cells and bodies are perceived as genuinely unnatural acts. As various authors already pointed out, the "un-natural is not simply non-natural" but represents "the other side of the norm."[1] The idea of unnaturalness has the power to solicit emotional responses of which the most powerful one is horror.[2] Bioethical debates thus almost always take place in an emotionally heated environment to say the least. As Robert Edwards, pioneer of *in vitro* fertilization, thus not an impartial participant of one such debate said, his work was perceived in the public imagination as "dramatically doom-lit and gaudily coloured by science-fiction fantasies and visions – fantasies of horror and disaster, and visions of white-coated, heartless men, breeding and rearing embryos in the laboratory to bring forth Frankenstein genetic monsters."[3]

I would like to focus on two questions. First, how *does* bioethics deal with this fear surrounding biotechnology? In answering this question I will immediately reflect on my second question, that is, how *should* bioethics deal with this fear? When I refer to bioethics dealing with fear in one way or another, I not necessarily

1 Helmut Puff, cited by Philip, 2011a: 3.
2 Ibid.
3 Cited in by Ball, 2011b http://newhumanist.org.uk/2474/playing-god-by-philip-ball-januaryfebruary-2011, accessed 1 Dec 2012.

refer to professional bioethicists but to every participant who assumes the moral authority to influence public opinion and policy in these topics. So what I am going to say applies to scientists, NGO activists, medical doctors, politicians and professional bioethicists alike. However, when I speak about how bioethics *should* handle fear, my concern is professional bioethics as such. Of course, it would be great if all participants enumerated above conformed to certain norms of conduct, but it does not seem to make much sense to prescribe norms for concerned citizens regarding how they should manage their deepest anxieties. Bioethicists carry more responsibility in this regard and I believe it is their task to show good examples and influence other participants in an indirect manner.

It is also important to bear in mind that although in many cases fear first is expressed by the public and then professionals try to deal with it in a response, there are occasions where the roles are different. Just think of the case of the recombinant DNA techniques back in the 1970s, where concerns were voiced by the scientist themselves, among them James D. Watson and David Baltimore, and they effectively self-imposed research restrictions.[4]

In principle, bioethics can deal with fear in three ways, although in practice they seldom appear in a distinct and pure form. First it can *alleviate* fear, second it can *acknowledge* fear, and third it can use or *utilize* fear. What I mean by *alleviation* is quite straightforward. It may be the case that a fear appears to be unfounded. In this case bioethics justifiably tries to dispel fear by pointing out false premises or contrary evidence, etc. A case in point is the controversy over the alleged potential of certain childhood vaccines to cause autism and other severe disabilities.[5] What is not justifiable is to sweep worries off the table as unscientific and thus illegitimate. Unfortunately, as we all know, this happens regularly. Sir Peter Medawar the eminent biologist who opposed the restraints on recombinant DNA technique found that the fear of scientists is irrational while that of the laymen stems from "their deep-seated scientific illiteracy."[6] I do not wish to deny that scientific illiteracy exists and is a problem, neither do I claim that each opinion is equally respectable. However, scientific-minded people should appreciate that

4 The most famous document of this affair was the Berg-letter published in 1974 in the prestigious journals *Science* and *Nature*. Berg et al., 1974: 175.

5 On vaccine denialism, see Specter, 2009: especially Chapter 2.

6 Turney, 1998: 4.

the grounds on which a technology can be justifiably rejected are not necessarily scientific.

By *acknowledging* a fear I do not the mean the reinforcement of it but the realization that the dangers are real, concerns are justified and precautionary measures are to be taken. This does not necessarily involve the complete prohibition of the procedure or technology in question, it might result in the introduction of regulatory procedures and safety checks. This approach is discernible in most bioethical controversies. In the ideal case ethical considerations lead to wise precautionary measures thereby preventing misuse and potential harm. Of course, in real life consensus is seldom reached, but still precaution is regarded as an effective means in bioethics which is capable of taking potential risks and dangers into consideration and to respond to them, in a sensible and proportionate way. Usually bioethical debates revolve around the degree of regulation needed. As I mentioned, the ways in which bioethics treats fear often overlap. Indeed, the acknowledgement of the legitimacy of a threat and its subsequent reasonable management leads to the alleviation of the fear. However, fear is rarely dispelled entirely, but it is not the primary purpose of bioethics either.

However, as in the case of alleviation, there are cases where acknowledging a fear by professional bioethicist can be harmful. I mean cases where precaution is due indeed but the fear motivating it should not be simply acknowledged. Let me clarify this point with an example. In a number of countries, controversies about genetic information led to legislation that effectively protects genetic data and regulates access to them.[7] Virtually nobody questions the validity of such regulations. But during the public discourse bioethicists, and scientists as well, tacitly accepted the concept that genetic information is a kind of code with the help of which all the secrets of a person can potentially be revealed. While arguing for the need for privacy, bioethicists inadvertently reinforced genetic determinism, the notion that our complete personality and future fate is inscribed in our genomes. Why else should we protect our genetic data so much? Bioethicists failed to point out that only a small minority of the genes can be held responsible for a single trait or illness, and a slightly greater minority indicates proclivity to some medical condition. Of course, we still have good reasons to protect genetic information.

7 On the problem of genetic privacy and potential threats posed by DNA fingerprinting, Hubbard and Ward, 1993: 145 ff.

Its suitability for personal identification or the fact that genetic data carry a great deal of information not only about the persons concerned but about their relatives as well, are good reasons for the protection of genetic data. Genetic determinism and reductionism have been great obstacles in the last two decades that hindered proper understanding of how the genes work and only recently, with the emergence of epigenetics can be seen some progression in this regard. Regarding our present purpose, the lesson from this is that bioethicists should not accept fears without critique, not even when precaution is really desirable. Bioethics can inadvertently maintain false beliefs and reinforce ungrounded concerns, thus it is potentially prone to fear mongering.

This leads us to the last way in which bioethics can deal with fears. This is the case when bioethics *uses* or *utilizes* fear. Here the worries and anxieties are not merely inputs to which bioethics, after due consideration, responds either by trying to alleviate it or by recommending suitable precautionary measures. Fear in this sense replaces consideration and is elevated to the rank of argument. Hence, fear is not an inducement for further enquiry how to deal with a problem, instead it is the evidence of its own truth.

In politics and public affairs it is often the case that the parties involved are not interested in rational discussion and negotiation; instead, they seek to maintain fear in its most uncontaminated form. The same can happen in the field of bioethics. For example, in the case of genetically modified organisms opposing activist groups are often engaged in the maintenance if not the escalation of fear instead of the articulation of the grounds for the opposition. To be sure, there are good reasons for caution regarding GMOs but opponents should clarify these reasons, whether they be ecological, religious or philosophical. Although fear is perfectly legitimate, it cannot replace reflection. When a debate goes in this direction, it is the responsibility of professional bioethics to lead the argumentation back on the right track. Thus, in my opinion it is all the more inexcusable when it is a bioethicist who follows this strategy. Unfortunately it is not without precedence. Leon Kass, a leading American bioethicist, once the advisor of President George W. Bush on bioethical matters, has spoken of the wisdom of repugnance as the ultimate guide in such controversial issues as human cloning or stem cell research. Although he states that "revulsion is not an argument," he hastens to add that "in crucial cases (…) repugnance is the emotional expression of deep wisdom, beyond reason's power fully to articulate it. (…) We are suspicious of those who think that they can rationalize away our horror (...)"[8] So far, so good. But after stating that cloning is a sort of "pollution" or "perversion," he adds that "to pollution and perversion the fitting response can only be horror and revulsion; and conversely, generalized horror and revulsion are prima facie *evidence* of foulness and violation" (emphasis mine – V. Sz.).[9] It is this last conclusion that I cannot accept. Kass and his wisdom of repugnance fuels fear and keeps it alive. Beyond the total rejection of the object feared no alternative is acceptable for him. In this scheme any effort to alleviate or rationally handle fear would be straightforwardly harmful, for it is horror itself that spells out the truth about the matter, so to speak. Furthermore, Kass declares that the burden of demonstration and refutation is on those who do not share his revulsion, while he very well knows that an inarticulate emotion cannot be refuted. This approach hinders the possibility of rational discussion and thus plays bioethical issues in the hands of fear mongers.

Aside from the fact that this argument can be self-defeating whenever someone fails to feel the appropriate revulsion, it is a category mistake to place fear on a par with arguments. Fear is the fuel and inducement of much that is going on in bioethics; and of course, as something so elementary, instinctive and often subconscious, it can never be rationalized away. Neither it is needed to do so. Neither alleviation nor precaution means the complete rationalization or eradication of our fears. These are legitimate ways by which we can manage them and learn how to live with them tolerably well. It must be the purpose of bioethics to help us towards this end. We need fear to keep us alert, but we should not let it have dominion over us.

References

Ball, P. 2011a. *Unnatural: The Heretic Idea of Making People.* London: Bodley Head.

Ball, P. 2011b. Playing God, *New Humanist* 1, http://newhumanist.org.uk/2474/playing-god-by-philip-ball-januaryfebruary-2011 (Accessed at 1st Dec 2012).

Berg, P et. al. 1974. Potential Biohazards of Recombinant DNA Molecules, *Sciences* 185, 303.

8 Kass and Wilson, 1998: 18-9.

9 Ibid. 23.

Hubbard, R. and Wald, E. 1993. *Exploding the Gene Myth: How Genetic Information is Produced and Manipulated by Scientists, Physicians, Employers, Insurance Companies, Educators, and Law Enforcers.* Boston: Beacon Press.

Kass, L. and Wilson, J. Q. 1998. *The Ethics of Human Cloning.* Washington, D. C.: AEI Press.

Specter, M. 2009. *Denialism: How Irrational Thinking Harms the Planet and Threatens Our Lives.* New York: Penguin.

Turney, J. 1998. *Frankenstein's Footsteps: Science, Genetics and Popular Culture.* New Haven – London: Yale University Press.

BIOETHICS: NEUTRALIZING THE POWER OF FEAR

Tadej Strehovec, Ljubljana

Introduction

With the development of medicine and technologies new ethical issues arise like, what is the meaning of human life and death? What should we do in the face of suffering and pain? Do we have a right to make decision about the life of others? What are the responsibilities of others in the case our life is threatened and our wellbeing is diminishing? All these dilemmas are taking part in bioethics which is based on the radical transformation of old medical ethics and moral theology. Today's bioethics is a crossroad of different kind of sciences and is a political factor in medicine, biology, philosophy, theology. It is a phenomenon based on the development of modern technologies and influences law, public policy, literature, cultural and history studies, pop-media, philosophy and religions. Bioethics in general is an intellectual and social phenomenon that has grown extremely rapidly over the past several decades and now represents a significant cultural and political force. Today's bioethics is a spectacular intellectual and public success. One of the most important engines for the success of bioethics is fear, which could be found in different kinds of forms and in different bioethics issues.

I. Bioethics is fear motivated multidisciplinary space

Fear in general is an unpleasant emotion many times caused by the belief that someone or something is dangerous and likely to cause pain, or a threat. It is one of the basic inner emotions of humans as joy, sadness and anger. Fear is often related to the specific behaviors like escape and avoidance. Many times fear is related to future events. People believe that the situation will be worsening and that such unacceptable condition will continue. This kind of understanding of fear is present in bioethics where appears over and over again in different fields of medicine and society. People facing bioethical dilemmas like in the case of the use of genetically modified organisms, are afraid for their health and the future of society as well. Politics and economy are often well aware of the power of fear and its manipulating role in the life of an individual or society. Fear in today's bioethics could be identified at least in seven basic areas:

1. The fear of human life. This kind of fear is possible to identify in the case of abortion and contraception where human life could be seen as a threat to the individual liberty, economy, politics and peace (Thomson 1999, 36-37; Pabst Battin 1998, 156-158). The organizations like The International Planned Parenthood Federation, United Nations, and World Health Organization etc. are the most important political and economic powers to control and reduce the world human population. The promotion of sterilization, abortion, contraception and women employment is the face of fear of life. On the other side in the case of infertility another form of fear of human life could be recognized. Especially in the West hundreds of thousands of couples suffer of non-having their own children. They feel the fear of life without their children. Their perception and meaning of life are threatened and many times common life is no longer possible. In this area the whole industry of fertility treatment is present and many ethical issues like in vitro fertilization, freezing of human embryos, selling human ova and sperms arise. Life in bioethics is not always the intrinsic value, sometimes it is an opponent or ally which causes different kinds of fear related dilemmas.

2. The fear of dehumanization of human life. Another form of fear in bioethics could be seen in different kind of issues linked with the euthanasia, palliative care, assisted suicide and aggressive medicine treatment. The so called "dehumanization of human life" is for some people one form of fear which could be overcome with the use of technology and premature death. Death as a solution for this kind of fear is a part of different kinds of ideologies like radical liberalism and utilitarianism (Kuhse 1999, 236-237).

3. The fear of violence, loneliness, ageing and suffering. Bioethics is dealing with the ethical issues linked with terrorism, bioweapons, medicalization of human behavior and plastic surgery. People are often afraid of violence due to the political instability and are in favor of appropriate control and use of modern technology for weapon production. This kind of phenomena could be recognized as well in the field of the asocial behavior where people could be attacked, killed or kidnapped. The medicalization of human behavior for example with the use of Ritalin in public schools could be seen as one form of dealing with this kind of problem. Another form of fear is linked with the loneliness and dissatisfaction with our appearance. The loneliness is one of the biggest problems of human society. Depression as a related consequence of fear of loneliness can be treated with special drugs and therapies. The case of non-medical plastic surgery where people have fear of their appearance is another source of fear and issue of bioethics.

4. The fear of mixing different kinds of natures. With the invention of technology for producing genetically modified organisms and food, creation of hybrid animals and vegetables or making half human and half animal bio structures, the new kinds of fears appeared among people. People many times feel anxiety where unnatural forms and products enter into their lives. This is especially true in the case of Monsanto, the biggest multinational GMO company which was many times lobbying in Brussels or Washington to legalize the production and use of GMO food. The issues with the patentability, licensing, safety and the reduction of biodiversity are some of the main concerns in the field of bioethics.

5. The fear of epidemics and human or animal experimentations. The media covering pan epidemics like SARS and BSE produced a large amount of fear over the world. People were afraid for their lives and pressed their government to protect their citizens. Similar logic could be seen in the case of HIV and in animal and human experimentations (Schuklenk in Aschcroft 2007, 245-246). The fear of animal suffering is present in modern society due to different kind of animal rights groups which promote the termination of animal experimentation and the use of alternative experiments (Singer 1999, 466; Rollin 1998, 411-414).

6. The fear of defining the personal ethical position in this global and multicultural world. The main challenge of modern (wo)man is to select and define his or her ethical position and values system. Due to the lack of proper formation, knowledge and political correctness people do not like to make decision and prefer to leave it to the professionals and politics. This is in particular true for socially very sensitive topics like abortion, euthanasia, in vitro fertilization and redefinition of marriage and family. People are many times afraid not to be politically correct and different from other minded people.

7. The fear of publicly speaking about ethics and values. This kind of emotion is rooted in ideological, verbal or media violence of other minded people, groups, organizations and ideologies. Many times bioethics issues are extremely sensitive and create different kinds of convictions, beliefs and emotions. Therefore people and even bioethicians are not always enough protected from internal and external pressures and many times prefer to avoid expressing their beliefs and publicly speaking about morality and ethics.

Nevertheless in bioethics there are even more aspects of fear. Fear or fears are the leading force to make bioethics visible and present in media, science and politics. But at the same time it is important to underline that fear in bioethics is its basic problem. Many times the society expects that bioethics experts will identify the roots of fear and neutralize them with the rationalization and use of more peaceful terminology. But doing this kind of neutralization is not the final aim of the bioethics process. Bioethics is aware to acknowledge the right of individual and society to be in so called "bio-fear." People and society expect from bioethics to make social boundaries where fear is legitimate like it is in the case of human experimentations, cloning or in the use of bio-weapons.

II. Bioethics: Neutralizing fear through dialogue

Bioethics as a "super discipline" came into being as it began to generalize all these different kinds of fears, raising systematic theoretical issues like the distinction between killing and letting die, the criteria of personhood and the assessment of quality of life. These have been accompanied by attention to still more general background of moral issues that arise in many fields of bioethics based in the frame of dialogue: truth telling, confidentiality, informed consent and paternalism. With all these dialogical tools bioethics neutralizes the fear of negative consequences of problematic practices in medicine and in society. Bioethics main task is therefore to create the public space of non-violent dialogue between various ethical and religious traditions, groups and ideologies. This meta-dialogue is possible due to the four main pre-conditions:

1. Bioethics terminology. One of the basic characteristics of bioethics is to create and to use such type of language and terminology which are accessible to professionals from different kinds of sciences, media and general public. The use of this kind of professional terminology helps to create the frame of confidence, respect, terminological clarity and avoidance of misunderstanding.

2. Bioethics is multicultural space of equality. For the bioethical process is significant that basic equality exists among various ethical and moral theories and traditions. Every moral conviction is appropriate and dialogue between different kinds of theories is a basis of bioethical process. Therefore bioethics remains deeply interdisciplinary and multicultural. This multicultural and multi ethics perspective of bioethics is important for neutralization of fear.

3. The main characteristic of bioethics is its methodology. In its academic role, bioethics makes no claims to truth and solutions, rather claims especial expertise in the capacity of analysis of patterns of reasoning and logical implication, assessing the validity of arguments for a specific moral conclusion. Therefore bioethics as a philosophical and theological reflective enterprise cannot yield either agreement or truth. Many times bioethics plays a role more like that of a counselor: it helps parties at odds with each other to understand the nature of their disagreements; it distinguishes between empirical disagreement and disagreement of values. Therefore bioethics uses methods like values clarification and does not decide cases like a court; it assists the parties involved in deciding how to resolve their disagreements. It does seek answers, but makes no pretense of reaching the solution. The solution - from bioethical perspective – is more the domain of individual convictions, politics and religions as well. Therefore bioethics does not and cannot play an authoritative role in public life and it cannot pretend to offer the solutions, even though it plays an important public role.

Bioethics has a significant role of neutralizing fear through the creation of its own basic terminology, creating multicultural space of dialogue and the awareness of limits in searching the solutions. The non-violent dialogue is therefore the basic way how bioethics explains fears and resolves ethical problems in a non-conflict manner.

III. Bioethics as a science of neutralizing fear in public space

Politics and media are very sensitive for the bioethical issues like abortion, euthanasia, genetically modified organisms and food, bio-safety etc. The media often (un)intentionally create the atmosphere of fear in public space to get public attention. The most evident cases of such reports are linked to the epidemic of SARS, human cloning and cosmetic surgery (Kruvand in Vanacker 2011, 138-140). These issues are often presented as a conflict between different kinds of human rights, ideologies and groups. Many times the bioethics experts are invited to publicly present their views, comments and suggest solutions. This kind of task could be very challenging due to the difficult use of appropriate language, terminology and to speak in a non-conflict manner in media. The interest of media is often to focus in bipolar perspective highly controversial issues and to confront different kinds of people, politicians, experts and bioethicians (Zylinska 2009, 102-109). To avoid the creation of atmosphere of fear it is important to emphasize the educational role of bioethics. The media and schools should in proper time "normalize" different bioethical issues, give good ethical knowledge, underline the importance of human dignity and non-violence, and to grant people the right to decide by their own. People are many times faced with the bioethical issues like embryo experimentation or GMO, and are not capable to define their ethical position due to the lack of authentic information and proper education. Therefore the bioethics experts should be well aware of their public responsibility and should take into account that speaking in public space is a part of their neutralization of fear in public space.

Conclusion

The main aim of bioethics is to help people and society to deal with difficult issue of fears and to suggest such policies that negative consequence of fear will be avoided. The three fathers of modern bioethics Joseph Fletcher, Paul Ramsey ad Richard McCormick, all theologians, gave basic Christian background to modern bioethics (Kuhse in Singer 2001, 4-8). In the crisis of secular bioethics, the modern Christian bioethicians facing with fear-dilemmas are invited to emphasize the basic Christian values like human dignity, personhood, dialogue and compassion (Brody 1998, 41-44; Engelhardt Jr 2009, 234-235). With this ethical orientation, bioethics could be an important partner to neutralize and to normalize the importance of fear in modern society and establish safe and constructive space of searching the truth, compromises and political solutions.

Literature

Brody, Baruch. 1998. Religion and bioethics. In *A Companion to Bioethics*, edited by H. Kuhse in P. Singer. Malden (USA): Blackwell Publishing Ltd.

Engelhardt, Jr, H. Tristram. 2009. Moral Pluralism, the Crisis of Secular Bioethics, and the Divisive Character of Christian Bioethics: Taking the Culture Wars Seriously. *Christian Bioethics: Non-ecumenical Studies in Medical Morality* 15 (3), 234-253.

Kruvand, Marjorie and Bastiaan Vanacker. 2011. Facing the Future: Media Ethics, Bioethics, and the World's First Face Transplant. *Journal of Mass Media Ethics* 26 (2),135-157.

Kuhse, Helga. 1999. Why killing is not always worse - and sometimes better - than letting die. In *Bioethics: an anthology*, edited by H. Kuhse and P. Singer. Malden: Blackwell Publisher Ltd.

Kuhse, Helga and Peter Singer. 2001. What is bioethics? A historical introduction. In *A Companion to bioethics*, edited by H. Kuhse and P. Singer. Oxford: Blackwell.

Pabst Battin, Margaret. 1998. Population issues. In *A Companion to Bioethics*, edited by H. Kuhse and P. Singer. Malden (USA): Blackwell Publishing Ltd.

Rollin, Bernard E. 1998. The moral status of animals and their use as experimental subjects. In *A Companion to Bioethics*, edited by H. Kuhse and P. Singer. Malden (USA): Blacwell Publishing Ltd.

Schuklenk, Udo and Richard Aschcroft. 2007. International research ethics. In *The bioethics reader: editors' choice*, edited by R. F. Chadwick. Oxford: Blackwell.

Singer, Peter 1999. All animals are equal. In *Bioethics: an anthology*, edited by H. Kuhse and P. Singer. Malden: Blackwell Publisher Ltd.

Thomson, Judith J. 1999. A defense of abortion. In *Bioethics: an anthology*. Malden: Blackwell Publisher Ltd.

Zylinska, Joanna. 2009. *Bioethics in the Age of New Media*: Cambridge, MA: MIT Press.

INTELLECTUAL HISTORY, POLITICS, TRADITION AND AUTHORITY

FEAR IN 16th CENTURY CROATIAN RELIGIOUS LITERATURE

Krešimir Šimić, Osijek

I.

At the end of the famous novel *Name of the Rose* by Umberto Eco, William of Baskerville and blind librarian Jorge meet in the library-maze. Father William has finally found the second book of Aristotle's *Poetics*, a book about comedy. Even though he had not read it, he rebuilt almost the entire content of the book about comedy using examples from the first part of *Poetics* and *Rethorics*. William then asked Jorge why he wanted to protect this book more than any other. Jorge's answer is resolute: "Because it was by the Philosopher" (Eco 1986: 276). This is understandable: The philosopher – Aristotle – built the foundation upon which the whole medieval and even later western educational system is developed. Jorge his own critique of the science based on Aristotelianism summarizes in the following thoughts:

> "Every book by that man has destroyed a part of the learning that Christianity had accumulated over the centuries. The fathers had said everything that needed to be known about the power of the Word, but then Boethius had only to gloss the Philosopher and the divine mystery of the Word was transformed into a human parody of categories and syllogism. The book of Genesis says what has to be known about the composition of the cosmos, but it sufficed to rediscover the *Physics* of the Philosopher to have the universe reconceived in terms of dull and slimy matter, and the Arab Averroës almost convinced everyone of the eternity of the world. We knew everything about the divine names, and the Dominican buried by Abo — seduced by the Philosopher — renamed them, following the proud paths of natural reason. And so the cosmos, which for Areopagite revealed itself to those who knew how to look up at the luminous cascade of the exemplary first cause, has become a preserve of ter-

> restrial evidence for which they refer to an abstract agent. Before, we used to look to heaven, deigning only a frowning glance at the mire of matter; now we look at the earth, and we believe in the heavens because of earthly testimony. Every word of the Philosopher, by whom now even saints and prophets swear, has overturned the image of the world. But he had not succeeded in overturning the image of God. If this book were to become ... had become an object for open interpretation, we would have crossed the last boundary" (Eco 1986: 276–277).

For Jorge, laughter is "weakness, corruption, the foolishness of our flesh. It is the peasant's entertainment, the drunkard's license; even the church in her wisdom has granted the moment of feast, carnival, fair, this diurnal pollution that releases humors and distracts from other desires and other ambitions ..." From Aristotle's book, says Jorge, corrupt minds could draw the extreme syllogism, that laughter is man's end! Jorge continues: "This book could strike the Luciferine spark that would set a new fire to the whole world, and laughter would be defined as the new art, unknown even to Prometheus, for canceling fear" (Eco 1986: 277). The law is imposed by fear.

Eco's novel is undoubtedly reminiscent of Mikhail Bakhtin's theory of carnivalisation. According to Bakhtin, carnivalisation – reshaping the Carnival into the language of literature – is a central feature of Renaissance literature (Bakhtin 1967: 186). Carnival's laughter and expressions – intimate, cynical, eccenetric – penetrated into the geners of Renaissance literature and remodeled them. Moreover, during the Renaissance, carnivalisation removed many barriers and became a kind of worldwiew – worldwiew marked by laughter (Bakhtin 1978: 80, 116).

The importance of laughter in Renaissance culture speaks to many humanistic and medical treatises, for example: Baldessare Castiglione's *Libro del cortegiano* (1528); Juan Luis Vives' *De anima et vita* (1539); Laurent Joubert's *Traité du risu* (1579); Cels Mancini's *De risu, ac ridiculis* (1598). Renaissance authors predominantly rely on ancient sources, primarily on Aristotle's definition in *De patribus animalium* (III, 10): "Of all creatures, only for man is peculiar to laugh," Aristotle's *Poetics* and *Rethorics*, the second book of Cicero's *De oratore*, the sixth book of Quintilian *Institutio oratoria*, and finally Hippocrates treatise and novel (Skinner 2007: 142–176). According to Bakhtin, however, ancient authors and individual opinions were not sufficient to change the medieval belief in the immutability of the world. For the final change, a powerful culture of laughter, which has been developing for thousands of years, was needed. On this basis occurred carnivalisation's consciousness (Bakhtin 1978: 291–291). This has manifested in the literary works of G. Boccaccio, W. Shakespeare, M. Cervantes and Rabelais' novel *Gargantua and Pantagruel* (Bakhtin 1978: 293). Bakhtin concludes that this laughter began to abolish medieval fear, fear of God, moral, commandments, death and afterlife.

Bakhtin's perception of Renaissance literary culture has insightful observations; however, he leaves us with the question: does not the emphasis of the liberation aspect of Renaissance laughter against "medieval fear" actually affirm his own position needed for his own struggles against the dogmatism? It seems that Bakhtin not only emphasizes the Renaissance theory of laughter but overstates it.

It is well known that, apart from Burckhardt's image of Renaissance culture that is opposed to the Middle Ages – which coincides with Bakhtin's vision – there are other views. For example, one can see Henry Thode's incentives for changes in the work of Francis of Assisi. Arnold Hauser has pointed out that there is certain continuity between the Middle Ages and the Renaissance, which is looming in the medieval nominalism (Burckhardt 1997: XXXI–XXXII).

As the new historians gathered methodological principles in the journal *Annales d'historie économique et sociale* – they started to research, amog other things, mentality or collective psychology. Jean Delumeau argued that in the Renaissance culture, the predominante feelings were feelings of fear and gulit. In the book *La Peur en Occident (XIV–XVIII sièles)*, Delumeau says that a pessimistic view of the world coincides with appearance of the plague, the Turkish invasion and religious discord (Stojanović 2003: 5–17). From such a viewpoint, it seems that Renasissance laughter is the other side of Renaissance fear. This was clearly shown in the Croatian Renaissance literary culture, particularly in its important segment – religious poetry.

II.

Literary historiography knows that the Croatian Renaissance literary culture is significantly marked by laughter. For example, Nikola Nalješković and Marin Držić wrote comedies that, in a broad sense, colud be interpreted as *mundus inversus*: the central place of carnivalesque logic of inversion (Plejić Poje 2009: 521). That religious poetry has comic elements is less known. It is found in the humorous lyrics of Marko Marulić (*Spovid koludric od sedam smartnih grihov*, *Anka Satira*, *Poklada i Korizma*), the songs of Horace Mažibradića *Da bogat u gori poklikne zvat' koga* and *Od kud tako gladan i suha* and the song *Sedam opačina* by Miho Bunić Babulinov, which has misogynistic elements. However, within religious poetry, which is an important aspect of European and Croatian Renaissance literary culture, fear dominates.

Images of fear are most frequent in songs that are thematically related to death. These songs reflect the fear that the world would collapse. Celan's *Dies irae, dies illa* is the best example (Hercigonja 1975: 166). This kind of religious poetry in Croatian literary culture is known already by verses from Novak's Missal. In poetic meditations on death, eshatological motifs of final judgment, heaven and hell are frequent, but in these meditations motif of rotting bodies can also be found (Hercigonja 1975: 168). In the song *Od suda versi*, paraphrased from the latin song *Dies irae, dies illa*, there are many motifs that belong to Biblical apocalyptic literature (wars, eclipse, bloody moon, fire, eshatological vision of the court). From the eschatological motifs – the final judgment – two songs from Klimanović's rituals are composed. In the sequence *Pokle zakopaju človika* after the introduction, the lyrical subject is Jesus, who is the Judge (v. 13–20). In the sequence *Pokle se zakopa človik* after the warning of life's transience, comes the verses in which Jesus is also the Judge (v. 35–42). Frequent images of macabre and naturalistic "scene" of decay emerge from the songs: what was once a proud human body, now, eaten by worms, lies in a damp and dark grave (Hercigonja 1975: 167). For example, in sequence *Nad grobom kada telo u grob položet'* from Klimanović's rituals (v. 1–22).

With songs about death there is often a related motif *memento mori* (Hercigonja 1975: 166). This call is often imposed through the voice of the dead man. For example, in the sequence *Nad mladim junakom* and in the song *Martac govori* from *Zagrebački zbornik*,[1] the lyrical subject is a young man who suddenly died. A dead man is also a lyrical subject in the song *Glava marteška govori* from *Vartal* (v. 3–4) and in songs *Počine veras pustošniem mladcem* (v. 14) and *Pjesanca Gospi* from cyrillic anthology *Libro od mnozijeh razloga*, which recalls the medieval thought *Memento, nostris iungenda ossibus ossa tua*. To the songs written in the spirit of *memento mori* belong two songs written in the form of an epitaph: Nikola Nalješković's *Jedan mrtac ali kosti od mrca govore putniku* and Nikola Dimitrović's *Ti, koj putem greš, za mal čas nu postoj*. To the same group of songs – in which the lyrical subject is a dead man who encourages the addressees to believe in Christian eschatology – belongs Nalješković's songs *O, žene, o,*

1 In Croatian lierary historiography *Zagrebački zbornik* sometimes is called *Marulićev zbornik*.

ljudi, nu pamet jedan čas and *Gospođe izbrane, koje ste na lipos*. However, this time the lyirical subject is a woman and the addressees are women. In the songs *Smarti i života razgovor* from Splitsko-trogirska pjesmarica and *Najprie strašno prijećenje od smarti* from *Libro od mnozijeh razloga*, the lyrical subject is death. Death is the lyrical subject also in song *Smart govori*, Marulić's paraphrase of Latin epigram *De morte*.

In many songs we can finde motifs *mors nivelatrix* and *mors omina aequat*, which is also the *topos* of religious poetry. For example, this is seen in the dialogical song *Smarti i života razgovor*. A motif of death with a scythe is common in religious poetry of Mavro Vetranović (*Remeta*, v. 97–104, *Pjesanci moru*, v. 105–108, *Na noć od božjega poroda*, v. 115–116, *Pjesanci smrti*, v. 19–20). In the oniric structured song *Pjesanci san*, the lyrical subject represents an eshatological vision (v. 7–12), where a mythological being Meger, one of the three Erinyes (goddess of revenge), emerges from a muddy lake and punishes people (v. 25–78). Vetranić's song *Pjesanca suda napokonjega* is based on the apocalyptical image of the end of the world. This is actually a catalog of apocalyptic images (v. 28–32, v. 37–43, v. 49–58, v. 61–74, v. 115–132). One very interesting image is the "big barn", based on the topos *mundus inversus* (v. 136–162). This picture is even more interesting because the eschatological pictures of the end of the world are mainly related to water catastrophe, such as the biblical flood (Genesis 7, 17– 24). Vetranović sometimes used images of decay of the human body in his satires directed against the arrogance and greed. The song *Pjesanca protiva oholasti* where he recommends a consideration of human inanity, illustrates this point (v. 15–20).

III.

Although comic genres were popular, Croatian Renaissance literary culture has retained many images of fear. It is mostly about the eshatological fears – fear of death and the final judgment. At first glance one might think that this is a relic of the "dark" Middle Ages that was used for some kind of social discipline. The blind librarian of the aforementioned Eco's novel says: "To the villein who laughs, at that moment, dying does not matter: but then, when the license is past, the liturgy again imposes on him, according to the divine plan, the fear of death." (Eco 1986: 277) Of course, the aspect of social discipline by cosmic and eschatological fear – against which, according to Bakhtin, people struggled using prophetic parody and folk-Festive – certainly to some extent emerges in the images of fear (Bakhtin 1978: 253). It is well known that fear is an important theme in the history of political theory. According to Thucydides, the Athenians already argued that one of the three most important motives of human action, together with honor and interest, is fear (Thucydides 1982: 44). Aristotle wrote about fear and timidity in *Nicomachean Ethics*. He associated courage and timidity with virtue and vice. Succumbing to fear and acting cowardly means to be unchaste. The political theory of Thomas Hobbes is the apogee of the political theory of fear. He pointed out three political dimensions of fear. Firstly, contrary to the view that poeple naturally fear death, Hobbes believes that the fear of death comes from the moral importance of self-protection. Secondly, the fear of death makes man rational agents and political entities. Thirdly, one must be taught to fear death through a system of moral education, organized by the social elite. Finally, Hobbes believes that fear lies at the very fundations of civilization: The great and enduring societies are not founded on the goodwill people have towards each other, but on the fear that they have of each other (Hobbes 1991: 113).

Whatever political theories influenced literary production, interpreting literary images of fear only from this aspect would be reductionism and therefore would obscure other aspects. Besaides those already mentioned, *Nicomachean Ethics* and of course *Poetics* (the aim of tragedies is to guide feelings of pity and fear to catharsis), Aristotle developed some kinde of "philosopy of fear" in the second book of *Rhetorics* (V, 1–15). For Aristotle, fear is anxiety caused by impending evil that can destroy or cause suffering, but only when these evils are not too far away. "Everyone knows that he will die, but if death is not on the doorstep, no one thinks of it" says Aristotle (Aristotle 1989: 96). Further (2–11) Aristotle says that everything that is scary becomes scarier if it is caused by something that can not be changed (12). Finally, Aristotle pointed to the mental state of people who experience fear (13–15).

When Jean Delumeau was asked why the feeling of the fear and a pessimistic view of the world came in times of economic prosperity before Black Plague, he answered: because Augustine's theology, parts of patristic literature and some Biblical passages. Whether or not Delimeaue is right, it is hard to say. But that images of fear in religious poetry were motivated by theology of fear, seems quite possible. Thomas Aquinas developed theology of fear in the first part of the second book of *Summa Theologica* (q. 41–45).

When discussing the object of fear, Aquinas addresses many questions about fear: whether fear is a passion of the soul, whether fear is a special passion, whether there is a natural fear, whether the species of fear are suitably assigned, whether the object of fear is good or evil, whether the evil of nature is an object of fear, whether fear itself can be feared, whether sudden things are especially feared, for which there is no remedy. In the chapter 43, which tells about the causes of fear, Aquinas asks the following questions: Is love or defect the cause of fear? Finally, in the chapter on the effects of fear (q. 44), Aquinas answered following questions: whether fear causes contraction, whether fear makes one suitable for counsel, whether fear makes one tremble and whether fear hinders action (Aquinas 1920: 764–775). According to Thomas Aquinas, fear is a mental excitement, especially regarding the onset of evil (*Summa Theologica* I–II. 41. 1–2). The basic fear is natural fear (*Summa Theologica* I–II. 41. 3). Humans and animals have natural fear. However, according to Aquinas, the human sense of fear is not only instinctive but also depends on his rational powers. This kind of fear can be much more powerful because it involves the will which judges things according to good or evil. Man can therefore be afraid of theoretical situations, concepts, and ideas.

Starting from six types of non-instinctive fears outlined in John Damascene *De fide orthodoxa*, Aquinas divided fears into two groups. In the first group are fears which consider evil in men's actions. There is laziness, or as Aquinas defines it, the fear of too much toil. Next, there is shamefacedness, which is the fear of damaging one's reputation through disgraceful actions soon to be committed. Finally, there is shame which is the fear of damaging one's reputation through disgraceful actions previously committed. The second group of fears concern those evils encountered with respect to external things, that is, those things that exceed a person's power of opposition. First of them is wonder, then stupor, and finally anxiety.

Although fear is primarily described in terms of the shrinking from a thing judged as bad or evil, Aquinas notes that fear is also concerned with good, albeit indirectly. In this respect, one can fear a thing which is good in itself, not with respect to its goodness, but rather as that which causes the affliction of evil or harm to oneself. The example that Aquinas offers is that of a righteous and good judge who is feared by the criminal not with respect to the judge's goodness, but rather for the punishment that he can inflict. According to Sthepen Loughlin, this observation has a two-fold importance. It introduces a distinction necessary to Aquinas's discussion concerning the forms of fear encountered in the religious domain, and second, it reveals what the primary cause of fear is: love. A central feature of Aquinas's doctrine concerning the emotions is that each of them finds its root in love. Love establishes the context out of which the emotions might arise. And so, with respect to fear, love binds a person to a good, which then allows him to desire it. The context has now been established wherein fear can possibly arise, namely when something prevents or endangers the fulfillment of one's desire for this good. Without love, no fear would arise. Indeed, as Aquinas states, fear is born from love.

Aquinas, among other things, tried to show the place of fear among Christians. This he does inderectly. He talks about four kinds of fear: wordly, servile, filial and initial. Worldly or human fear arises in one whose love is centered primarily on the world and its goods. Given the orientation of this love and the context it establishes, the fear it produces is something which is always reprehensible to the Christian whose love must be centered on the things of heaven. Although worldly fear, in its proper sense, is something to be avoided, this does not extend to the remaining three fears. In fact, Thomas argues that these three are required for a full Christian life. The way in which Thomas distinguishes these three is to build upon one's love of God, and, in this context, to identify some evil which causes the person to adhere all the more to God. And so, with respect to servile fear, this evil is simply that of God's punishment, while filial fear considers the evil of committing an offense against God. Initial fear considers both evils together. Since servile fear regards punishment, the love at work here is not so much a love of God, but rather a love of self. However, servile fear has the good effect of drawing one to the things of God, and of keeping one from sin through fear of punishment. It is not something desired by the mature Christian, that is, by one who wishes to draw nearer to Him in love. Filial or chaste fear is the ideal fear for the Christian in his relationship to God. This fear does not regard God primarily as the dispenser of judgment and punishment. It arises out of a well-ordered and mature love for God. Its depths are revealed in the two acts it engenders, namely, a profound reverence for God, and secondly, a great concern that one's activities will have the effect of separating one from God. Thus, one fears offending God, not to avoid any punishment that may result, but rather to avoid the separation that results from sin and guilt. Finally, initial fear relates to filial as the imperfect does to the perfect. In this respect, initial fear is that which is exhibited by the neophyte as he begins his growth in charity. He acts with the love of God and justice, as well as the fear of punishment which eventually fades through the acquisition of charity. The more a man loves God, the less he fears punishment (Loughlin 2002: 1–16).

If we now return to the images of fear in Reanissance literature, we can say that the role of fear is not only social discipline but a release, parhaps more radical then liberation by laughter. Carnivalization can be a subversive force, but, like any revolution, leads to a "revolutionary rules", which is *contradicto in adjecto*. In other words, carnivalisation does not lead to complete freedom (*aurea aetas*), but only to temporary releas (*mundus inversus*). So, the "dark" eschatology of medieval and Renaissance literary culture are not necessarily in conflict with Renaissance aspirations of freedom. Perhaps it is just a case of looking at freedom from a different angle.

Literature

Aquinas, Thomas. 1920. *Summa Theologica*. Westminster, Maryland: Christian Classics.

Aristotel. 1989. *Retorika*. Zagreb: Naprijed.

Bakhtin, Mihail. 1967. *Problemi poetike Dostojevskog*. Beograd: Nolit.

Bakhtin, Mihail. 1978. *Stvaralaštvo Fransoa Rablea i narodna kultura srednjega veka i renesanse*. Beograd: Nolit.

Burckhardt, Jacob. 1997. *Kultura renesanse u Italiji*. Zagreb: Prosvjeta.

Delumeau, Jaean. 2003. *Strah na Zapadu (od XIV do XVIII veka): opsednuti grad*. Sremski Karlovci: Izdavačka knjižarnica Zorana Stojanovića.

Eco, Umberto. 1986. *The Name of the Rose*. New York: Warner Books.

Hercigonja, Eduard. 1975. *Srednjovjekovna književnost*. Zagreb: Liber – Mladost.

Hobbes, Thomas. 1991. *Leviathan*. New York: Cambridge University Press.

Jagić, Vatroslav – Kaznačić, I Antun. 1871. *Pjesme Mavra Vetranića Čavčića*. Zagreb: Jugoslavenska akademija znanosti i umjetnosti.

Kolendić, Petar. 1912. *Dvadeset pjesama Mavra Vetranovića*. Zagreb: Jugoslavenska akademija znanosti i umjetnosti.

Loughlin, Stephen. 2002. *The Complexity of timor in Aquinas's Summa Theologiae*. In: *Fear and its Representations in the Middle Ages and Renaissance*, Arizona Studies in the Middle Ages and the Renaissance, Volume 6, ed. by Anne Scott and Cynthia Kosso, Brepols.

Lucić, Petar. 1990. *Vartal*. Split: Književni krug.

Plejić Poje, Lahorka. 2009. *Leksikon Marina Držića*, ed. Slobodan. P. Novak, Milovan Tatarin, Mirjana Mataija, Leo Rafolt. Zagreb: Leksikografski zavod Miroslav Krleža.

Skinner, Quentin. 2007. *Vision of Politics*, Volume 3. Cambridge: Cambridge University Press.

Strohal, Rudolf. 1916. *Zbirka starih hrvatskih crkvenih pjesama*. Zagreb: Tisak C. Albrechta.

Thucydides. 1982. *The Peloponessian War*. New York: Modern Library.

FEAR AND PRIDE AS FUNDAMENTAL ELEMENTS OF THE ANTHROPOLOGY OF EARLY MODERN POLITICAL PHILOSOPHY[1]

Béla Mester, Budapest

Fear of Death as the Basis of Hobbes's Political Anthropology

The emblematic work of the early modern political philosophy, Thomas Hobbes's *Leviathan*, by the most opinions, was established on an anthropology, which was focussed on the *fear of death* as the fundamental emotion of every human being. It is dominant in the state of nature, when, amongst other torments, "which is worst of all, continual fear, and danger of violent death; and the life of man, solitary, poor, nasty, brutish and short" (I. 13. Hobbes 1651: 62). Later, the same emotion makes possible the establishing of the social contract: "The Passions that encline men to Peace, are Fear of Death; [...] And reason suggesteth convenient Articles of Peace upon which men may be drawn to agreement" (I. 13. op. cit. 63). In the end, the working peace made by the social contract could not be maintained without the subjects' fear of the violence of the ruler: "For by this Authority, given him by every particular man in the Common-wealth, he hath the use of so much Power and Strength conferred on him that, by terrour thereof, he is enabled to form the wills of them all, to Peace at home, and mutual aid against their enemies abroad" (II. 17. op. cit. 87–88). By the tool of fear, the ruler can limit and regulate the dangerous endeavours of humans, summarised in their inclination to vanities, or their *pridefulness*, in this system of ideas. We can see that in Hobbes's thought, fear is a universal phenomenon, both the illness and medicament of the human life.

The first question of interpretation concerns the foundations of this fear which penetrated the whole of social life of Hobbes's world. A biographical interpretation calls our attention to Hobbes's mother who was pregnant with Thomas in the time of the English national fear of the Spanish Armada. Another, more serious

1 This writing was supported by the Hungarian Scientific Research Fund (OTKA K 104794).

explanation of the fundamental role of fear is the social experience of the civil war. However, the real, conscious model of the state of nature was England in the time of the civil war, in many aspects for Hobbes; the image of the fundamentally *fearful* humans, with fearless rulers above them is based on a more ancient, culturally embedded anthropology. However, Hobbes's direct criticism of religious opinions, and his corpuscular natural philosophy are inevitable elements of his thought. The structural similarities between the anthropological basis of his political philosophy and the Christian tradition of political theology was clear for the scholars as early time as the middle of the last century. Michel Oakeshott in his introduction to Leviathan with great influence links the Augustinian tradition on the consequences of the original sin in political anthropology and Hobbes's opinions. The predicament of mankind enforcing the social state is the original sin in Augustine; *pride* or *vain-glory* has a similar role in Hobbes's system by Oakeshott: "Hobbes deprives Pride of moral significance, it still remains a defect. And since Pride (it will be remembered) it is the Augustinian interpretation of the original sin, his doctrine of Hobbes seems to approximate his view to the conception of predicament as springing from, not nature, but defect in nature." (Oakeshott 1975: 59–60.)[2] By the interpretation of Oakeshott, the Augustinian tradition has been combined with the novelties of the early modernity and the Reformation in Hobbes; his philosophy has "reflected the changes in the European intellectual consciousness which had been pioneered chiefly by the theologians of the fifteenth and sixteenth centuries" (op. cit. 58). Here is no place showing the large scale of interpretations of the parallelism between the concepts of pride in Augustine and in Hobbes, rooted in Oakeshott's reading of Leviathan; I can offer two characteristic instances, only. W. B. Glover described a more developed comparison between Augustine and Hobbes, emphasising the role of the Reformation in the Augustinian tradition (Glover 1993, first published in 1966). Recently, A. P. Martinich has evaluated Hobbes as "a very protestant thinker" of the Calvinist wing, in the larger context of the Augustinian tradition (Martinich 2005: 177, and *passim*).

By the evidences of his texts, interpreted in this sense by a significant part of scholars, Hobbes actually used the patterns of the Judeo-Christian tradition about the human nature after Adam's fall, in a special, secularised, rationalised

2 Oakeshott's writing was first published in 1946, as a preface for *Leviathan*, edited by him.

and systematised form. Human condition in the state of nature is equivalent with the human nature just after the fall. Signs of the sinful, corrupted human nature are the emotions of *shame*, with its counterpart, *pride,* or *vain-glory*; and the *fear of the Lord* has its roots in here. Fear of God has transformed to the fear of *ministers of God,* in the Scriptures (Rom. 13:4); and the term used for the rule by fear and that of *terror*, is the same in the *King James Bible* (Rom. 13:3), and in the *Leviathan* (II. 17. Hobbes 1651: 87–88; see above). Earthly power has a double function in this frame; it is both the punishment of the original sin, and the part of solution of the problems emerged by the corrupted human nature after the fall. The motto on the frontispiece of Hobbes's masterpiece describes this metaphor of political theology with a Latin Scriptural quotation: "Non est *potestas* Super Terram quae comparetur ei". Regarding the whole text; we should realise that the power of *Leviathan* is based on its *fearlessness*, and on the *pridefulness* of all other beings, as the cause of their *fearfulness*. By the English text of the King James Bible: "Upon earth there is not his like, who is made *without fear*. He beholdeth all high *things*; he *is a king over all the children of pride*". We can realise that the English version lacks the word *potestas [power].*[3] For Hobbes, it was a crucial expression; Leviathan in here is not an extraordinary animal, but a symbol of the extraordinary power of the earthly ruler given by God. It is the reason why he avoided the English Bible. Hebraism with *all the children of pride* refers to all the beings in the corrupted nature of sinfulness after the original sin, with its consequence of pride.[4] Fearfulness of the sinful people has appeared in its counterpart, in the uniqueness of the fearlessness of the great Leviathan. By my opinion the word *king* is not a merely symbolical expression in here for Hobbes; it is the bridge between the metaphor of Leviathan and the description of the really existing royal power, established on the anthropology of the original sin, and its consequences for the rule.

3 However, the text includes clear symbols of the earthly power; equivalents of *potestas* are missing from all the translations of the Scriptures, excluding the Latin. The terms of the Hebrew text I have consulted with György Gábor, professor of the Jewish University in Budapest, and my colleague in the Research Centre for Humanities.

4 All "children of pride [b'ni shachatz]" means all "the proud beings". The structure of this characteristic Hebrew expression was inherited by the translations, in Latin it is "(rex super universos) filios superbiae". Considering that the Latin equivalent of the "pride" in KJB is "superbia", connections with the Augustinian anthropology are clearer.

However, Hobbes used these elements of the Judeo-Christian theology in highly secularised and rationalised form, cleaned from direct theological references; the result is a darker and more closed anthropology than that of any denomination in his lifetime, including the strictest English Puritans. Hobbes's conceptual systematisation of the inherited elements of the religious tradition follows to a kind of mono-causal explanations, rooted in the dominancy of the fear of death. Here should be mentioned that other philosophies in the Western thought before Hobbes with a central concept of *fear of death* have focussed on the escape from this misery of human condition; the author of Leviathan is probably the first one who keeps it in the focus in his whole system, everywhere. This strictness is partly a consequence of his secular language; he could select the needed elements of the traditional anthropology, and disregard the features useless for him. This conceptual consequentiality of his system of ideas is good for the clearness and transparency of his argumentation; and it causes serious problems within the system, at the same time. It is the dichotomy of the states of nature and society, and the difficulty of the step of social contract made by the humans of the state of nature to create a civil society. From the consequent darkness of the description of the state of nature, based on the strict conceptuality of his anthropology, follows the problems of the human faculty of making societies. Hobbes's problem was solvable supposing a basic sociability of the human nature, existing in the state of nature, or, in religious language, in our corrupted nature after Adam's fall. Seemingly, Hobbes avoided this solution consciously, risking the problems appearing in his system following from his choice. The next question is that of the possible advantages of his choice for his political philosophy. Before discussing this question, we should see another historical solution of a similar problem of early modern political thinking within the theological conceptual framework. It is a feature of the political theology of John Calvin as a distinguished representative of the early modern Protestant Augustinian thought, a tradition, which was mentioned above, concerning Hobbes's intellectual background.

Original Sin and Antique Tradition in Calvin's Political Theology

Calvin's starting point in his *Institutes* is directly the question of human faculties under conditions of the original sin, and consequently our corrupted nature.[5] The surprising key word in here is the natural *sociability* of humans: "man is by nature a social animal [homo est animal natura sociale], he is disposed, from natural instinct, to cherish and preserve society" (II. 2. 13. Calvin 2009: 166).[6] However, his chain of ideas follows - in its vocabulary and in its system - the Augustinian tradition of the consequences of the original sin concerning the earthly power; the corn of his political thinking is based on this originally Aristotelian thesis of natural sociability of humans. From this positive feature of the human nature, remained after Adam's fall, follows a special sense both for political thinking, and adequate activity, the human faculty of *iustitia civilis*. In here Calvin risks the theologically consequent description of the universality and homogeneity of our corrupted nature, and provokes long and essential theological debates amongst his fellow-reformers. The importance of this foundation of political theology for him is mirrored in these conscious difficulties of the fundaments of his political theology. Calvin's personal interest as a renaissance humanist man of letters was in this anthropology to offer a possibility to save the ideas of his favourite antique studies in a Christian context, after his conversion.In the text of his *Institutes*, under conditions of the human faculty of *iustitia civilis* it is possible to study classic pagan political philosophers with a good Christian consciousness; he seemingly has rethought the old Christian cultural question of *Athens versus Jerusalem*, and saved the spirit of Athens in the church of Jerusalem.. By his words, "in reading profane authors, the admirable light of truth displayed in them should remind us, that the human mind, however, much fallen and perverted from its original integrity, is still adorned and invested with admirable gifts from its Creator. [...] How, then, can we deny that truth must have beamed on those ancient lawgivers who arranged civil order and discipline with so much equity?" (II. 2. 15. Calvin 2009: 167.) However, the role of the cultural embedment of the ideas cannot be overestimated in this case; Calvin's solution has more importance than an intellec-

5 I have recently discussed the problems of Calvin's political theology in my article published in the same book series earlier (Mester 2010).

6 For the correction of the modern English version of Calvin's work, I have used a standard edition of the original Latin text (Calvinus 1863–1892).

tual bias of an educated believer. The human faculty of political thinking based on our *natural sociability* is the elementary condition of the needed choice between the contested concepts of the earthly power, made by the Christian individuals, under condition of the chaotic political structure of the early modern Continental Europe; in here our civic obligation toward the magistrate is certain, but the identification of the legitimate magistrate is a question. This Aristotelian sociability is the deepest root of our political options in the political thought of Calvin, from the civil obedience to the right of resistance. Political thinking appears in the writings of Calvin as a description of modern phenomena by the tools of an antique republican vocabulary.

Exclusion of the Antique Tradition in Hobbes's Political Thought

However, Calvin's solution offered a special secularised public sphere of politics for the flock of believers; it supposed stability on the bottom of the chaotic system of institutions. Calvin's humans can make decisions about the concrete, existing forms of the earthly power, creation of a new political institution made by them *via* social contract is not possible; and it is not needed, because they live always in a form of society, which follows from their *natural sociability*. However, Calvin's solution is a step for establishing the individual choice in politics; it has an intrinsic limit to develop a more radical methodological individualism in a form of the social contract theory. It is an emblematic fact of the history of philosophy that Aristotle, who was referred by Calvin in this context, in his *Politics* developed his principle of the natural sociability of humans arguing against the proto-contractualism of Lycophron the Sophist. For the endeavours of Hobbes, this system of human faculties was insufficient. It was better for him to leave in obscurity the method of the choice of the individuals of the state of nature than give up the clear dichotomy between the states of nature and society. The cultural embedment of Hobbes's dilemma is the same as that of the problem of Calvin; it is the question of the role of the humanist knowledge read from the classics in the world of early modernity. Hobbes draw an opposite conclusion than Calvin, within a highly similar conceptual framework; by him, all the political knowledge of the classics is useless, and what is more, harmful under modern conditions. By the dark description of the *Leviathan*, in "these westeren parts of the World, we are made to receive our opinions concerning Institution, and Rights of Common-wealths, from *Aristotle*, Cicero, and other men, Greeks and Romans, that living under Popular States, derived those Rights, not from the Principles of Nature, but transcribed them into their books, out of the practice of their own Common-wealths, which were Popular; [...] And by reading of these Greek, and Latine Authors, men from their childhood have gotten a habit (under a false shew of Liberty) of favouring tumults, and of licentious controlling the actions of their Souveraigns, and again, of controlling those controllers, with the effusion of so much blood; as I think I may truly say, there was never any thing so deerly bought, as these Western parts have bought the learning of the Greek and Latine tongues." (II. 21. Hobbes 1651: 110–111.) Hobbes in here made a personal choice, which concerned the core of his cultural identity; he sacrificed the antique intellectual and political ideas of his youth for the conceptual clearness of the contractual model invented by him, risking the harms of the strictness of his system of ideas. If Calvin's choice can be summarised metaphorically in the sentence of "spirit of Athens in the church of Jerusalem, for the flock of the believers in the early modernity", the epitome of Hobbes's choice can be that "no Athens and no Jerusalem, but the people of the marketplace of London, only, and their adequate Commonwealths in the next century".

Consequences for Our Time

Searching the roots of the modern political thinking, and its anthropological foundation, we have observed two emblematic systems of the early modernity, both are based on the concept of the fear inheriting the ideas of the Judeo-Christian religious tradition about the *fearfulness* of the corrupted human nature under conditions of the inherited sin. Calvin's political theology has achieved the possibility of the relatively free political choice and acting of the people by the method of the partial sacrificing of the unity of the corrupted human nature, saving the usage of the republican vocabulary of the classical political writers. Politics in Calvin's conceptual framework always has a certain degree of the *ethos* of the antique republicanism that is the active participation in Christian form, but it is limited in its tendencies of methodical individualism. The second one, Hobbes's contractualism is based on the elements of the same religious anthropology in secularised and rationalised form. Hobbes's methodological systemacity radicalised the dominant role of fear in his anthropology, and a strict methodological individualism followed from it, excluding the forms and vocabulary of antique republicanism based on another anthropological basis - that of natural sociability of humans. However, Hobbes's system is the first consequent description of a modern political society with its intrinsic individuality; he could not describe the political acting in the same society, partly because of the same strict methodological individualism. The dilemma which emerged from the counter-theories of the early modernity is surprisingly modern, and we can trace it directly in the distinction of Benjamin Constant between *the liberties of the ancients and moderns*, and Isaiah Berlin's concepts of *positive and negative liberties* (Constant 1980; Berlin 1969). Participation with the *ethos* of the ancients, risking the individuality on the one hand, and the violence, on the other, or freedom of privacy, risking the active participation, they are the Scylla and Charybdis of the modern public people from Calvin to our time.

References

Berlin, I. 1969. *Four Essays on Liberty.* Oxford: Oxford University Press.

Calvin, J. 2009. *Institutes of the Christian Religion* (trans. H. Beveridge). Peabody/MA: Hendrickson Publishers.

Calvinus, I. 1863–1892. Institutio Religionis Christianae [Institutio maior]. In G. Baum – E. Cunitz – E. Reuss (eds.), *Ioannis Calvini Opera quae Supersunt Omnia.* Brunswig: Schwetschke. Vol. 2. [*Corpus Reformatorum*, Vol. 30].

Constant, B. 1980. *De la liberté chez modernes. Écrits politiques* (ed. M. Gauchet). Paris: Libraire Générale Française.

Glover, W. G. 1993. Human Nature and the State in Hobbes. In P. King (ed.), *Thomas Hobbes. Critical Assessments,* London – New York: Routledge. Vol. 4. *Religion,* pp. 50–72.

Hobbes, Th. 1651. *Leviathan, or, The Matter, Form, and Power of a Commonwealth Ecclesiastical and Civil.* London: Andrew Crooke.

Martinich, A. P. 2005. *Hobbes.* New York & London: Routledge Taylor & Francis Group.

Mester, B. 2010. The Beatitude of Souls amongst the Things Indifferent. Adiaphora in the Stoical Ethics and in the Christian Thinking. In J. Juhant & B. Žalec (eds.): *Art of Life. Origins, Foundations and Perspectives*, Münster: Lit Verlag, pp. 147–154.

Oakeshott, M. 1975. Introduction to *Leviathan.* In M. Oakeshott, *Hobbes on Civil Association,* Oxford: Blackwell, pp. 1–74.

FEAR, POLITICS, POWER – CIVILIZATION AS THE EDUCATION OF COURAGE[1]

Gábor Kovacs, Budapest

"*Qui n'a pas vécu avant 1789, ne connait pas la douceur de vivre*" – He who didn't live before 1789 could not experience the joys of life – says Talleyrand's famous bon mot. It doesn't seem to be an overstatement, in the early 21st century, to risk thathe who didn't live in a totalitarian political system could not experience what means to live in the state of fear. The fact that both thinkers who are the heroes of my paper, Guglielmo Ferrero (1871–1942) and István Bibó (1911–1979), attributed an essential role to fear which was the consequence of their life experiences about the nature and operational mechanisms of totalitarianism. Their walks of life crossed each other at the Graduate Institute of International Studies of Geneva in 1934-35. Ferrero, the emigrant Italian thinker who had escaped from the Fascist Italy to Switzerland acquired a professorship of the Institute and Bibó was his disciple attending his professor's lectures dealing with the problem of political power.

Guglielmo Ferrero was a many sided thinker with a significant achievement in the field of literature, journalism and historiography. (To the influence of Ferrero exerted on Hungarian culture see: Ferenczi, 1990) His personal encounter with fear induced by a new kind of political regime was in the post-war Italy after Mussolini's taking over of power. Ferrero gave an interview to an American reporter with criticizing remarks concerning the Italian fascism. The text was cabled to Rome by the Italian Consulate. (Ferrero 1942: 6) The telegram came to find its way to Mussolini and incensed him against the Italian intellectual. The authorities threatened Ferrero who was deeply astonished by the discrepancy between the insignificance of the case and the pathologically exaggerated reaction of political power. How is it possible that a political regime possessing the means of power to an extent unknown in previous modern history feels being threatened by an interview given to a remote foreign newspaper? Ferrero found the cause of this strange phenomenon in fear which emerged because of the lack of legitimate po-

1 This paper was supported by the Hungarian Scientific Research Fund (OTKA K104643).

litical power. This personal experience stimulated his researches focusing upon the principles of legitimacy. Here it is not enough space for a detailed investigation of his theory (about this problem see: Kovács 1999: 321–323) but it is not necessary for us; what we are interested in is his conclusion according to which if a political power doesn't arise from the actually valid principle of legitimacy or abuses this principle it inevitably becomes illegal inciting ever increasing amount of fear dispersing in whole society. Fear permeates whole universe but human being is in a privileged position because of his awareness of death:

"Knowing that he may die at any moment and that one day or another he will have to die, he sees the danger of death everywhere. Unbalanced by this fear, his imagination darkens the face of the universe with imaginary dangers that he adds to the real ones, with fantastic beings or monstrous forces against which he is powerless."(Ferrero, 1942: 30)

Ferrero draws - from the mental fragility and precariousness of human being - a Hobbesian conclusion according to which fear prompts some kind of social contract reducing the amount of this fear of anarchy and war to the as possible least level. (Hobbes, 1958: 104–109) Progress of a civilization means its ability to develop the principles of legitimacy ensuring lasting fearless existence for the ensuing generations of human beings living within the frameworks of it. Civilization, seeing from this aspect, is the educational process of courage. A historical event, the Jacobin phase of the French revolution, in the theory of Ferrero, derailed this educational process. (Ferrero, 1951) Instead of decreasing of the amount of fear, existing in French society after the collapse of royal power, the Jacobins elevated it to the position of a power legitimating means. Terror became an ideology; Jacobin dictatorship, in the interpretation of Ferrero, was a proto-totalitarian kind of political regime and Napoleon for him was the historical prefiguration of the totalitarian dictators of the 20th century.

To the life of Istvan Bibo, the middle class origin intellectual, whose intellectual socialization bore on itself the imprint of Ferrero' thought, totalitarianism cast its dark shadow as well. Communist takeover in 1949 broke into two his carrier; he was stripped of the membership of the Hungarian Academy of Sciences end removed from the University of Szeged where he had previously acquired a professorship. He was relegated to the margin in the early 1950s, during the Communist dictatorship which was one of the darkest periods in the 20th century for Hungary. In 1956, during the Hungarian anti-Stalinist revolution he became the state-minister of the last revolutionary government; after the putting down of the revolution, in the period of reprisals the court of the Kadarite puppet government condemned him to a life imprisonment with the charge of conspiracy against the legal political power, i.e. the Stalinist dictatorship. By an amnesty, in 1963, he was released from the prison and the last period of his life was spent in inner emigration. Unlike many of his contemporaries he never made a compromise with the government of the so called 'soft dictatorship'.

Bibó originally was dealing with the philosophy of law but his interest, from the 1930s on, turned to political philosophy and political science. Fear played a central role in his thought – the notion avowedly was borrowed from Ferrero's political philosophy and Bibó adapted it into his own theory. Bibó's main field of interest was Central and Eastern Europe, the region which, for him, because of specific constellations of social, political and socio-psychological factors became the theatre of political-communal hysterias induced by fear concerning the existence of national communities. (Kovács, 2010, Kovács, 2012)

It is not an easy task to classify Bibó as a political thinker; his thought bears on itself the imprint of socialism, conservatism and liberalism and his thought is imbued with characteristically Christian values. This seems to be embarrassingly eclectic composition but this is the consequence of his *synoptic method* learnt from his former master Barna Horváth, professor of legal philosophy and sociology at Szeged University where Bibó got his doctorate in 1934. Synoptic method in the sociology of law of Horváth inspired by neo-Kantianism involves a strict separation of the field of facts and values but means at the same time the synopsis i.e. viewing together facts and values. (Berki, 1992: 518, Csepregi, 2003: 78–79) These are two spheres of reality having their own characteristic inner laws; the inner law of the sphere of facts is causality, the inner law of the sphere of values is normativity. Facts must be viewed according to their inner law, i.e. causality but, at the same time, must be viewed according to the law alien to them, i.e. normativity and vice versa.

Bibó enlarges the scope of this Kantian origin method using it in a wider sense; it means for him not only viewing together facts and values but viewing together different value systems without striving for a synthesis of them. Some elements of conservatism, socialism, liberalism and Christian thought, in his opinion, are all vital important for European civilization but the exclusive dominance of one of them would enforce reality into a cage of ideology. At the root of Bibó's thought there is a phenomenological-pragmatic approach. What is important for him is the *healthy sense of reality*; different people with different ideological departures will conclude to the same conclusion supposing they possess this healthy sense of reality. Similarly to pragmatism the validity of truth, for Bibó, can be proved or disproved by the action of a human agent. The experience of reality will be distorted if we approach to reality around us with ideological presuppositions. This is the meaning of the claim that we have to see the thing, the phenomenon itself.

There are two basic requirements for Bibó which are beyond particular political value-systems or ideologies: *human dignity* and *fearless human existence*. They are interconnected requirements; it is not possible to ensure human dignity for human beings if their existence has been burdened and distorted by fear. The most respectable achievement, in Bibó's theory, of the European civilization is the making of political democracy ensuring the possibility of fearless life.

There is an ambivalent criticism of modernity in Bibó's thought; it is one of the most interesting characteristics of it. Bibó, one the one hand, highly appreciates the political principles of modernity embodied in the institutions of representative democracy and, on the other hand, strongly criticizes the modern history having run to deadlocks from time to time. (Kovács, 2010) The content of European civilization, it is the deepest conviction of Bibó, is the *humanization of power* but it has been endangered from the beginning by the recurrent waves of power-concentration. Bibó, similarly to conservatives, prefers small evolutionary changes to rapid revolutionary transitions but, according to his opinion, in certain circumstances revolution is the only means for dispersing a petrified power concentration burdened upon society.

The problem of violence leads to another problem, namely to the connection of political action and morality. It is a crucial point in our train of thought because it leads us to the problem of *fear-management* and its relation to the calculative rationality of modernity. One of the basic axioms of modern political thinking is the separation of morality and politics; it, in Weberian terms, has been part and parcel of the process of rationalization and compartmentalization of modern life since early modernity. This separation was the core of Machiavelli' thought whose approach was determined by his anthropological pessimism. Human beings, Machiavelli declares, are bad by nature, unless they are enforced to be good by outer factors. Love of the subjects is a good thing for the Prince but it doesn't depend on him. Fear, contrary to love, is in the power of the Prince; he has only to take care so that fear doesn't change into hate. (Machiavelli, 2012: 82) Prince, in other words, is able to use fear for his own purpose with the help of calculative rationality. So, fear, in the theory of Machiavelli, appears as a serviceable means of power-technique; the Prince who has acquired the art of good rule can keep it under control. To avoid the frequently heard misunderstanding it must be pointed out that Machiavelli, as one of the founding fathers of modern republicanism, doesn't teach inherent immorality of politics; what he talks about is the amoral nature of political action. His thesis is that the inner regulative principles of the fields of morality and politics are different; but he doesn't think that both fields are totally independent from each other; excessive cruelty unmakes the moral fabric of society demolishing everything around itself. When such thinkers as Machiavelli and Hobbes drew line between morality and politics it was the consequence of the special constellations of early modernity; the politics of the Late Middle Ages saturated with Christian morality had resulted in devastating religious and civil wars and to separate these two fields seemed to be the best medicine for religious hate with its devastating aftermaths.

But this medicine, as medicines usually do so, produced undesirable long term side-effects. The Jacobin phase of the French Revolution of 1789 was the second step in the history of fear-management of modernity. Its novelty was the intertwining of terror and fear. The terror induced fear couldn't be domesticated: it converted into irresistible force destroying everything around itself. The rational fear-management transformed into enemy-seeking political hysteria leading whole society into the self-perpetuating and ever expending circle of fear. That is why French Revolution of 1789 was, in Bibó's opinion, the most successful and the most unsuccessful revolution at the same time. It was a success because it had removed the power concentration of the *ancien regime* and it was a failure because using terror as a governmental technics unleashed fear, letting it loose on European civilization.

The second stage of the French Revolution, Bibó argues following Ferrero's interpretation, is the historical prefiguration of the totalitarian revolutions of the 20th century. The fabric of the European civilization has been woven with three threads; the Graeco-Roman organizational practicality, the Christian program of social organization based on the idea of non-violence, and the modern technique of freedom and rights embodied in the institutions of parliamentary democracy are equally important constituents of it. Political method emerging from the connection of terror and ideology, i.e. totalitarianism, threatens with the unmaking of this intricate fabric. Bibó rejects, on the one hand, socialdarwinism with its implications resulted in Nazism, and the concept of class-struggle, the basic ideological tenet of Stalinism.

The humanization of power and the lessening of fear implied by it, in Bibó's thought, require a connection between the fields of morality and politics. This doesn't mean the flat preaching of morality but the moral grounding of political institutions. Politics, albeit it is a self-contained field of human action with its own inner regulative principles, should have its roots in the soil of morality. If these roots were cut off politics would pervert into some kind of power technology and politicians would become mere technicians of power as it happened in the case of totalitarianism and its personnel. Bibó's intellectual position concerning the relation of morality and politics has adequately been described by one of its interpreters as the realism of moralism, an "almost flawless synthesis of a deeply radical, morally infused vision and value-system with the hard-nosed, unsentimental realist's insights into enduring problems of politics and society" (Berki, 1992: 513).

Conclusion

Christianity is a requisite historical component of the European fear-lessening political program, Bibó argues, and he refers, first of all, to Jesus' exemplary gestures concerning the fear-lessening power of neighbourly love: "He had an extraordinary gift of using word and gesture for quelling people whetted to hate, strike, judge, scold, or to vent other wretched forms of fear, and opening their eyes to the futility of their intention or conduct." Bibó, 2012 a: 12) Christian love, for Bibó, doesn't mean a passive kind of behavior, surrender or helpless submission to violence and injustice but an activity looking for the possibility of applying violence-stopping human gestures. There are, of course, situations, when such kind gestures are ineffective and we are enforced to use violent means facing violence and injustice but in this case we have to aware of our failure and we shouldn't forget that violence is the last means and it can't be glorified as a panacea for solving social and political problems. Violence always generates more violence and increases the amount of fear circulating among the members of society. Democracy, for Bibó, means a special kind of political system which is based on the institutional methods of fear-lessening, and to be a democrat "is first and foremost not to be afraid; not to be afraid of those who have a different opinion, speak a different language and are of another race; not to be afraid of revolution, conspiracies, the unknown evil intentions of the enemy, hostile propaganda, disdain, and generally all those imaginary dangers that become real dangers because we are afraid of them" (Bibó 2012 b: 15).

References

Berki, R. 1992. The Realism of Moralism: The Political Philosophy of István Bibó, *History of Political Thought,* vol. XIII., (3), pp. 513–534.

Bibó, I. 2012a. *The Meaning of European Social Development* (translated by P. Pásztor), manuscript.

Bibó, I. 2012b. *The Miseries of Eastern European Small States* (translated by P. Pásztor), manuscript.

Ferenczi, L. 1990. Ferrero on Hongrie (1905–1918). In: *Venezia, Italia e Ungheria tra Decadentismo e avangardia.* A cura di Zs. Kovács et P. Sárközy. Budapest: Akadémiai Kiadó, pp. 221–227.

Csepregi, A. 2003. *Two Ways to Freedom.* Christianity and Democracy in the Thought of István Bibó and Dietrich Bonhoeffer. Budapest: Acta Theologica Lutherana Budapestinensia.

Ferrero, G. 1942. *The Principles of Power.* The Great Political Crises of History. Translated by Theodore R. Jaeckel. New York: G. P. Putnam's Sons.

Ferrero, G. 1951. *Les deux révolutions françaises* 1789-1796. Paris: Monnier.

Hobbes, T. 1958. *Leviathan Parts I and II.* New York: The Bobbes–Merril Company, Inc.

Kovács, G., 1999. Can Power Be Humanized? The Notions of Elite and Legitimation in István Bibó's Political Philosophy, *Studies in Eastern European Thought*, 51 (4), pp. 307-327.

Kovács G. 2010. Region of Deformities? – The Image of Central-Eastern Europe in the Political Philosophy of István Bibó. In Jurova J., Jozek M., Kiepas A., Machura P., (eds.), *Central-European Ethos or Local Traditions: Equality, Justice*, Boskovice, Czeh Republic: Albert, pp. 133–140.

Kovács, G. 2012. Rationality and affectivity in Politics – the Role of Fear and Hysteria in the Political Thought of István Bibó. *Archiwum Historii Filozofii I Mysli Spolecznej* Archive of the History of Philosophy and Social Thought. Vol. 57/2012, Supplement, pp. 65–82.

Machiavelli, N. 2012. *The Prince.* http://www.constitution.org/mac/prince.pdf

This paper was supported by the Hungarian Scientific Research Fund (OTKA K104643).

ANTI-POLISH MIGRANT MORAL PANICS AND TRADE UNIONS IN THE UK[1]

Paul Chan, Manchester; Ian Fitzgerald, Newcastle; Rafal Smoczyinski, Warsaw

Defining the problem

Over the last decade, the growth of cross-border migration has stimulated considerable research into its effects on culture and society. In Europe, the enlargement of the Union has not only resulted in growth of an economic and geographic area known for its most extensive free movement of workers, but also renewed interests in researching the conditions and consequences of this new wave of migration. In times of economic boom, migration was essentially emphasised by politicians as a positive development, aimed at plugging skills shortages and promoting growth (Dench *et al.* 2006); yet in current times of austerity, anxieties surrounding migration are mounting leading to increasing precarity for migrants and the retreat of the political rhetoric of the 'good migrant' (see e.g. Anderson 2010). The intensification of migration has certainly, as Santos (2006) highlighted, "led social scientists and politicians to view them as a *rupture* with previous forms of cross border interactions, a new phenomena termed 'globalization' (p. 393; *emphasis* added)." In recent times, governments across the world – especially in the developed world – appear to be keen to contain this rupture by fortifying national borders through the tightening up of routes to immigration and laying the rhetorical blame on immigrant workers displacing the indigenous population in the labour market (Anderson 2010). Slogans such as 'British Jobs for British Workers' is just one such example.

Immigration has certainly fuelled the rise of nationalistic and protectionistic sentiments, and stoked the growth of the far-right political movement in Europe. The contemporary case of Anders Breivik – the Norwegian who carried out a bomb

1 It is acknowledged that this paper was produced while carrying out the Polish National Science Centre's funded project "Societal Reactions towards Polish Economic Migrants in Northern England after 2004", project nr. 2011/01/D/HS6/04257.

attack on government buildings in Oslo and a mass shooting that killed 69 people on the Norwegian island of Utøya – illustrates the contentious and potentially explosive nature of immigration dynamics. Yet, as Goodwin (2009) observed in the evolution of the far-right movement in Europe, the rise of nationalist sentiments has taken a 'cultural' turn in that anti-immigration discourse has moved from one that is against economic migration to one that focuses on the threat of immigration to cultural identity and integrity. Indeed, Anders Breivik claimed that his actions were motivated by his desire to quell the tides of European multi-culturalism.

However, in spite of recognising the marginalisation of migrants, or the 'silencing' of migrants in the encouragement of assimilation, it is argued that scholars have implicitly treated migrants as a distinct social category of the 'stranger' living in a foreign land and having limited resources to alter their destinies. It is this tacit assumption of the inevitability of migrants acting as passive recipients of what life throws at them that our article attends to. We render the relative 'silencing' of migrants as problematic, and join contemporary interests in explicating the struggles and resistance of marginalised groups (see e.g. Parnaby 2003) through narrowing our observations of the treatment of the Polish migrants in the UK.

With the 2004 enlargement of the EU the United Kingdom witnessed an unprecedented inflow of economic migrants from Central and Eastern European countries (A8 countries) (Salt, Millar 2006). Due to this many British public institutions including those involved with housing, labour policy and social cohesion have experienced significant pressure. The UK, though, did introduce a limited registration scheme for these workers and over one million A8 migrants, the majority Poles (66 percent) registered as being employed in mostly low paid jobs. It is also not known how many others were self-employed or did not register with the scheme. Although, again it is estimated that large numbers were in these categories (Harvey, Behling 2008). Because of the growing number of A8 migrants, in some parts of indigenous British society there has developed a complex set of anxious societal reactions triggered by this challenge. The following article will analyse anti-migrant societal reactions understood as moral panics drawing mostly on Carby-Hall (2007), Mawby and Gisby (2009) and Robinson (2009). Further, it will explore the crucial role of British trade unions who campaigned on behalf of migrants and were committed to give them a voice.

Anti-Migrant Moral Panics

The concept of moral panics explores the dynamics of collective concern towards an alleged menace to social order. According to Cohen (1972: 9), who introduced this concept into field of social sciences, modern societies appear to be subject to periods of moral panics: "*A person or group of persons emerges to become defined as a threat to social values; its nature is presented in a stylized and stereotypical fashion by the mass media, politicians, and interest groups*". The classic definition of this concept states that panics serve to reassert the dominance of an established value system, provide ontological security at a time of social anxiety, and target those who are considered folk-devils as an external threat. The development of anxious social reactions towards A8 migrants in Britain during 2000s followed a similar pattern to that identified by moral panic scholars (e.g. Ben Yehuda, Goode 1994; Thompson 1998; Critcher 2003). The typical features displaid are – concern, hostility, dis-proportionality, symbolization and then the intervention of social control agents. Firstly, as the data demonstrate a heightened level of concern over A8 migrants, and consequently over A2 migrants (Bulgarians and Romanians) has been detected from the news media prior to the accession (BBC 16th April 2003) and then in its early stages at both national and local levels (The Morning Star – October 26th 2004; The Sun - August 23rd 2005; Daily Telegraph - November 2nd 2005). Carby-Hall (2007) in his report "*The Treatment of Polish and other A8 economic migrants in the European Union Member States*" quotes a Financial Times/Harris Poll which indicates that British citizens expressed more concern than citizens of the other EU States towards arriving A8 migrants. Forty-seven percent of the British respondents considered that A8 migrants constituted a negative factor for the economy (with only 19 percent thinking that it had been positive), 76 percent of respondents argued that there were too many foreigners in Britain and 76 percent of respondents wanted the British authorities to impose new measures to limit economic migrants arriving from the A8 countries (ibid).

Mawby and Gisby (2009) have also recognised the symptoms of moral panic towards Eastern European migrants. They cite media reactions and manufactured news, which were appearing especially in the tabloid type British media. They explore the discursive strategies of the mass media which constantly linked migration with crime. According to their argument the growing concern of the public was systematically fed with stylized and stereotypical headlines such as "floods of migrants taking our jobs". Another permanent issue that contributed to a moral panic concern was the social housing policy theme. Robinson (2009) shows how moral panic proponents (e.g. Migration Watch UK, and the British National Party) were producing dubious claims that migrants acted as a major reason for social housing shortage and were allegedly responsible for the rise in house prices. These rumours about obtaining social housing at the expense of British citizens in need resonated with the social imaginary and contributed to the rise of a moral panic concern (ibid). At the same time as this political support for the BNP began to increase, notably in the North of England, particularly in Burnley and its neighbouring borough Pendle. Interesting it was not only indigenous white communities but also established Asian and other black minority ethnic communities that have reacted negatively to the A8 migration (Slough Borough Council 2008: 277). As a consequence of moral panic claims a rise in hostile attitudes have occurred. Carby Hall (2007: 260) describes incidents near Hull and Lincolnshire of hate crimes committed against Polish migrants who were targeted as folk devils because "… *they were allegedly taking the jobs of local citizens*". Migrants in different areas fell prey to acts of verbal abuse, assaults, property damage, arson and even murder (Carby Hall 2007: 259; see also McIlwaine et al. 2006; Thorp 2008).

The emergence of A8 migrants in the British social field has triggered not only a moral panic ideology circulating in the form of tabloid rumours, urban legends, and political agitation but further the negative framing of economic migrants has also evoked the intervention of social control agents. According to Mawby and Gisby (2009) the fear of migrant crime fuelled by the tabloid press has affected policy making responses. For instance in October 2006, the UK government declared that it would restrict labour migration from the A2 countries (Bulgaria and Romania). The symptoms of social control involvement was visible also during the heated debate over the consequences of the new immigration for housing policy in the UK. The UK Independence Party and British National Party were addressing British Government to "restore proper control" over housing policy and immigration, in 2007 the Cabinet Minister Margaret Hodge in *The Observer* stated that migrants should not be prioritized over indigenous population for social housing (Robinson 2009). Whilst in the same year in his speech as Labour Party leader and Prime Minister Gordon Brown whilst speaking about his Britain introduced the now infamous phrase 'British jobs for British workers'.

Finally, we may also reveal the major indicator of moral panic, namely, the potential of disproportionality embedded in the anti-migrant claim making. According to existing data the alleged threat posed by Eastern European migrants was not corroborated by the empirical evidence on the actual risk to social cohesion. For example, claims that A2 enlargement would mean a flood of crime was not evidenced by criminal records (Mawby and Gibsy 2009). Similarly the allegations about social housing abuses committed by new migrants were not justified. Governmental reports revealed that less than five percent of social lettings in England in 2006/07 were provided to foreigners and less than one percent of social houses received A8 and A2 migrants (Robinson 2009). Further, a study commissioned by the Department of Work and Pensions (Gilpin et al. 2006) questioned the moral panic thesis that A8 economic migrants were taking the jobs of British citizens. This report showed that there was no statistical evidence to support claims that migrants from Eastern Europe have expanded the scale of unemployment in the UK. In fact, Carby-Hall (2007) provides a significant amount of information that economic migrants from the new EU member states contributed to growth as they filled labour shortages.

Polish Migrant Workers and UK Trade Unions

Before discussing the trade union response to new Polish migrants and the path taken by UK trade unions, it is worth reminding ourselves of the past reaction of UK trade unions to new migrants. Wrench (2004) discusses this in some detail, including noting that ex-Polish servicemen were recruited following the Second World War but under strict TUC (The UK trade union federation) guidelines. However, the main bulk of engagement here was with ex-colonial mainly black workers who were sometimes excluded from union membership and openly discriminated against. Overall though there was a negative response to new migrants, until the introduction of trade union anti-racist education and initiatives to support black and new migrant workers. What must be considered though is that whilst the national trade union response evolved a more complex situation existed at the workplace where some anti-migrant attitudes remained (see Jefferys, Ouali 2007). Thus as Penninx and Roosblad (2000) remind us it is not just that trade unions should support or not oppose migrants introduction into a national labour market. It is more that they are willing to include these workers into membership and indeed into organisational structures.

Hence entering the period of the new Polish migration of 2004 it is not surprising to report that UK trade unions at a national level supported the entry of Polish workers into the UK labour market through policy documents, statements and some initiatives. Indeed there was already underway, following the death of Chinese migrant workers, a national and sector campaign to introduce the Gangmasters Act 2004. This would make it illegal to operate a business that supplied labour, often mostly migrant, without a licence in the agriculture, food processing and packaging sectors. The trade unions, in particular the T&G, were at the forefront of this successful campaign. Following the A8 accession at a regional level, trade unions, and in particular the regional divisions of the TUC, supported new migrants through a number of policy and campaign initiatives (see Fitzgerald, Hardy 2010). Policy and campaign initiatives often supported already emerging local ad hoc meetings and activities which were jointly organised by trade unions, local government, community activists and NGOs. Here advice and information were provided to new Polish migrants with regard to housing, social benefits, wages, bank accounts etc. (see Fitzgerald 2008).

We have to bear in mind that for a large number of Polish workers the early migration meant suffering quite horrendous conditions both in the workplace and in the community. This included unpaid wages, poor working conditions, poor housing and indeed destitution, as well as reported slave and forced labour (see Fitzgerald 2006; Carby-Hall, 2007; Craig et al., 2007). This situation did improve due to the assistance provided by a number of Polish community activists (including the long standing ZPWB). Trade unions and NGOs also supported action and often provided a growing amount of targeted Polish language information. However, these bodies were often constrained either by resources or a failure to understand or accept the needs of newly emerging communities (see Fitzgerald 2008). There were also cases of workplace action. For example one group of 21 Polish building workers in North Tyneside did take direct action against employer violence and exploration. Ucatt had spent some months trying to unsuccessfully organise these workers. But following violence by the employer to one particular Polish worker they walked off site and formed a picket line. The employer was forced to contact Ucatt who then negotiated a return to work settlement (Fitzgerald 2006). Further, a Solidarnsc international officer reports that they have received numerous requests from UK Polish migrants for details of UK trade unions. This includes a South East based group who were at the time in dispute with their employer over wages and conditions.

The agency of community based Polish activists is most noticeable where the growth of networks brought together sometimes dispersed migrants. This included a growing network of Polish language, Polish administered community websites (see Fitzgerald et al. 2012) and the rise, as noted of Polish community associations. Activity here was often based around Polish cafes, pubs and shops that had opened in town and cities throughout the UK. Trade unions and other organisations did support some of these developments but often this has relied on the agency of these newly emerging Polish community activists and some individual Polish workers. They have taken a central role in organising community events and inviting trade unions and other organisations to attend. The key issue with this is how successful this is in expanding union boundaries to encompass the more fluid developments in the new Polish communities. One of the more interesting developments here was the GMB establishment of a separate Polish branch (the member level democratic structure of a UK trade union) which was established in a learning and organising centre in Southampton (Branch M-48). This branch had Polish elected officials and was conducted in Polish which allowed people to communicate effectively and to gain the confidence to engage in debate.

Discusion and Conclusions

Moral panic occurrences seem to confirm a tacit assumption of the vulnerable migrants who acted as passive recipients of hostile attitudes of some sectors of the indigenous British population. However, we argue that the stigmatized identities of Polish migrants were open to new rearticulations, that is to say, migrants with the help of external agents (e.g. trade unions) were able to a large extent fight back and overcome their plight. The evidence shows that UK unions have shown an inclusionary approach to new Polish migrants that, particularly at a national level, was based on three noticeable factors. First, it is not surprising given a more open acceptance of migration in a multicultural UK. Second, the UK had a number of skill shortages and new migrants were not seen as displacing indigenous workers. Indeed early on it was estimated that a manageable number of A8 workers would come to the UK (Dustman et al. 2003). Third, Fitzgerald and Hardy (2010: 137) report a more open union approach to new migrants given that these were European and of course white. However, by 2006 both the scale and scope of the accession migration were believed to be unprecedented, affecting most areas of the labour market. This meant that most UK organisations were ill-prepared to deal with new Polish migrants. The overwhelming initial response was crisis management, so for trade unions when they encountered Poles there were questions and needs outside of their main collective bargaining duties. So this necessitated involvement in collaborations with organisations that they would not normally deal, hence the large number of local ad hoc meetings and activities (Fitzgerald 2008). There were in essence a number of 'marriages of convenience' to deal with and support Polish workers and their families in the community.

Finally then this paper whilst acknowledging anti-migrant moral panic in the the UK has emphasized that migrants were not passive recipients of the hostile societal reactions but indeed contested and negotiated their stigmatized identities. This is not to deny that migrants had limited possibilities of fighting back. Sedimented structures of power which limited migrants possibilities of accessing material and symbolic resources required external agency that would help them to challenge stigmatization. This assistance was provided by British trade unions as well as a growing number of Polish migrant organizations.

Bibliography

Anderson, B. 2010. Migration, immigration controls and the fashioning of precarious workers. In *Work Employment & Society*, 24(2): 300–317.

Ben Yehuda, N., Goode, E. 1994. *Moral Panics*, New York: Oxford University Press.

Carby-Hall, J. 2007. *The Treatment of Polish and Other A8 Economic Migrants in the European Union Member States*. Report for the Commissioner for Civil Rights Protection of the Republic of Poland.

Castles, S., Kosack, G. 1973. *Immigrant Workers and Class Structure in Western Europe*. Oxford: Oxford University Press.

Cohen, S. 1972. *Folk Devils and Moral Panics.* London: McGibbon and Kee.

Craig, G., Gaus, A., Wilkinson, M., Skrivankova K., McQuade, A. 2007. *Contemporary slavery in the UK.* Joseph Rowntree Foundation.

Critcher, C. 2003. *Moral Panics and Media.* Buckingham: Open University Press

de Sousa Santos, B. 2006. Globalizations. In *Theory, Culture and Society*, 23(2-3), 393 – 399.

Dench S., J. Hurstfield, D. Hill, Akroyd, K. 2006. *Employers' use of migrant labour.* Online Report. 04/06, London: Home Office.

Dustman, C., Casanova, M., Fertig, M., Preston, I.,Schmidt, C.M. 2003. *The impact of EU enlargement on migration flows*. Home Office Online Report 25/03, London: Home Office.

Fitzgerald I. 2006. Organising Migrant Workers in Construction: Experience from the North East of England. Newcastle upon Tyne: Northern TUC.

Fitzgerald, I. 2008. *A Moving Target: The Informational Needs of Polish Migrant Workers in Yorkshire and the Humber*. Leeds: Yorkshire and the Humber TUC.

Fitzgerald, I., Hardy, J. 2010. Thinking outside the box? Trade union organising strategies and Polish migrant workers in the United Kingdom. In *British Journal of Industrial Relations*, 48(1): 131–150.

Fitzgerald, I., Martinez Lucio, M., Hardy, J. 2012. The internet, employment and Polish migrant workers: Communication, activism and competition in the new organisational spaces. In *New Technology Work and Employment* 27(2): 93-105.

Gilpin, N., Henty, M., Lemos, S. Portes, J., Bullen, C. 2006. *The impact of free movement of workers from Central and Eastern Europe on the UK labour market.* Department for Work and Pensions, Working Paper No 29, London: HMSO.

Goodwin, M. J. 2009. The radical right in contemporary Europe: past, present and future. In *Political Studies Review*, 7(3), 322–329.

Harvey, M., Behling, F. 2008. *The Evasion Economy: False Self-Employment in the UK Construction Industry*. London: UCATT.

Jefferys, S., Ouali, N. 2007. Trade unions and racism in London, Brussels and Paris public transport. *Industrial Relations Journal*, 38:5, 406–422.

Mawby, R., Gisby, W. 2009. Crime, Media and Moral Panic in an Expanding European Union. In *The Howard Journal* 48(1): 37-51.

McIlwaine, C., Datta, K., Evans, Y., Herbert, J., May, J., Wills, J. 2006. *Gender and Ethnic Identities among Low-paid Migrant Workers in London.* Queen Mary University of London, June 2006.

Parnaby, P. 2003. Disaster through Dirty Windshields. Law, Order and Toronto's Squeegee Kids. In *Canadian Journal of Sociology* 28(3): 281-307.

Penninx, R., Roosblad, J.(eds). 2000. *Trade Unions, Immigration, and Immigrants in Europe, 1960–93*. Oxford: Berghahn Books.

Robinson, D. 2009. New Immigrants and Migrants in Social Housing in Britain: Discursive Themes and Lived Realities. In: *Policy and Politics*, 38 (1), pp. 57-77.

Salt, J. and Millar, J. 2006. Foreign labour in the United Kingdom: current patterns and trends. *Labour Market Trends*, 114 (10): 335–55. Office for National Statistics.

Slough Borough Council. 2008. *Memorandum*, to the House of Lords, Select Committee on Economic Affairs, 1st Report of Session 2007–08, April 2008.

Thompson, K. 1998. *Moral Panics.* London: Routledge.

Thorp, A. 2008. *Impacts of immigration.* House of Commons Library Research Paper 08/65, 25 July 2008.

Wrench, J. 2004. Trade union responses to immigrants and ethnic inequality in Denmark and the UK: the context of consensus and conflict. In *European Journal of Industrial Relations*, 10 (1): 7–30.

CULTURE OF FEAR AND THE MEANING OF AUTHORITY; WHAT ARE WE AFRAID OF?

Mateja Pevec Rozman, Ljubljana

Introduction or what are we afraid of?

Modern times are denoted with various changes as for instance the fall of the European Communism, the rise of ecological crisis, the collapse of financial market etc. Uncertainty arises in all areas of human life, which is the basis for the prosperity of fear. Even if human being is a being of hope, we all have our fears too. We are afraid of losing someone we love, we are afraid of losing our human dignity, health, job, life, freedom, love, faith etc. Everyone and each of us have his or her own fears, which we are afraid they will be realized. Sometimes we are also afraid to except the truth, we are afraid to start healing the wounds, to start the process of reconciliation … we are afraid of being weak and small, vulnerable, we are afraid of not being loved and accepted. We are afraid of the darkness and emptiness … And there is nothing wrong with that! We don't have to be afraid of being afraid; fear is an expression of human non-necessity and incompleteness. Human is a being whose life is not in his possession (Stres 1985, 76). A man is not a perfect (total) being so he/she cannot totally escape from fear. On the other hand, fear is a vital part of human self-preservation and survival (Juhant 2012, 16), together with love, fear is a basis of morality (Žalec 2012, 21) so it would be wrong to overlook or ignore it.

What is fear?

Some authors distinguish between the terms fear in its narrowest sense (*Ger. Furcht)* and anxiety or dread (*Ger. Angst*), but others use both terms interchangeably as synonyms, namely, a clear-cut distinction between them in real life is difficult to make. Fear is a reaction to something concrete, e. g. fear of a dentist, fear of an exam, fear of the loss of property or assets, and as such has nothing to do with anxiety which is something undetermined – a state which essence and meaning can be comprehended only as a presentiment of the fact of life which is called death.

Slovenian psychologist and psychotherapist Miran Možina finds there is a terminological confusion in Slovenian psychology regarding terms fear (*Slo. strah*) and anxiety (*Slo. bojazen, tesnoba, anksioznost*) (2010, 40-44). In Slovenian literature, the term anxiety disorder is most frequent (Erzar 2007), whereas in Serbian literature the term fear is used the most. Both terms are similar; however, fear includes also anxiety but not the other way round (Možina 2010, 40). The main distinction between them is that fear is an emotional response to a definite threat (for instance, when seeing a snake), whereas anxiety can occur without an identifiable trigger stimulus (ibid., 41). Fear is a basic emotion of each individual, which main role is to protect and to adapt (Erić 2004, 534). For many authors, distinction between fear and anxiety has become unclear, so both terms have been equated more and more.

To sum up: fear is an emotion induced by a threat. Psychotherapist Milivojević describes fear as a person's response to a dangerous object or situation – the person assesses that he or she cannot cope adequately with the object or situation endangering him or her or that some of the person's values are endangered. Anxiety is a common name/term for fears that relate to future events (worry, stage fright, anxiety) (Milivojević 2008, 490-491). The purpose of fear is very clear: it helps to survive and protect the individual and it also offers a protection of individual values. It is an inner signal (ibid., 491) that warns us to realize that the situation we are situated in is surpassing our abilities.

Hope as the opposite of fear

Already the earliest antique philosophers were concerned about "fear topics", but it became most popular in the 19th century with Søren Kierkegaard (Petkovšek 2012, 32). His attempt is to define human existence confronting with absolute free choices, also unfounded; consequently they fill us with anxiety (Vattimo 2004, 20). Kierkegaard was convinced that fear essentially defines human being. How can a man then confront fear? What is the opposite of fear? Is there anything stronger than fear that could define a human existence?

The opposite of fear according to some authors is courage; courage as a force that helps overcome individual's weakness and reduce the dread of the unknown of what is to come. Aristotle treats fear in connection with courage (fearlessness) in the III. Book of his *Ethika Nikomacheia* (cf. also Juhant 2012, 13):

"The man who exceeds in fear is a coward; for he fears both what he ought not and as he ought not, and all the similar characterizations attach to him. He is lacking also in confidence; but he is more conspicuous for his excess of fear in painful situations. The coward, then, is a despairing sort of person; for he fears everything. The brave man, on the other hand, has the opposite disposition; for confidence is the mark of a hopeful disposition /.../ As we have said, then, courage is a mean with respect to things that inspire confidence or fear, in the circumstances that have been stated; and it chooses or endures things because it is noble to do so, or because it is base not to do so" (Aristotle 1116 a).

In a sense, we can agree with Aristotle, but this is not the last and final answer.

However, courage is not really adverse to fear, but just a subcategory of fear. The true opposite of fear is hope. Without hope a person is a slave to fear, without hope a person is limited, unfree. No power, except faith, hope and love which are grace (gift of God), can save a person from the horror of existence; no power, not even courage (Kermauner 1985, 33). A similar response to experiencing fear or horror can be seen in war and post-war times when totalitarian regimes were in place. War as the state of absence of peace and freedom and the state of a constant threat of an end, is an example of how violence over people maintains a state of a general existential anxiety which role is to force people to surrender and to accept another, alien authority. Today, it is difficult to imagine the terrifying horror or fear from inhumane cruelty (inhumanness), but one can slightly sense it at the sites of mass grave in Slovenian Teharje or remains of mass execution in Huda jama, where the victims of the Slovenian Communism were thrown. Not just courage but faith in God and hope of being rescued from distress help a person in overcoming fear of inhuman situations.

Guernica, a painting by Pablo Picasso (1937), is an expression of fear in the tragedies of war. It shows suffering and violence over individuals, especially innocent civilians. Guernica was created in response to the bombing of this village (Guernica) in Basque Country (northern Spain) by German and Italian warplanes at the behest of the Spanish Nationalists forces, on 26th April 1937, during the Spanish Civil War. This work has gained a monumental status, becoming a perpetual reminder of tragedies of war (Wikipedia, Guernica (painting)). Picasso's Guernica is an anti-war symbol and also an embodiment of peace.

What happened on that horrible day in Guernica? This was a quiet village. The nearest military target of any consequence was a factory on the outskirts of the town, which manufactured various war products. The factory went through the attack unscathed. Thus, the motivation of the bombing was clearly one of intimidation. Furthermore, a majority of the town's men were away as they were fighting on behalf of the Republicans. Thus, the town at the time of the bombing was populated mostly by women and children (Preston 2007, 12-19).

After the bombing, it was through the work of the Basque and Republican sympathizer and *The Times* journalist George Steer that propelled this event onto the international scene and brought it to Pablo Picasso's attention. Steer, who rushed to town, compiled his observations into an article that was published on 28th April 1937 in both *The Times* and *The New York Times*, and which on the 29th, appeared in *L'Humanité,* a French Communist daily (Wikipedia, Guernica (painting)). Steer wrote:

"Guernica, the most ancient town of the Basques and the centre of their cultural tradition, was completely destroyed yesterday afternoon by insurgent air raiders. The bombardment of this open town far behind the lines occupied precisely three hours and a quarter, during which a powerful fleet of aeroplanes consisting of three types of German types, Junkers and Heinkel bombers, did not cease unloading on the town bombs weighing from 1,000 lbs. downwards and, it is calculated, more than 3,000 two-pounder aluminium incendiary projectiles. The fighters, meanwhile, plunged low from above the centre of the town to machinegun those of the civilian population who had taken refuge in the fields." (Preston 2007, 12-19).

Why this example? It is to remotely grasp the fear and horror of the innocent inhabitants of that Spanish village. How can one challenge such fear, horror in fact, when one is uncertain of the fate that awaits one or one is afraid that the menacing threat is unavoidable? The words of an eyewitness Luis Aurtenetxea reveal fear and horror but also hope and faith (people were praying) during Guernica bombing:

"We were hiding in the shelters and praying. I only thought of running away, I was so scared. I didn't think about my parents, mother, house, nothing. Just escape. Because during those three and one half hours, I thought I was going to die" (Treasures of the World, Bombing of Guernica 2013).

These words indicates that courage is not the only opposite of fear. There is also hope which is a much stronger opposition.

Traditions as transmitters of hope

Hope and faith are the opposite of fear. Fear can be overcome with the help of one's own inner force (faith, hope and love), which could be supported by external factors, such as religion, family, friends, strong personalities, habits and tradition. Authority plays an important role in tradition. Further on, I will concentrate on tradition and authority within tradition, which can offer support to an individual in overcoming fear or at least subduing it.

What is tradition and what is its importance today? Traditions are, above all, bearers of values and standards of excellence. Traditions are the repositories of the standards of rationality, which enable moral deliberation and action. In that sense, tradition is not conservative (MacIntyre does not use the term in a conservative sense). If tradition is vital, it contains continuities of conflict (MacIntyre 1985, 222) and a mutual discussion on good, which gives it its special meaning and purpose. Whether a tradition is adequate depends on whether it can be passed on. Here, authority plays an important role. In his book *Three Rival Versions of Moral Enquiry* MacIntyre points out two requirements where authority is vital for the tradition to function: authority (the teacher) and the student must establish trust (confidence) and the student must accept the teacher's authority; the second is rational authority, in which teacher must be capable of passing his/her knowledge on to the student and help the student develop and one day become the teacher himself and above all a critical thinker (MacIntyre 1990, 61-62).

It is crucial that the initiate or learner – the person who wishes to be initiated into certain tradition – and the authority (master or teacher) establish a relationship that is based on trust. The master or teacher is someone who is able to evaluate and judge the quality of the initiate's work and must also be able to direct and stimulate him or her on how to go further (MacIntyre 1990, 65-66). The learner must trust the teacher completely and, at least initially, must be prepared to act on the teacher's directions without him- or herself being able to grasp the point of those directions; that is to say, initiation into intellectual enquiry is possible only on the condition that the learner is prepared to accept some form of intellectual authority (MacIntyre 1990, 89-93). Although the learner progresses safely and under the protection of the master's intellectual authority, he or she must be open for developing certain personal qualities, such as adherence to the goods that constitute that tradition, and willingness to develop virtues in accordance with those goods.

Authority plays a vital role in transmitting the meaning for traditions which are bearers and transmitters of meaning, virtues, knowing and certain types of practices. Through all these practices people can cope easier in crises (e.g. faith gives meaning to losing a loved and the latter is therefore easier to accept). Authority plays also a very significant role in supporting an individual (a student or others) in overcoming fear or at least subduing it. When a student or learner is at the beginning of a process of "acquisition" of knowledge, sometimes he feels a personal weakness and some kind of fear in front of all that new knowledge that must be discovered- fear, that there will be not enough time to read all the books and get all the necessary knowledge to be a proper carrier of certain tradition. Also a fear of not being a good critical thinker appears sometimes and an authority plays a vital role at overcoming that fear.

As it was already mentioned, it is important that the relationship between a master and learner is based on trust. There are other types of relationships that exist between them which must also be pointed out.

We must also distinguish: 1. Fear of authority: a fear of lack of trust and confidence, a fear that a pupil couldn't fulfil expectations of authority and 2. Fear to lose authority: in a sense that pupil must carry on alone (without teacher) and/or in a sense, that sometimes also authority- teacher must acknowledge imperfection or even mistake. An authority could be capable to show a student that fear is a vital part of human self-preservation but at the same time hope is stronger and fear can be defeated- also by relying on the strength of tradition (values, knowledge, standards of excellence and practices).

Concluding thoughts

Fear permeates on all spheres of human being and paralyzes our ability for living a flourishing life. On the other hand fear is an emotion that plays an important and also positive role in the question of human survival. We don't have to be afraid of "being afraid"; fear is a signal and we should not ignore it. It is a basic emotion which can help us move from the standing position toward the goal. We must accept fear as a part of our non-necessity. Tradition and authority can help an individual to overcome fear. Hope, faith and love cannot totally eliminate fear but ennoble it. Among many fears we have, the most noble and pure anxiety is, "like Paul Ricoeur said: a fear that we haven't loved enough!" (Stres 1985, 77).

References

Aristotle. *Nicomachean Ethics* (transl. W. D. Ross), available at: http://classics.mit.edu/Aristotle/nicomachaen.3.iii.html, (obtained 26th November 2013).

Erić, Ljubomir. 2004. *Seksualne disfunkcije* (Sexual Disfunctions). Zemun: A-Š Delo.

Erzar, Tomaž. 2007. *Duševne motnje: psihopatologija v zakonski in družinski terapiji.* (Mental Disorders: Psychopathology in Marriage and Family Therapy). Celje: Celjska Mohorjeva.

Juhant, Janez. 2012. *Strah in kultura strahu.* (Fear and Culture of Fear). In: J. Juhant, V. Strahovnik and B. Žalec (eds.), *Kako iz kulture strahu? Tesnoba in upanje današnjega* človeka, Ljubljana: Teološka fakulteta Univerze v Ljubljani, pp. 9-20.

Kermauner, Taras. 1985. Med strahom in pogumom; vprašanje strahu v novejši slovenski literaturi (Between Fear and Courage; the Question of Fear in Slovenian Modern Literature). In: J. Gril (ed.), *Strah in ljubezen: Zbornik predavanj s teološkega tečaja o aktualnih temah za* študente *in izobražence 1984-1985*. Ljubljana: MOŠ, pp. 32-49.

MacIntyre, Alasdair. 1985. *After Virtue; a Study in Moral Theory*. London: Duckworth.

MacIntyre, Alasdair. 1990. *Three Rival Versions of Moral Inquiry*. Notre Dame Ind.: University of Notre Dame Press.

Milovojević, Zoran. 2008. *Emocije; Razumevanje* čustev *v psihoterapiji*, (*Emotions; Understanding Emotions in Psychotherapy)*, transl. Igor M. Ravnik and Slavica Ravnik. Novi Sad: Psihopolis Institut.

Možina, Miran. 2010. *Uvodna* študija *k slovenski izdaji* (*Preface to Slovenian edition*). In: L. Erić *(ed.), Psihodinamična psihiatrija II* (*Psychodynamic psychiatry II*)*; Teorije strahu in stanja* strahu. Ljubljana: Hermes IPAL, pp. 9-139.

Petkovšek, Robert. Strah in pogum v eksistencialni analizi (Fear and Courage in the Existential Analysis). In: J. Juhant, V. Strahovnik and B. Žalec (eds.), *Kako iz kulture strahu? Tesnoba in upanje današnjega* človeka. Ljubljana: Teološka fakulteta Univerze v Ljubljani, pp. 32-41.

Preston, Paul. 2007. George Steer and Guernica. *History Today* 57 (2007), pp. 12–19. Available at: Wikipedia.Http://en.wikipedia.org/wiki/Guernica_(painting) (obtained 29th November 2012).

Treasures of the World. 2013. Bombing of Guernica. Available at: Http://www.pbs.org/treasuresoftheworld/a_nav/guernica_nav/gnav_level_1/1bombing_guerfrm.html (obtained November 28th 2013).

Stres, Anton. 1985. Ali ljubezen premaga strah (Does Love Conquers Fear). In: *Strah in ljubezen: Zbornik predavanj s teološkega tečaja o aktualnih temah za* študente *in izobražence 1984-1985*, Ljubljana: MOŠ, pp. 65-77.

Vattimo, Gianni. 2004. *Filozofska karta 20. stoletja: Tehnika in eksistenca (Philosophical Map of the 20th Century: Technics and existence)*, transl. A. Šušulić. Ljubljana: Sophia.

Wikipedia.Guernica (painting). Available at: Http://en.wikipedia.org/wiki/Guernica_%28painting%29 (obtained 24th October 2012).

Žalec, Bojan. 2012. *Strah in ljubezen kot osnova etičnosti: od sv. Tomaža Akivnskega do Alberta Schweitzerja (Fear and love as the basis of ethics: from St.Thomas Aquinas to Albert Schweitzer)*. In: J. Juhant, V. Strahovnik and B. Žalec (eds.), *Kako iz kulture strahu? Tesnoba in upanje današnjega* človeka. Ljubljana: Teološka fakulteta Univerze v Ljubljani, pp. 21-31.

(POST) COMMUNIST SOCIETIES: THE SLOVENIAN CASE

FEAR AS AN INSTRUMENT OF REPRESSION IN COMMUNIST REGIMES. "UDBA" AND "STASI". A COMPARISION

Tamara Griesser-Pečar, Ljubljana

A totalitarian system is more than a dictatorship of one party based on an exclusive ideology. According to the Oxford dictionary it is a "*polity which permits no rival loyalties or parties*". A totalitarian regime is "*a system of government that is centralized and dictatorial and requires complete subservience to the state*" (http://oxforddictionaries.com). But that is not enough. A totalitarian regime interferes with all pores of society and human life and requires active engagement following the dictate of a certain ideology. The totalitarian authority expects a permanent mobilization in mass organizations and excludes everything that contradicts its authoritative aspiration — by all means up to the mental and physical liquidation. But this can only be achieved by brain-washing through all kinds of media in control of a certain party and with means of repression, with terror. According to definition terror implies the most extreme degree of fear. And totalitarian regimes are based on fear. They actually use fear as an instrument of repression. And the organization that tracked down and eliminated the hostile elements in the society was the secret political police: Udba in Yugoslavia, Stasi in East Germany, KGB in Soviet Union etc. And it is absolutely essential to evaluate the totalitarian regimes under the same criteria, to point out similarities and differences.

Slovenia is the only member of the European Union that experienced all three totalitarian regimes in the 20th century: Fascism (the Slovene Littoral came under Italy right after the First World War, respectively after the Treaty of Rapallo 1920), National Socialism (1941-1945 –Slovenes in Austrian Carinthia from 1938 on) and Communism. During the Second World War in Slovenia two levels of events have to be considered, that of the occupation and resistance on one side and that of communist revolution that caused a civil war on the other side. Its beginnings lie in 1941 when the communists monopolized the resistance and declared everyone outside the "Liberation Front" and the partisan units to be a traitor. And such a traitor had to be sentenced to death. The revolutionary side killed 4.230 civilians during the war (*Delo,* 31st May 2012). The unit that "liquidated" the opponents, many patriotic Slovenes, many Catholics, among them also priests, was the "Security and Intelligence Service", called VOS, recruited solely out of the members of the Communist party and communist youth organization SKOJ. It has to be pointed out that Slovenian VOS was the first such organization on the territory of Yugoslavia, organized after the Soviet model. VOS was the predecessor organization of Ozna (Department for the Protection of the People), founded in 1944 as a part of a military structure responsible directly to the Supreme Commander Tito. Its task was to control and eliminate all opposition of the liberation movement. Special military units were called KNOJ (Korpus narodne odbrane Jugoslavije – Popular defence Corps of Yugoslavia). By spring 1946 Ozna was incorporated into Ministry of Interior and was renamed to Department for State Security, called Udba (Uprava državne bezbedbosti, Uprava državne varnosti), but its employees kept the military status until 1952 (Šubelj, 2009, 333). The military part KOS (Kontraobveščevalna služba, Counterintelligence service) remaind under the army control. KOS changed its name in 1955 to Organization of Counterintelligence (Organ bezbednosti) and Udba in 1967 to State Security Intelligence (Služba državne varnosti, UDV) (Wikipedia.org/wiki/Stasi). It is no secret that the Soviet secret police officers came to Yugoslavia to help to organize the secret police and that OZNA officials were send to Moscow for training. And there is also some evidence that the reorganization was advised by Soviets in 1946 when the reorganization took place.

Germany experienced two different types of totalitarian regimes, Nazism – the so-called "Third Reich" between 1933 and 1945, and Communist regime in Eastern Germany: first, 1945-1949, during the Soviet military occupation and then in German Democratic Republic. The East-German Ministry for State Security, called Stasi, was established in 1950. It was like Udba a domestic secret police organization, an investigation authority and foreign intelligence agency. Its organization was strictly military and it was under the control of the Soviet regime. Stasi was supposed to be one of the most effective secret polices in the world. In the time between 1950 till 1989 it had 274.000 full-time employees. At the end it still had 91,015 employees (Wikipedia.org/wiki/Stasi). By 1989 Stasi had about 189.000 unofficial informants, which means one for every 90 citizens of GDR (Stasi, 21). 1,553 informants were in the federal Republic of Germany, "Bundesrepublik Deutschland" (Gieseke, 2001, 58). Stasi probably had a higher percent of intelligence operatives in comparison to the population than any other communist country in Europe. Stasi was not a usual intelligence service, it was a secret police with its own pretrial detention prisons (for example Berlin/Hohenschönhausen), with its own investigation apparatus, with own judges and prosecutors. Stasi had no special goals, it was, like Ozna/Udba the executor of Party's instructions, or as it was said "Shield and Sword" of the German Communist party, that is Socialist Unity Party (SED; Sozialistische Einheitspartei). It acted in a tradition of red terror, similar as the Soviet 's "Tscheka" during the October Revolution (Reiprich, 2002, 14).

Many documents in Slovenia were destroyed. At every national or international crisis Udba began with destroying of documents. A huge amount of archive files were destroyed also just at Slovenian independence. Like in Slovenia the German secret police Stasi began to destroy sensible documents after the fall of the Berlin Wall. Documents were shredded and since they did not have enough shredding machines, Stasi bought all that it could get in Western Germany, especially in Berlin. But because there were not enough of them in stock, Stasi-employees began to tear paper in two by hand. The pieces were collected in huge bags. Approximately 5% of documents were destroyed. In comparison to that in Slovenia probably 80% of documents are lost forever. In Germany destruction of documents was stopped first upon a women's initiative called "Women for Change" (Frauen für Veränderung) in Erfurt, in Thuringia. First regional Stasi offices were taken over. The Stasi headquarters followed on January 15, 1990. Since 1995 the single pieces of papers collected have been composed like a jigsaw puzzle.

Unfortunately we still do not know either how many employees Ozna/Udba had, or how many unofficial collaborators and informers worked for the secret police, because practically no systematic research has been done on this subject yet. There are only some partial studies about VOS and OZNA and there are partial numbers, some document files, testimonies of people involved, victims and a few offenders. We for example know that in the period 1945/46 there were 4.198 unofficial collaborators that controlled 25.770 so-called "*antinational elements*" (Starič, 14.3.1998). We know for example that 1945 ten clergy-members collaborated (priests, members of the religious orders, theologians), the number increased in 1947 up to 66, in 1949 to 310, at the end of 1950 up to 340 etc. (Pučnik, 1996, 146, 429). We still have the problem that victims often do not want to talk, because they are still frightened and the offenders do not want to talk, because they swore an oath to keep silent. One of the reasons why our knowledge about Udba is still on such a low level is also, that there was no cut between totalitarian regime and democratic Slovenia, like it definitely was in Germany and that many people especially those involved, or their adherents, either deny or minimalize the crimes committed by the communists. On the state level there was no condemnation of communist regime, which puts Slovenia in a unique position in the European Union. Also in Slovenia there was no lustration, with one exception. Officials and judges from the former regime retained their post Article 8 (3) of The Law on Judicial Office of the Republic of Slovenia. Article 8 determined that those who were involved in the violations of human rights are incapable to become judges. In Germany the former Stasi employees, collaborators and unofficial informers were considered a state risk and were therefore removed from all higher public offices, courts and universities. And because in Slovenia there was no clear division between the totalitarian Yugoslav regime and Slovene democratic system, even many employees of former Udba remained in office of the Slovene intelligence service Sova. We even experienced that the last head of the secret police was awarded a medal by the present president of the country. Nobody has been committed for the crimes against humanity, Slovenian courts refuged to open an investigation.

The record of the secret police victims in Slovenia is very high. At a population of approximately one and a half million at the beginning of the war to about two million people at Slovenia's independence, Slovenia had, according to estimates of collegue Milko Mikola in his newest book, more than 100.000 victims of communist repression: 15.000 were murdered, 25.000 were imprisoned because of political reasons, 16.000 persons were sentenced in political or show trials, 60.000 lost their property, 10.000 people of German nationality were deported to Austria as well as 245 Hungarian families to Hungary. About 17.000 people escaped persecution and fled across the border. And not only Slovenes, also at least 100.000 people of other nationalities were after the World War II. killed on Slovene territory (Mikola, 2012: 371). The regime forced many Slovenes to leave their homes and settle in a certain area inside the country. Many people were also shot on Slovenian borders, the estimation is that there were between 500 and 1.000. The last person that was shot was some days before Slovenia became independent, i. e. June 16th 1991. From 1945 on people tried to cross the border illegally and got caught in the clutches of secret police.

In East Germany the exact number of killed persons or those who lost their lives in camps and prisons is not known. The exact number of killings at the Berlin War and the intra-German border in not known yet. The numbers that are quoted vary between many hundreds to up to one thousand. So far 126 deadly incidents at the Berlin Wall are confirmed (Coming to Terms, 2011: 33). We can say that at least 265 people were killed by mines or shooting on state border between 1949 and 1989, several hundreds were injured (Schäfgen, 2011: 302). Those who were caught landed in Stasi prisons and their families and friends were also under strict Stasi-control and had to cope with severe consequences. There were approximately 205.000 political prisoners in German Democratic Republic (GDR) in 40 years and 105.000 cases of professional discriminations because of political reasons that can be verified. 170.000 persons were since 1992 rehabilitated. It is also known that 13.500 Germans were sentenced on political grounds after 1945 by Soviets in the Soviet zone. German Foreign Office tries to reach an agreement with the authorities of the former Soviet Union for cancelling the court decisions (Coming to Terms, 2011: 33).

Ozna collected files of all potential adversaries, was responsible for prosecution – pretrial investigation – for military and civil courts. Churches especially Catholic Church, remained the enemy number 1 till the break-down of communist regime. With constructed and false material Udba leaned on priests, monks and nuns, members of congregations, theologians and their friends and relatives. Many were forced to collaborate. The cases of those who suffered professional discrimination for political or religious reasons (beside the clergy) have not been investigated yet, except for some partial investigations for local areas like the region of Celje. In all those cases Ozna/Udba was involved as investigation authority. In fact till 1951 Ozna/Udba the pretrial investigation was completely in Udba's hand, the courts did not begin their work till Udba passed the prosecution records over to them. And the documents and witnesses that spoke for the accused were sorted out. Udba kept special prisons, was in charge of concentration and labor camps. Ozna/Udba was the instrument of the Communist party to supervise all areas of public and private life. Udba violated basic human rights if the needs of the Communist Party so dictated. This meant physical liquidation, brutal treatment in prisons – never-ending interrogation, deprival of food and sleep, dirt, bugs, isolation –, all kinds of different threats. Those who committed themselves to work unofficially for Udba had several motives for doing so. There were only few who collaborated because of political conviction or a sense of duty, some hoped for material and professional advantages, but most of collaborators did so because they were forced to do so or because they feared reprisals for themselves, family members or friends. They were told that they would land in prisons, or that their relatives and friends will be imprisoned or that they will have to cope with consequences. Also family members, friends and professional colleagues were put under pressure, so it is no surprise that there were all kinds of denunciations. The net of collaborators was growing and one never knew who belonged to it. Udba also followed prominent emigrants, broke in their homes, kidnapped some of them. Yugoslav Udba also killed several Serbian and Croatian emigrants in 1969s and 1970s.

Because of international echo in Slovenia the methods changed somewhat in the 1960s, in GDR in 1970s. Methods like torture and arrest were too obvious, so the secret police turned to "softer" methods, those that at the first side seemed less brutal. They no longer focused on "liquidation" of the opponents, in the foreground came then "physic demolition", in German called "Zersetzung". This term comes from the field of chemistry and means "corrosion" or "undermining". To prevent dissident ideas that endangered the Communist party system, the secret police began to spread rumors about individuals and certain groups, brought into public manipulated information, began to ruin reputations, to criminalize and isolate certain individuals and groups, to break in people's homes, to disturb them with strange phone calls and so on. Friendships and families broke, professional careers were ruined. It is also a fact that Udba helped to organize the priest's society, the Cyril-Methodius Society (CMD, Cirilmetodijsko društvo katoliških duhovnikov), that had the purpose to deepen the conflicts in the Church, or as they said, "differentiate" between high and low clergy and between the dioceses. Although Udba had unofficial informants in clergy, it was not as successful against the Catholic Church as was Stasi against the largest church in GDR, the Protestant Church. Both churches were a harbor for those whose attitude was critical to communist regime, but Catholic Church was internationally organized and therefore Udba was less successful in controlling it as was Stasi in East Germany with the Protestant Church. Both Udba and Stasi were omnipresent and omnipotent. They had access to all information, they penetrated into people's homes, observed their lives, bugged their phones, used all possible methods to threaten people and force them to collaborate, to spy on their neighbors, friends, relatives, colleagues, fellow pupils. The civil rights activist Vera Längsfeld for example found out that her husband, with whom she even had children, married her in order to spy on her. Unofficial informants penetrated in all spheres of society, infiltrated the opposition groups, churches, sport, youth and cultural organizations. One of the leading politicians of the party The Left (Die Linke) Gregor Gysi is said to have been an unofficial Stasi-informer. As lawyer he is supposed to have given over information about his clients.

In Germany the foreign espionage division of the Ministry of State Security Stasi also infiltrated West German government offices – an example is a senior aide to chancellor Willy Brandt Günter Guillaume. Stasi supported the Red Army Faction or Baader-Mainhof Gang (Rote Armee Fraktion or Baader-Meinhof Bande) organization that killed dozens of people in West Germany, Stasi used private information about sexual lives of those who worked in Western governments to get important information, demonstrations in Germany were supported by Stasi. Beno Ohnesorg was killed in a demonstration against the Schah by a West-German policeman Kurras, what radicalized the student movement in the late 1960s in Germany. It turned out that Kurras was an unofficial agent of Stasi. Stasi gave money to Neo-Nazi groups, ordered smearing of Nazi symbols on Jewish cemeteries etc. Here there are also parallels to Udba. Let us just think of the bomb-attack that was perpetrated by Udba agents in Völkermarkt/Velikovec in Austria 1979, the infiltration of Slovenian minority in Carinthia. Udba broke in the homes of emigrants, so it made an illegal investigation in the home of the known Slovenian priest in Paris, Ignacij Čretnik in 1984 (SI AS 1931, 2340).

Archive

AS 1931, šk. 2340, Ignacij Čretnik.

Literature

Camphausen, Gabriele et al. 2011. *Stasi. The exhibition on the GDR's State Security.* Federal Commissioner for the Records of the State Security Service of the former German Democratic Republic, Berlin.

Civilne žrtve v Sloveniji. *Delo*, 31st May 2012.

Coming to Terms: Dealing with the Communist Past in United Germany. Bundesstiftung Aufarbeitung, Berlin.

Dümmel, Karsten; Schmitz, Christian (ed.). 2002. *Was war die Stasi? Einblicke in das Ministerium für Staatssicherheit der DDR (MfS).* Zukunftsforum Politik, Nr. 43, Sankt Augustin.

http://oxforddictionaries.com/definition/english/totalitarian?q=totalitarian

Gieseke, Jens. 2001. *Die DDR-Staatssicherheit.* Bundeszentrale für politische Bildung.

Mikola, Milko. 2012. *Rdeče nasilje. Represija v Sloveniji po letu 1945.* Celje: Celjska Mohorjeva družba.

Pučnik, Jože (ed.). 1996. *Iz arhivov slovenske politične policije.* Ljubljana.

Reiprich, Siegfries. 2002. Eroberung und Konsolidierung der Macht – zwei Phasen in der Geschichte der Stasi. In: Karsten Dümmel, Christian Schmitz (ed.): *Was war die Stasi? Einblicke in das Ministerium für Staatssicherheit der DDR (MfS)*, Sankt Augustin.

Vodušek Starič, Jerca. 1998. Vladavina komunistične v Sloveniji po drugi svetovni vojni. In: *Zgodovinarji o komunizmu*, *Delo*, 13rd March 1998.

Schäfgen, Christoph. 2011. The prosecution of communist crimes in Germany. In: *Crimes of the Communist Regimes – an assessment by historians and legal experts.* Prague.

Šubelj, Ljuba Dornik. 2009. Vloga Ozne za Slovenijo po prevzemu oblasti 1944-1946. Dissertation, Ljubljana.

SOME SOCIOLOGICAL ASPECTS OF FEAR IN SLOVENIA: COMMUNIST REPRESSION AND CONTEMPORARY CONSEQUENCES

Igor Bahovec, Ljubljana

1. Introduction

The Communist system in Slovenia was essentially total and totalitarian. This could be seen already during the Second World War, when communists liquidated numerous civilians (Jančar 1998). That kind of approach was an integral part of the revolutionary method of taking over power. After the war, the postwar mass slaughters were the highest acts of violence. Over the decades the workings of the Communist system softened somewhat; brutal methods were mostly replaced by other means of control. At a comparable phase of development of the revolution, Sorokin (1947, 487-495) had already observed that this was not surprising, for despite changes the essence of party power remained the same.

Communist violence and the total nature of power engendered fear in people. Because of the violence, constraint and suppression of the freedom of speech and association and thanks to almost half a century of such conditions, there was great fear which had strongly influenced people both consciously and subconsciously. In this contribution we will endeavour to answer the question of whether after 20 years of democratic government people are still influenced by fear resulting from the previous system - and if so, whether in certain people this fear is so strong as to exert a significant influence on their life. Our data comes largely from our own research, but we will also use data from some other researchers.

Our own survey took place between the 1st and 5th of October 2012. Using computer-assisted telephone interviewing (CATI), we interviewed a representative sample of the Slovene adult population (multi-stage random sample), the final sample size being 904. Replies received are broken down by sex, age, education and type of residence area. [1]

2. Attitude to the past

We have put forward above the hypothesis that the Communist system was totalitarian and did not allow complete freedom. Of course, this does not mean that everyone was oppressed; on the contrary, there were many - especially in the last decades - who lived pretty well under Communism.

In our enquiry into attitudes to the period between WW II and the democratic change (Slovenia's independence), almost half of those surveyed (48 %) opted for "mostly positive", while "mostly negative" was chosen by 9.5 %. The most positive attitude to that period was expressed by people with a professional education, with incomes between €500 and €1000, least positive were those with elementary schooling aged over 55 and with incomes up to €500.

Other surveys have shown similar results. In 2005 and 2006 three surveys were carried out, and in all of them the majority (a little above 60 %) the „nearest"answer was „there were some good things and some bad things"; in a survey in1992 the proportion of such answers was 70 % (SJM05/1; SJM05/3+4; SJM06/2; SJM992/3). Around 20 % (1992 however 15 %) of them thought that this was „period of progress and good living conditions", between 6 % and 7 % were of the opinion that „that time was a time of fear and repression"

In a 2003 survey (SJM03/1) a good fifth of respondents (22 %) agreed with the statement that: "Slovenia after 1945 until its independence (1990) was governed by dictatorship"; however, almost half (45 %) disagreed with this. A third chose another possibility or didn't know how to answer.

The period from the war to the independence is usually viewed pretty positively by Slovenes - especially if they compare it with other periods of our history. By 2003, respondents described it as the least problematic for the existence of division and disagreement in Slovene society (Table 1). They had the same good opinion of the democratic period, a somewhat poorer one of the period between the start of the 20th century and the outbreak of the Second World War. The major-

1 The questionnaire was prepared by Igor Bahovec and Vinko Potočnik. The author of this article would like to give special thanks to Janez Juhant for the invitation to do the research.

ity, some 60 % of all respondents (and 74 % of those who declared their views) were of the opinion that during the Second World War "things happened which fatally divided the Slovene people"; as for the first five years of the Communist "dictatorship of the proletariat" that is the view of 50 % of respondents.

Table 1. *Were there, in any of the periods listed below, events which were significantly divisive of the Slovene people?*
Proportion of "yes" replies. Source: SJM 03/1.

a) around Christianisation	29 %
b) the period of the Reformation and Counter-reformation	40 %
c) the dawn of the 20th century, when the political parties came into being	41 %
d) the period between the two world wars (the Kingdom of Yugoslavia)	44 %
e) during WW II	60 %
f) the advent of the communists to power after the 2nd world war	50 %
g) the period between 1950 and independence	29 %
h) the period of independence, after 1990	31 %

This data shows clearly that with regard to the understanding of divisions in the Slovene nation the key periods are the 2nd World War and the first five years after that war. Therefore, in considering fear which has its roots in the past it is sensible to look first at these periods, especially the post-war period.

2.1 The post-war mass slaughters

Slovenes have different views on the post-war slaughter. According to research carried out in 2003 (SJM 2003-1), almost half of them (46 %) think that this was an "abominable crime". A good fifth thought that it was "a serious political mistake" (22 %). Other responses were chosen by fewer respondents: "understandable acts of revenge" (7 %), "tragic but unavoidable result of civil war" (9 %), "punishment for betrayal of their own country" (10 %).

In our survey, however, we put the questions slightly differently. What we wanted to discover was not what they thought of these events, but what effect they had on the current life of individuals and families and on how we confront, deal with, this tragic period.

To the question "does it seem to you that people who know about it are afraid to talk about post-war slaughter" (Graph 1), almost 30 % replied "yes", 44 % said "no", 20 % said "people whom we know are simply not interested". Amongst those who know people who are afraid to talk, most are over 55 years old, have only an elementary education and are regular Mass-goers.

Graph 1. *The past regime forbade talking about the post-war homicide. Does it seem to you that people you know feel afraid to talk about the topic? Which of the following statements describes your opinion? People you know are ...*

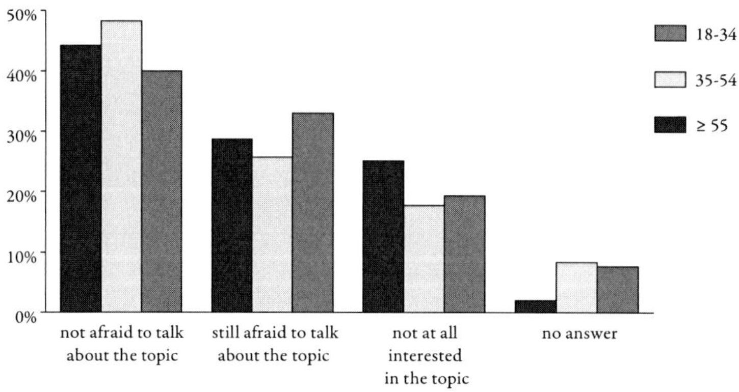

At first sight the number of "yes" answers appears very high. What are the reasons for such a situation after two decades of democracy, why are people still afraid? How is it that the transition has not brought a greater reconciliation of the people with the past? How can this be, since we have shown that the period after the 2nd world war is viewed negatively by less than 10 % of the people? It appears to us, that it is not easy to explain; therefore we looked in greater detail at some of the findings of our survey.

The great majority of respondents (63 %) believe that "there is an urgent need to speak openly of the darker side of that period". A further 13 % believe that it is time to break the silence on these subjects. These response patterns did not vary with sex, education etc. Similarly, to the great majority of people, it seems necessary that the younger generation should be informed of the dark side of our past (Graph 2). The correlation with age is interesting here - it is especially the younger people, those under 35, who would like to see a public discussion, while those over 55 are opposed to it.

Graph 2. *Does it seem necessary to you that younger generations should be informed about the dark side of the past?*

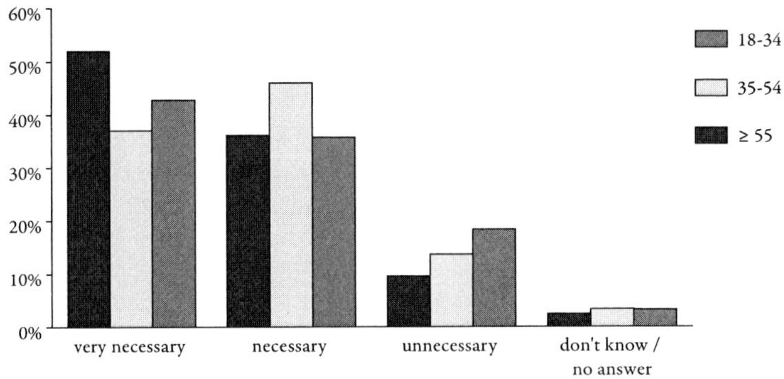

There is a similar level of agreement with regard to attitudes to history. In our survey almost 9 out of 10 people questioned were "generally proud" of our Slovene history (89 %), while 6 % were ashamed of it. A similar result was found in the previously mentioned 2005 survey, in which 87 % replied that they were (very or generally) proud (SJM05/3+4). In the following year's survey 70 % were (very) proud, 6 % not proud; the remainder is somewhere in between (SJM06/2).

However, while on the one hand we are very proud of our history, on the other hand data shows that it will not be easy to resolve the differences of attitude to the war and postwar periods. The great majority of people, some 64 % of respondents, consider that "conflict and enmity from the past are still very high in Slovenia" (Graph 3). There is an age correlation in the responses: younger people see fewer conflicts than do older people. The greatest difference is between those who have a professional education and those with only elementary schooling or less - the former see many less conflicts than the latter.

Graph 3. *Are conflicts and enmities from the past still strongly present today?*

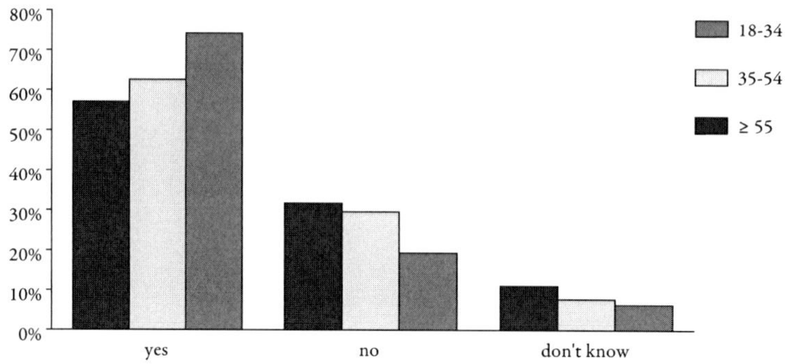

2.3 Difficulties and barriers conflict resolution

With regard to existing conflict among Slovenes, it is appropriate to ask whether the public wants to resolve them. We asked the question "whether the present atmosphere in Slovenia makes it possible to seek the truth with regard to our past and present?" Responses show that: less than one fifth (17 %) feel that the current atmosphere makes it possible to seek the truth, more than half (53 %) "not at all" and a further quarter (26 %), only partly (Graph 4). There were considerable differences between groups, such that there are a number of correlations: men see a better atmosphere than women, less educated than more educated, those with lower incomes more than those with higher incomes; no observable difference, however, between age groups. Those who have a religious faith are more optimistic than non-believers - whether this faith takes the form of personal faith (existence of a personal God) or religious activity (how frequently they attend religious services). Finally, those who support the present government consider the present atmosphere significantly better than those who don't.

Graph 4. *Would you estimate that the present atmosphere in Slovenia supports searching for the truth about our past and present?*

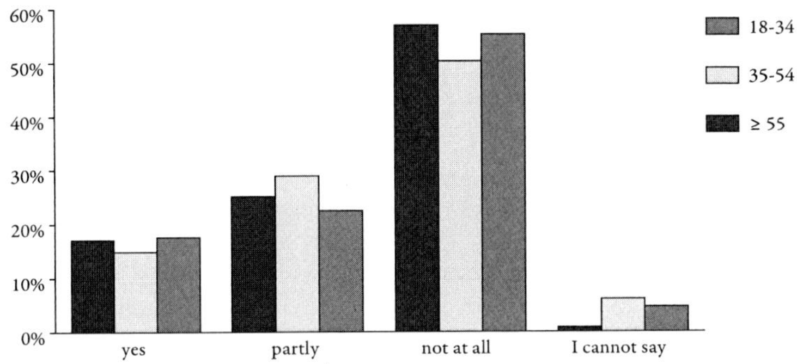

With regard to the question "How would determining the truth of Slovenia's recent past influence the current divisions in the Slovene area?" a good half (55 %) think that it would have no effect or simply didn't answer the question. Almost a quarter (24 %) were of the opinion that this would "contribute to reconciliation", which was somewhat greater than the number who thought the opposite, that this would lead to "even deeper divisions" (20 %) (Graph 5).

Men were more inclined to say it would lead "to reconciliation" than women (although the correlation is weak); supporters of the present government are more "optimistic" than their opponents; with regard to education levels, the most "pessimistic" group were those who had completed professional education. Responses to this question correlate fairly strongly with the two questions on religious beliefs: the most "optimistic" are practising believers (the boundary being those who attend Mass at least once a month) and those who believe in a personal God.

Graph 5. *How would further uncovering /establishment of truth about Slovenian recent history affect present divisions in Slovenian society? Would it contribute ..*

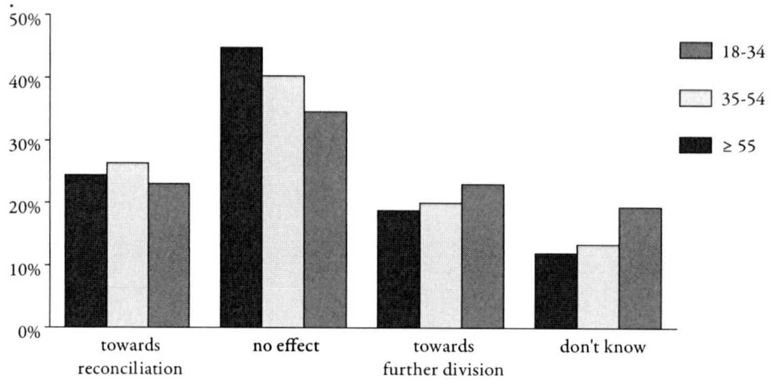

Such a spirit may partly explain the large proportion who think "that Slovenia still has a network of people, related to the previous regime and who are very powerful". That this is "absolutely true" is believed by 30 % of respondents, a further 42 % however, believe that this "is partly true" (Graph 6). Correlations are as follows: that this is true is the view mainly of men, supporters of the current government and those who regularly attend religious services.

Graph 6. *Some people think that networks of people connected with the past system exist in Slovenia and that they still enjoy huge influence. Do you consider this is ...*

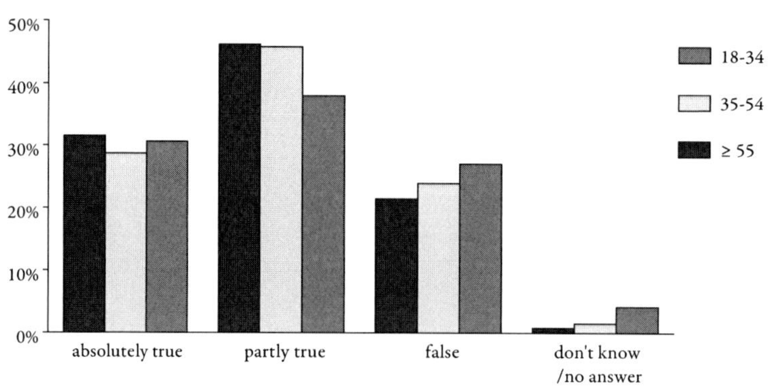

Many people also think that these networks still wield a lot of power in society. More than half of them believe that "those who oppose such networks have problems, even today (for example that this may lead to them having vexations at work or even losing their job)"; "very likely" was chosen by 18 %, "possibly" by 39 %

of those surveyed. The numbers who think otherwise come altogether to less than half (14 % think that this is impossible, 6 % of them don't know and 24 % that such networks don't exist).

3. Final observations

We think that what we have mentioned above shows the following:

(1) In Slovenia there is, on the one hand, a fairly strong popular view, or you could call it an attitude, an approach, that one should also be "objective" about the negative aspects of the past (and in particular about the period after the 2nd World War) and the present. Most people agree that the younger generations should be informed of the negative aspects of history; this is especially emphasised by the young.

We can take this to be a fairly positive approach. However, it must be added that some themes from those periods remain taboo to the wider public. Some post-communist circles do not support free technical and scientific investigation of those periods. We believe that until these taboos are abolished and proper reflection on past times takes place (polarised explanations are not good enough) we can expect that memories will be manifested in uncontrollable forms, in outbursts (which are more or less polarising).

(2) There are serious obstacles to the continuance of the reconciliation process in Slovenia. People sense that "conflicts and hatred from the past are very strong" even today, that there is a climate which "does not support the seeking of the truth". The more so since many people suspect that there are "old boys' networks" surviving from the old regime and that these networks are fairly powerful.

We believe that in this we have partly succeeded in explaining why so many people continue to be afraid to speak of the post-war mass slaughters. To a certain extent such an attitude is unsurprising also because it seems many people think "that people who speak up in favour of open discussion of such subjects [discussion of these murders] risk attracting negative consequences or difficulties". Some 23 % of respondents believe that this is fairly likely and 44 % that this is unlikely; the opposite opinion, that this is "impossible", was held by only 27 %. There are few significant differences in the replies of different categories of people to these questions, the exceptions being: the more "pessimistic" are those who attend religious services at least once a week, are over 55 years of age.

Therefore we consider that in Slovenia, with regard to certain aspects of the past, there is a certain duality, ambivalence and difference of opinion. On the one hand, replies show that there is fairly uniform support for objective sharing of knowledge of negative aspects of history, on the other hand, regarding (sentimental) relations to them and their significance, society is very divided. Since public opinion is not expressly in favour of research into the truth, it is hard to expect that things are likely to improve in the near future. Without openness to the truth, without a sensitive search for truth and an endeavour to ensure that truth will be suitably respected, in Slovenia certain people will continue to speak fearfully of the past.

Finally, we would like to point out that given the high degree of polarisation in the region of Slovenia we need to devote a lot of effort to seeking suitable ways of increasing mutual trust and resolving differences. We believe that a central task is to encourage moderation, "the middle ground" and genuine dialogue. If this is not just to be a wish but also a possibility it seems to us to be necessary to fulfil certain important conditions:

(1) Every social group must contribute its part to change, to the best of its ability. If we take as an example the process of reconciliation, the task for Christians is more demanding than for others, since the Christian message carries more hope in itself, stronger reasons for mercy and forgiveness, more benevolence, etc. than do other world views. It is interesting that in a certain way Christians are already succeeding in this, since many respondents have shown that those who regularly participate in services and/or believe in a personal God, have a more optimistic attitude.

(2) It is probably a good idea to look at how similar difficulties have been resolved in different societies and cultures. Western civilisation places a lot of emphasis on individual responsibility, justice and court proceedings to punish crimes, etc. This serves as our cultural model. We know, however, that it would also be well to recognise that we all suffer because of injustice - thus we could paraphrase Dostoyevsky, that all is linked in this world, that our lives are all interrelated. If we consider the problem from this angle, it is good to look at cultures in which there are strongly bonded societies/a strong community spirit. In this context we would like to draw your attention to the South African or sub-Saharan concept of *ubuntu*. The heart of the principle lies in accepting the interdependence of all people, other creatures, nature and also the souls of the dead. Because divisions cause the whole community to suffer, the search for solutions is also a matter for the whole community. According to the *ubuntu* principle, the truth must be uncovered and the guilty must admit their guilt, however, the driving motive is not punishment but a new opportunity for increased reconciliation (more on this: Bahovec 2012).

(3) Replies show that no subgroup included in the survey (whether by age, party affiliations, faith, etc.) has a uniform attitude or opinion. Therefore it seems

important to us to recognise that the difficulties discussed affect not only individuals of certain groups (Christians, ex-Communists, politicians, those principally responsible for discord, etc.) but are (to a certain extent) a matter for society as a whole, as well as for individual groups and persons in society.

References

Bahovec, Igor. 2012. The meaning of culture for reconciliation: dialogue, memory and community. In Juhant, Janez and Bojan Žalec (eds.). *Reconciliation : the way of healing and growth.* Zürich; Münster: Lit, 249-258.

Jančar, Drago (ed.). 1998. *Temna stran meseca: kratka zgodovina totalitarizma v Sloveniji 1945-1990 : zbornik člankov in dokumentov*. Ljubljana: Nova revija.

Sorokin, Pitirim A. 1947. *Society, Culture, and Personality. Their Structure and Dynamics. A System of General Sociology*. New York: Harper and Brothers.

* * *

SJM = Slovene Public Opinion Survey. Distribution: Arhiv družboslovnih podatkov (= ADP) = Social Science Data Archive [Ljubljana: Faculty of Social Sciences]. http://nesstar2.adp.fdv.uni-lj.si/webview/ (October 2012)

SJM92/3: Slovene Public Opinion Survey 1992/3: The Process of Democratization. Ljubljana: ADP.

SJM03/1: Slovene Public Opinion Survey 2003/1. Ljubljana: ADP.

SJM05/1: Slovene public opinion survey 2005/1: International Comparative Study Work Orientation, ISSP 2005. Ljubljana: ADP.

SJM05/3+4: Slovene public opinion 2005/3+4: World Value Survey; Attitudes Towards Reforms. Ljubljana: ADP.

SJM06/2: Slovene public opinion 2006/2: Role of government, ISSP 2006; Leisure and sport, ISSP 2007. Ljubljana: ADP.

FEAR AND INHIBITED INITIATIVE

Tomaž Erzar & Katarina Kompan Erzar, Ljubljana

1. Fear and reduced initiative

One of the most subtle, but key aspects of fear and fearfulness that shows itself on both personal and social level only gradually, is the inhibition of initiative. Inhibition and initiative are the stop and start buttons for our behavior, but also signs how we learned to react to danger and how secure we feel in our everyday life. When a child is afraid, he stops exploring the surroundings, he stops thinking about what he needs or wants, and quite spontaneously seeks shelter. The child strives for physical closeness with the caregiver, clings to the mother, grabs her skirt, is pressed to her with fear and glances around in the direction from which danger is expected (Robertson and Bowlby 1952). While this behavior is quite easy to spot in children, it is much more difficult to recognize it in the adult, because adults usually do not express distress or ask for help by clinging to someone. Instead, they reduce their activity, become numb, slow down their movements, and look for a place to withdraw, all the while being fearfully aware of their surroundings.

2. Long-term effects of fear and fearfulness

Experiences of fear and fearfulness in the childhood can have long term consequences, if, due to their impact, child's activity and spontaneous exploration and interest for himself and the world around him is reduced to a minimum. It is important to know that the child's exploration of the world is not just about discovering new aspects of his physical environment, but even more exploration of his interpersonal and inner world, of what he feels and experiences when connecting with other people and himself. A key consequence of chronic fear is not only poor knowledge and handling of material things, such as poor dexterity, poor maneuverability or agility, but also reduced knowledge and tolerance of own emotions and less confident behavior in social contacts. In a world that is chronically overwhelmed with fear and events that aim to incite and spread fear, people begin to behave rigidly, suspiciously and servant-like. They only rarely speak openly of themselves, and even when they do so they do not express their personal opinion or experience, but hide behind general statements and descriptions. Such behavior is no doubt sometimes a matter of judgment or tactical restraint, because people do not want to expose themselves further and suffer consequences by which certain political or economic systems want to compel their obedience.

What happens more often, however, is that people go silent also "internally". People who learned in their families of origin that seeking support when in trouble is not a desirable form of behavior and emotion, because their parents found such behavior excessive, inappropriate, embarrassing, immature, or annoying, will also in adulthood experience their own feelings of distress and helplessness as intrusive, embarrassing and inappropriate. Since these feelings have been avoided for years and have not been connected either with people's inner states nor with conditions in their surroundings, people will eventually become completely incapable of adequately distinguish emotionally between the present and the past experiences of fear and distress. In this way, unsafe conditions of their adult life will awaken their most painful childhood experiences of insecure attachment to their parents and mix with them (West and Sheldon-Keller, 1994). The same holds true for those children who have been covertly filled with fear because their parents did not recognize it or even fled from it, while seeking protection with their own children. They as well will in adulthood be unaware of the degree to which past experiences of fear and distress contribute to their current feelings of fear, physical discomfort and emotional rigidity and frozenness.

3. Fear and the internal schema of the self-with-the-other

When fear subsides, the child's interest in the world around him normally increases, as well as the interest in his own desires and needs. When Mary Ainsworth studied children's behavior in a laboratory situation, she observed that she can reliably distinguish between securely and insecurely attached infants only if she compares their ability to re-engage in exploration of the surrounding area in the moments after the return of the mother to the room from where she was previously unannounced gone (Ainsworth and Bell 1970). The criterion of the child's internal sense of security thus turned out to be not the amount or intensity of the crying upon mother's leaving or duration of crying or frightened behavior, but quickly recovered capability for further exploration and taking initiative. The same holds true for adults. In everyday life, we often observe that successful individuals, groups and companies do not necessarily win in all situations, but are always able to quickly pick up after being defeated and learn new strategies and skills from the experience of defeat. The phrase "Learning from defeat" hides a profound truth. Loss does not imply an experience of profound shame and unworthiness, nor it is necessarily a sign of carelessness, laziness or lack of readiness, but is an opportunity to get in touch with hard emotions, deal with them and get through them. On the other hand, signs of perfectionism, humiliation of opponents and rapid fluctuations back and forth from complete euphoria to complete brokenness betray the precarious sense of self-worth which stems from a number of past experiences in which growing children were forced to rely on themselves for an adequate emotional evaluation of their efforts. Negative emotional background of such childhood conditions forms the basis for many forms of adult behavior and reactions for which neutral observers justifiably believe they are childish and immature (Brennan and Shaver 1998).

When fear insists, it gets, as we say, under your skin and eats away at the core of your life. Even in the absence of immediate danger, people fearfully persist in passivity and frozenness. Their fragile internal image of the world and of themselves tells them 'You alone are to blame', 'Nobody will help you', 'You're completely helpless and there is nothing you can do to save yourself from this', 'The world is not worthy of confidence, it preys on your weaknesses and will make you pay high price for your mistakes.' Listening to this inner voice, people are left feeling helpless and wait to be delivered from the situation by some higher power or exceptional intervention by some kind-hearted person or force. They rarely relax to the extent that they could use their creativity and take initiative in the world and interpersonal relationships, since they do not consider themselves to be able to change anything in the world or even express their opinion. They have a feeling of being a victim of permanent terror, coercion and mean people in their surroundings, whom they experience as inaccessible, sullen, contemptuous and opportunistic (Martens, 2005).

4. The Slovenian culture of fear

That said, one can easily understand why internalization of fear prevents sincere connection between people. It awakens deeply rooted feelings of loneliness and helplessness and numerous experiences of defenselessness when one was left on his own. "Help yourself and God will help you," says Slovenian proverb suggesting that in our region we had been for centuries experiencing not only feelings of insignificance and smallness, which in themselves are not harmful, but also feelings of insecure attachment, which had merged with our current experience of the world, God and our fellow human beings, to the extent that they formed up into the advice older generation had always passed onto younger ones. Proverb explains that man must help himself first, which means that her/his close and intimate relations are not perceived as a place of comfort in times of distress.

Accordingly, God's help is only due after you have already resigned to the fact that you can rely only on yourself and that spontaneous support is not what you deserve (Clinton and Straub 2010).

A related long-term result of internalized fear which is extremely difficult to overcome is pseudo-bonding. Seeking to feel normal in their own eyes and in society's, internally scared individuals become experts in pretending to feel true attachment to parents, relatives, friends, and intimate partners. Even when they come together and connect with one another in the fear of impending danger, as this could have been the case during the World War II, this does not mean they are genuinely connected to each other or feel each other's distress, and that these bonds will make them feel less helpless. For them, the transition from insecure to secure form of attachment is very slow and gradual and can only take place in safe and sincere relationships which for them are out of reach. This transition requires personal initiative and perseverance (Erzar and Kompan Erzar 2011) and that is exactly what extreme war circumstances do not allow. In such circumstances personal initiative hides behind group practices that seemingly absolve people of responsibility and personal risk. So if we judge our society by the personal initiative of its people in seeking support and creating safe interpersonal world, we must observe that our society has not yet left behind exceptional and dangerous circumstances and is still living in the past mixed with the present (Juhant 2011, 36).

In his partly autobiographical prose for adolescents entitled *The Village Command* Vladimir Kavčič (b. 1932) describes the events in the villages in the Poljanska valley during the first days after the collapse of the Yugoslav Army in April 1941. In these dangerous and uncertain days adults in the village react with caution and are more or less passive: they stay hidden in their houses and wait in fear, listening to every little bit of information, no matter how reliable it may be. The world stalls and hangs in uncertainty. Without usual care and control, children in the village, whom the author takes as heroes of his story, are on the contrary unusually active. In their ventures on the one hand they feel that they should take care of domestic needs and demands of parents; on the other hand, they sense that the circumstances give them an opportunity of free research and hikes. While they ride on the trolley bringing home food and stuff from abandoned military depots, they stuff their pockets with ammunition and weapons. All this ends after a few days when a foreign army walks into the village. *The Village Command* is a very felicitous title for the times in which children are growing up without adult protection, and must, in a world that is full of uncertainty, fend for themselves. Thus they get the feeling that everything depends on them, they are the 'command', while adults (especially men, fathers, who once seemed to lead the world and know what to do) are either absent or completely passive and just helplessly wait for a change to happen. And so it happens that the story about children's exploration gradually grows into a play about real weapons, dangerous fights with boys from neighboring villages and flirting with participating in the real war.

In our view, this story which is a miniature image of the developments of the World War II on our territory has a broader meaning. There is no doubt that at those times war generations of children were in distress, brought about by a sudden onset of war, and that their developmental as well as emotional needs were neglected. This neglect however reveals a deeper background of their insecure attachment to their parents: boys who are left without a father before the war feel more uncertain, but are bolder and less cautious in the boys' conflict. The boy most left to himself is the one who is attached to his mother only by fear of punishment and who cannot say for his mother that "she loves kids," as he is proud to say for the mother of one of his fellows. In children's own words, adults who love children seem to be in this valley in which everybody shoots on everybody "as rare as real tobacco". The overall impression is that, for adults and children alike, this war is a children's game, which in their view cannot have any serious consequences. Despite the fact that people in the narrative do in fact die, dying is perceived in the way adolescent boys perceive death. For them, war is basically an open space of research and experimentation where you don't get penalized. Symptomatically, the narrative ends with an explosion of a hand grenade, triggered by the two main characters of the story. They relied excessively on their war skills gained during their previous exploits with weapons. The explosion injures both of them, but none suffers any lasting consequences.

The key viewpoint for understanding the world described by Kavčič and the generations of young boys who were actively involved in the conflicts of the World War II, is the children's inability to recognize their own fear, rage and shame. Research on insecure attachment confirmed that if children do not get their basic psychological needs met, they survive by forming a false sense of self and by avoiding their innermost feelings. This causes several related psychological deficits, like excessive shame and guilt, major reality distortions and trust problems and difficulty empathizing and bonding with other people. Lacking adult guidance which would enable them to gain access to their genuine childhood feelings of helplessness, fear and abandonment, children in the story became premature adults and premature war heroes. They were dragged into the adult world of revenge and hatred they did not understand, or understood as a child. In the concluding chapter Kavčič's story describes how the children of the warring parties after the war shook hands and forgot the conflicts of the war, but one cannot help thinking that this portraying of violence and war is inspired by the children's self-perception which is characterized by overly simplistic black-or-white perception of justice. The question arises whether the generation of these young adults ever had the opportunity to recognize their childhood fears and insecurities and talk about them, without risking new humiliation and shaming either at home or in society. One may suspect the only thing they learned from adults was that internal uncertainty must be avoided at all costs. Eventually, the young generation lost touch not only with their fears and sense of shame, but also with their rage and sprouts of hatred which stem from internalized feelings of fear and shame.

From there, in our opinion, comes the insurmountable gap in the Slovenian public understanding of the World War II between the perspective of the participants and the perspective of today's generations. From today's point of view, the initiative of adolescent children in times of war appears to be in the first place the result of longstanding neglect and mistreatment in their families-of-origin and the fact that they were left alone in the world gone mad. This was, in no way, an initiative which could lead the world towards a more integrated and sincere trust. With this genuine initiative long gone, we still, after decades of postwar time, in Slovenia have no true words for the innermost feelings of our grandfathers and fathers. We must realize with regret that these feelings can only be verbalized and expressed in a sincere way by adults who have access to their fear and are not ashamed to admit their childlike vulnerability and deep feelings of shame, rage and hatred.

In this regard, we remain a society of children who must, even before they really grow up, not only take care of themselves, but find an explanation for our generations-old feelings. It is thus no wonder we still perceive the world through the eyes of our fathers and describe it in words which are inappropriate to express our insecurities and vulnerabilities. And no wonder that we still live in a very unpredictable and threatening world, just like the world in which our fathers found themselves "in command", alone on the village road with real weapons in their hands.

References

Ainsworth, Mary in Silvia Bell. 1970. Attachment, exploration, and separation: Illustrated by the behavior of one-year-olds in a strange situation. *Child Development, 41*, 49–67.

Brennan, Kelly and Phillip Shaver. 1998. Attachment styles and personality disorders: Their connections to each other and to parental divorce, parental death, and perceptions of parental caregiving. *Journal of Personality, 66*, 835–878.

Clinton, Tim and Joshua Straub. 2010. *God Attachment: Why You Believe, Act, and Feel the Way You Do About God*. New York: Howard Books.

Erzar, Tomaž and Katarina Kompan Erzar. 2011. *Teorija navezanosti*. Celje: Celjska Mohorjeva družba.

Juhant, Janez. 2011. Sprava kot projekt slovenskega postkomuinističnega dialoga. In: J. Juhant, V. Strahovnik, B. Žalec (eds.), *Izvor odpuščanja in sprave: človek ali Bog? Spravni procesi in Slovenci*. Ljubljana: Teološka fakulteta: Družina, 13–41.

Kavčič, Vladimir. 1955. *Vaška komanda* [*The Village Command*]. Ljubljana: Mladinska knjiga.

Martens, Willem. 2005. Shame and Narcissism: Therapeutic Relevance of Conflicting Dimensions of Excessive Self Esteem, Pride, and Pathological Vulnerable Self. *Annals of the American Psychotherapy Association, 8*(2), 10–17.

Robertson, James and John Bowlby, J. 1952. Responses of young children to separation from their mothers. *Courrier of the International Children's Centre, 2*, 131–140.

West, Malcolm in Adrienne Sheldon-Keller. 1994. *Patterns of Relating – An Adult Attachment Perspective*. New York: Guilford.

CULTURE OF FEAR IN SLOVENIAN SOCIETY

Jernej Letnar Černič, Ljubljana

Introduction

The shaping of communist identity and personality has left inerasable scars in the landscape of the present-day Slovene democratic society. The Republic of Slovenia (hereinafter Slovenia) was in the twentieth century subjected to three forms of totalitarian systems or regimes: fascism, National Socialism and Communism. Slovenia is therefore the only EU member state that has been subjected to all three totalitarian regimes, fascism, National Socialism and Communism. All three forms of totalitarian regimes in Slovenia had common and comparable characteristics. It must be noted that all three forms of totalitarian regimes in Slovenia attempted to monitor and regulate every aspect of public and private life by every means wherever feasible. What is more, it must be noted that fascism, Nazism and communism in Slovenia differed in their duration. Whereas Nazi occupation of Slovenia lasted from 1941 to 1945, the fascist totalitarian system governed Slovenia from 1919 to 1943. The long-lasting totalitarian regime in Slovenia was the Communist totalitarian regime which officially terrorized Slovenia from the end of Second World War in 1945 to the first democratic elections in April 1990, when the opposition political parties united in *DEMOS* movement. However, the Communist totalitarian regime began much earlier already during the Second World War when the Communist Party monopolized the Resistance movement. In the last century Slovenia survived several crimes against humanity of totalitarian regimes. Such totalitarian crimes have in the contemporary Slovenian society domesticated culture of fear. This article examines how the Slovenian society deals with culture of fear and crimes against humanity. It analyses four key components of the transitional justice: an objective assessment of historical facts, the liability of the perpetrators and victims' rights and education for the future, and an assessment of the Slovenian transitional justice.

Section 3 of the present work briefly outlines the factual background of the Communist crimes committed in Slovenia. This is followed by a discussion and analysis of transitional justice measures in Slovenia in Section 3. Finally, Section 4 examines reconciliation measures in Slovenia and lays the basis for the argument that there exists a strong legal and moral ground for prosecuting perpetrators of crimes against humanity. In this way, this article thereafter analyzes the consequences and influences of the shaping of culture of fear in Slovenia, trying to draw out lessons concerning the understanding of current ideological divisions in Slovenia.

The Communist totalitarian regime in Slovenia

The Communist regime was the longest-lasting totalitarian regime regulating and terrorizing the territory of Slovenia. The Communist totalitarian regime officially governed Slovenia from the end of the Second World War until the first democratic elections in April 1990. However, the beginnings of the Communist regime can be traced back to the World War Two, i.e. late 1930s. The Communist totalitarian system gradually assumed more control from Nazi occupation of Slovenia in 1941, when it monopolized the resistance movement against the occupation and commenced the Communist style revolution (Hančič et al., 2009) The Communist totalitarian regime maintained its power through revolutionary violence, culture of fear, crimes against humanity against civilian population, show judicial proceedings, nationalization and confiscation of property, labour and concentration camps, elimination of political opponents by prohibiting and type of opposition. The Communist totalitarian period can be divided in two main periods: the period from the end of the war in 1945 until first months of 1950, and second period from the beginning of 1950s until the fall of the Communist regime in 1990.

The Slovenian Liberation Front won the armed conflict with German and Italian forces and liberated Slovenia. In this way, the Slovenian Communist Party seized the opportunity to turn a national liberation movement against the Axis forces from a resistance struggle to a civil war, and prohibited from fighting against the occupiers by those who did not accept leadership of the Communist party. In other words, the partisan movement led by the Slovenian Communist party won in the civil war. The most common Communist totalitarian crimes during the period 1945-51 included: mass extrajudicial killings or crimes against humanity, construction of concentration and labour camps, forced deprivations of liberty, arranging show and political trials, deportations of inhabitants to abroad, and suppression of religion and persecution of the church and clergy.

Picture 1– Identified secret mass graves on the territory of Slovenia

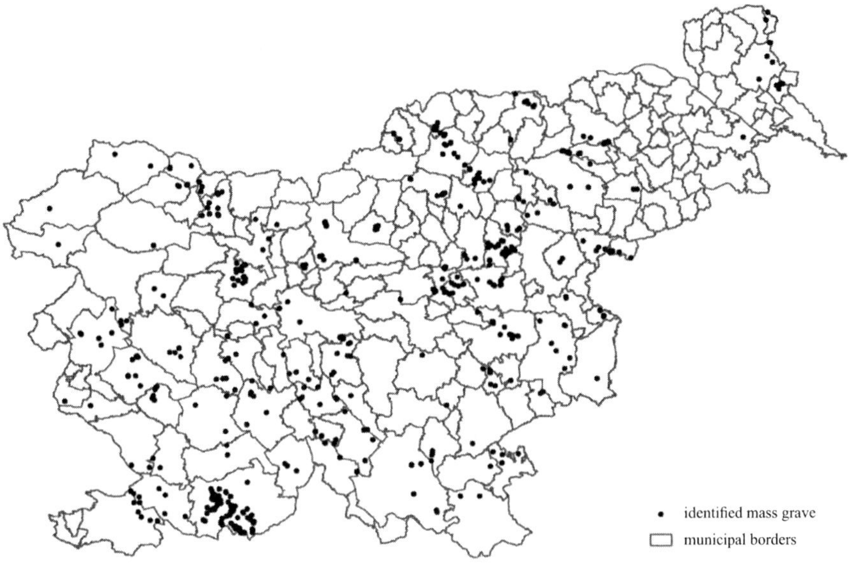

Source: Ferenc, 2008, p. 25.

Mitja Ferenc notes that for most of secret mass graves, individual graves and victims 'it is not even known where they lie, and they never received a burial worthy of a human being.' He continues that 'crimes were exacerbated by forced silence and suppression of the right to a grave' and that 'their victims simply did not exist' (Ferenc, 2008, 157). The Communist regime was marked by the concentration and labor camps, widespread extrajudicial killings, violent confiscations of property, show judicial processes, the collectivization, forced deportations of population from the place of residence, etc. Labour camps represent one of the most heinous human rights violations of the Communist regime in Slovenia. They were first named as punishment camps and later, from the beginning of 1946 as public institutions of forced labor. Apart from forced labor labour camps, the totalitarian regime established in 1949 camps for rehabilitation work in camps for socially useful work, which is the official terminology of the time employed the term 'working groups'. The majority of those camps were established in the period 1949-1950, when a number of persons were sentenced and sent to perform socially useful work.

Transitional justice measures in Slovenia

Transitional justice has begun in Slovenia only after the fall of the totalitarian regime in 1990 and it is yet to be finished. It can be divided into three phases. No transitional justice measures were employed after the fall of the fascist and National Socialist totalitarian systems after the Second World War. Therefore, one can discuss transitional justice in Slovenia only after the fall of the last of totalitarian regimes. In other words, it appears that transitional justice measures can be employed during the functioning of a particular totalitarian regime but it is doubtful if they can prove successful.

A. Transitional justice in trasition from totalitarian regime to democracy (1991-1995)

The objective of Slovenian transition was to achieve peaceful transition from totalitarian Communist regime of the federal Yugoslav state into a democratic system of the newly created and independent state of Slovenia. In April 1990 first democratic elections were held where non-communist political parties won the majority. There was no consensus agreed for a radical rapture with the former Communist regime. It must be noted however that there have been many calls for adoption of measures of lustration, which would prevent former Communist officials from participating in public life of the Slovenian state. However, such proposals were rejected mainly by left-wing parties, which are mainly successors of the Communist party. Perpetrators of totalitarian crimes have therefore not been brought to justice and were left in peace to enjoy their retirement. There was not a single trial before Slovenian court for crimes committed during the Communist regime. In other words, persons were given an informal amnesty for crimes committed during the totalitarian regime. Again as in Spanish case, it was the policy of not explicitly remembering the totalitarian period and its crimes. Equally, there was no truth and/or reconciliation commission established. The networks of former Communist regime were too strong for any alternative mechanisms to be successful. Reconciliation was understood as not mentioning the former regimes as it would not have had ever existed. The measures adopted were scarce and only impressionistic. The lack of a clear and well-defined policy in this period can be explained through the presence of also very important task, the transition from totalitarian to democratic system and the creation and functioning of the newly independent state.

B. Transitional justice as a partial reparation/compensation for the crimes of the past (1995-2004)

In the second period, the newly independent state of Slovenia has successfully sailed from the port and it was the time to concentrate on the measures repairing the past. Nonetheless, the second phase, between 1996 and 2004 was again marked by the lack of a general, integrated and consistent policy where only few measures were adopted. They aimed at remedying damages and redressing injustices committed in the totalitarian regime. The Denationalisation Act, the Victims of War Violence Act and the Redressing of Injustices Act imposed a number of obligations to state authorities in relation to the memory of totalitarian crimes. Here the focus was more on repairing damage caused, particularly by the Communist regime. However, these measures have been employed only half way through. Again, no truth or reconciliation commission was established. No legal act on reconciliation measures has been adopted. The National Parliament has found neither the majority nor consensus for adopting a lustration bill.

C. New developments after 2004

The third period has been characterised by a slight change of the social and political perception of the issues. The first and only case was brought against former Communist dictator. Slovenian courts refused in *Prosecutor v. Ribičič* to open investigation in his alleged acts possibly amounting to crimes against humanity. It is not surprising that this decision has not sparked any legal commentary or even discussion from members of the academic legal community in Slovenia. In this way, a number of Slovenian intellectuals and politicians share the fear that opening the investigation for crimes committed so many decades ago would deepen disagreement between different parts of Slovenian society and would hinder the path towards reconciliation between members of the former Communist Party and the rest of Slovenian society. However, examples from other countries show that there cannot be catharsis of the respective nations without historically and legally addressing atrocities committed. It is highly unlikely that a single judicial decision can address 'collective trauma' of the past in which Slovenian nation was split. However, it may be argued that this is necessary as 'a kind of catharsis' to set the new century on a course based on principles of non-discrimination, tolerance, and diversity in the Slovenian society. The handful of reactions came merely from members of the media and individual journalists. Most of them agreed that prosecuting persons for crimes which were not criminalized at the time of commission does not violate the prohibition of retroactivity since those crimes were already at the time of commission contrary to fundamental principles of humanity. However, some authors also disagreed with that opinion. Moreover, the government of Republic of Slovenia in 2004 established the Commission for the Settlement of Hidden Mass Graveyards and the Study Centre for National Reconciliation was established in 2008.

Reconciliation Measures

It appears that violations committed in Slovenia after the Second World War and during the duration of the Communist regime must be addressed if reconciliation of Slovenian population is ever to be achieved. No specific reconciliation measures have been so far adopted. Alternatively, the truth and reconciliation in Slovenia may offer alternative to prosecution of crimes at national level. In this way, alternative mechanisms would emphasize apologies and compensation rather than punishment. Such system may contribute to the identification of perpetrators, but in the same vein to peace and stability in society. Truth and reconciliation contribute to solving conflict peacefully. The work of the South-African Truth and Reconciliation Commission illustrates that truth commissions can be valuable mechanisms for victims, provided that they adopt and implement the 'victim-centred' ideals. The reconciliation between different sides of Slovenian society appears very far away. No measures or policies have been so far adopted to reach reconciliation between perpetrators and the victims of totalitarian crimes, mostly Communist crimes. Whereas fascist and National Socialist totalitarian regimes and their crimes are widely condemned in Slovenia, there is no unity in the Slovenian political arena in condemning the crimes of Communism during and after WWII along with other two totalitarian regimes in Slovenia in 20th century. All dead persons deserve the right to a grave. Human dignity and piety towards the dead is one of the cornerstones of our society. No tolerance is possible without these basic requirements. Persons who died as victims of war violence and post-war summary executions deserve inscriptions on the grave that they were victims of war and that they have fallen in the name of Slovenia. Families deserve that death certificates of persons killed are issued and that monuments are established in the places of the hidden mass grave sites such as memorial parks in Kočevski Rog and Teharje.

Conclusion

Whereas the fascist and National Socialist totalitarian regimes are widely condemned in Slovenian society, the crimes by the Communist totalitarian regime are not fully recognized by the whole Slovenian society. The awareness of post-Second World War Crimes is one of the preconditions for avoiding similar crimes in the future in Slovenia and elsewhere. Discussion on crimes committed on Slovenian territory after the Second World War and secret mass graves is often underpinned by deeply-rooted emotions that suppress the argumentative dialogue and reasoning and has led to long-term polarization of Slovenian society on left and right forces. This has led to long-term polarization of Slovenian society along left and right lines of the political spectrum. The challenge posed by transition from oppression to democracy is to account for the totalitarian regime and then rebuild a new society in its wake. The Second World War in Slovenia was primarily a time of social revolution that saw the forceful takeover of authority by the then illegal Communist Party of Yugoslavia. In the end, legally, it seems unlikely that any former high Communist official will be prosecuted in the future by the Slovenian Court for these crimes. Discussion has shown that it is very difficult to show probable cause for opening a criminal investigation into crimes against humanity committed on the Slovenian territory in the months following the Second World War. The issues concerning crimes against humanity after the Second World War in Slovenia are rife with political implications, and none of the crimes themselves fall within the *rationae temporae* jurisdiction of the International Criminal Court or International Criminal Court for the Former Yugoslavia. Perhaps most importantly, it is unlikely that the Supreme Prosecution Office of Slovenia will take steps to prosecute more former high Communist officials due to the procedural obstacles.

It can perhaps be overly simplistic to suggest compromise for difficult legal and political questions. In the case of crimes against humanity in the Slovenian territory, the various constituent groups often do not listen to each other or allow for compromise. Until all politicians realize some form of justice is inevitable in the foreseeable future, and victims'-oriented political parties radically change they way in asking for nothing but justice, nothing will be done to effectively tackle these crimes. Though the present situation may appear grim, consensus does appear to be growing for meaningful and continued reform, which would settle the question of post-war killings and the secret mass graves of victims in a manner that will respect victims' right to a name and a grave. Many of the underlying weaknesses in the enforcing transitional justice in Slovenian legal order can be directly tied to the nature of normative framework as coherent system does not exist for prosecuting to crimes of former totalitarian regime. The main problems lie in lack of knowledge and understanding of among politicians, civil servants and experts in Slovenia. Surely, there are many knowledgeable professionals in Slovenia, but the vast majority does not possess sufficient knowledge to respond to the challenges of the crimes of the past. When the focus would be directed towards means rather than ends, the normative framework for the implementation of transitional justice in Slovenia could provide some more clear guidance. The current state of regulation in relation to the implementation and advancement of the memory of crimes committed by totalitarian regimes in Slovenia is neither advancing the cause of protection and promotion of human rights, nor of the operation of an effective normative framework.

References :

Arendt, Hannah. 2003. *Izvori totalitarizma.* Ljubljana: Študentska založba.

Dežman, Jože. 2008. Communist Repression and Transitional Justice in Slovenia. In: Peter Jambrek (ed.), *Crimes Committed by totalitarian regimes*, Slovenian presidency of the Council of the European Union. Bruxelles, Ljubljana.

Dovžan, Gašper and Tekavec, Urška. 2001. *Temne strani slovenske pravne preteklosti v luči slovenske ustave.* Ljubljana: Nova Revija.

Hančič, Damjan; Podberšič, Renato and Ivanc, Blaž. 2009. Slovenia: From Triple totalitarian occupation to freedom and independence. In: Ludger Kühnhardt (ed.), *The reunification of Europe, Anti-totalitarian courage and political renewal.* Brussels.

Ferrar, Marcus. 2005. *Slovenia 1945: Memories of Death and Survival After World War II, I.* London, New York: B. Tauris & Co Ltd.

Ferenc, Mitja. 2008. *Topografija evidentiranih grobišč, Poročilo Komisije Vlade Republike Slovenije za reševanje vprašanj prikritih grobišč 2005-2008.* Ljubljana: Družina.

Ferenc, Mitja. 2008. Secret World War Two Mass Graves in Slovenia. In Peter Jambrek (ed.), *Crimes Committed by totalitarian regimes*, Slovenian presidency of the Council of the European Union. Bruxelles, Ljubljana.

Griesser Pečar, Tamara. 2009. Generalni register pojavov in žrtev totalitarizma. In: *Totalitarizmi – vprašanja in izzivi.* Ljubljana: Študijski center za narodno spravo.

Jančar, Drago. 1998. *Temna stran meseca.* Ljubljana: Nova Revija.

Jambrek, Peter (ed.). 2008. *Crimes Committed by totalitarian regimes,* Slovenian presidency of the Council of the European Union. Bruxelles, Ljubljana.

Šturm, Lovro. 2012. Ustavnosodna presoja o razmejitvi totalitarnega sistema in svobodne demokratične družbe, temelječe na človekoven dostojanstvu. In: *Dignitas, Revija za človekove pravice, No. 53-54, pp. 12-25.*

Valič, Andreja. 2009. Zgodovina za prihodnost. In: *Totalitarizmi – vprašanja in izzivi*. Študijski center za narodno spravo, Študijski center za narodno spravo, Ljubljana.

Vodopivec, Peter. 2006. *Od Pohlinove slovnice do samostojne države : slovenska zgodovina od konca 18. stoletja do konca 20. stoletja.* Ljubljana: Modrijan.

Vodušek Starič, Jerca. 2004. Kako se čistila Jugoslavija? *Gordogan*, pp. 36-50.

(UN)JUSTIFIED FEAR OF DAMAGE CLAIMS

Stanislav Slatinek, Ljubljana

Sexual abuse of minors by priests or other pastoral workers indicate a profound crisis of moral values. These offences are ruinous for children and youths as they deeply hurt their dignity. Since this state of affairs imposes special duties on the Church, the Episcopal Conference of Slovenia issued special guidelines concerning conduct in case of sexual abuse of minors by priests or catechists (SŠK 2006, 64).

Sexual abuse means all those actions which in a concrete case represent physical violation of sexual integrity of minors, and have to derive from sexual initiatives by a priest or a pastoral worker. Only after this condition is met, the conduct of a priest or a pastoral worker acquires characteristics of sexual abuse of minors and thus signs of criminal offence according to the Penal Code of the Republic of Slovenia (Article 183/III). Decisive for judging such matters correctly are therefore the defendant's actions and not how his conduct was interpreted by alleged victims.

The Slovenian courts have recently recorded a dramatic increase in the number of reports concerning sexual assault on minors by priests and pastoral workers. Accompanying these reports is the increasing number of abuses by those reporting, who are guided by their self-interests (e.g. expectations of damages) or merely by their wish to injure others. Every criminal proceeding in connection with minors thus requires that the accusation is carefully and critically evaluated (Klemenčič 2011, 18). Criminal offences of sexual assault on persons below fifteen years of age are judged by the Slovenian courts according to the Paragraph 3 of the Article 183 of the Penal Code of the Republic of Slovenia, which states: "A teacher, educator, guardian, adoptive parent, parent, priest, doctor or any other person who through the abuse of his position has sexual intercourse or performs any lewd act with a person under the age of fifteen and whom he is entrusted to teach, educate, protect or care for shall be sentenced to imprisonment for not less than one and not more than ten years" (the Penal Code).

In most cases courts believe minors who say that a priest or a pastoral worker committed the alleged sexual offences against them. The courts do not doubt the veracity of such statements made by injured parties, according to which the actions concerned were carried out in exactly the same way as described. The courts believe that injured parties perceive physical contacts with individual parts of the body made by priests or pastoral workers as sexual acts. By touching, the accused priests undoubtedly interfere with both physical and sexual integrity of the injured parties. By committing criminal offences, priests undoubtedly abuse their position of proclaimers of faith, yet they at the same time lessen the security which children expect from the Church. "All this additionally diminishes the modern man's power of trust, which Christians or their communities could mediate" (Juhant 2012, 390).

The fact is that persons under fifteen years of age (in our culture from 11 to 14 years) are in the period of early adolescence. In this period, youths develop their self-image. They have not yet reached sexual maturity. Actions of physical contact (allusions, instructions, gestures, facial expressions, looks) are understood as sexual acts. Len Sperry says that children under fifteen years of age are not yet capable of a deliberate consent to any sexual actions. The consensual incapacity is in case of such children absolute (Sperry 2008, 50-51).

Touching intimate body parts is from the ethical point of view inadmissible for priests as catechists, and is prohibited also for lay teachers (Slatinek 2010, 187). It is difficult to believe that the accused priests and pastoral workers had not been aware that such conduct was unlawful. In view of their age, maturity, position and life experiences, priests should be aware how abject such conduct is.

Also according to the Congregation for the Doctrine of the Faith (KVN 2011, 23-24), resolving cases involving sexual abuses should be as just as possible. If a priest is found guilty, he can be condemned to a certain number of canonical penalties. The most serious of which is dismissal from the clerical state. Regardless of this, the perpetrator is obliged to compensate the victim with an adequate and appropriate indemnity.

1. Damage claims against the Church

Besides reporting criminal offences, victims of sexual assault also bring damage actions against perpetrators and against the Church. Slovenian courts are assessing whether or not the Church in Slovenia is responsible for the conduct of priests. Sometimes the victims of sexual abuse decide to bring damage actions against the Church even after the perpetrator died (Damage claims 2007-2012). In some cases the victims are of the opinion that the responsibility lies exclusively with the perpetrator of sexual abuse, and they consequently do not sue the Church for damages. The law firms representing the victims of sexual abuse are frequently convinced that the Church is in case of criminal offences of clerics bound by joint and several liability for damages. They say that the relationship between the diocese and the priest is similar to that between the employer and the employee, in which the employer is responsible for the actions of workers. In cases when a priest "abused children during the course of his work, i.e. in his parsonage and during catechesis", the Slovenian court practice holds it that "the responsibility for the damage does not go only to a person who committed a criminal offence, but also to the legal person for which the former worked" (Zorman 2010/a, 22).

Several priests in Slovenia have been convicted for paedophilia, yet the Church's liability for damages has not been proved in any of these cases (23). Damage claims against the Church are nevertheless multiplying. If a court in one case establishes that the Church is jointly responsible for the conduct of its priest (or a pastoral worker) who committed a criminal offence against a person below fifteen years of age, it will form a precedent for all victims of abuses by priests, which will undoubtedly occur in the future (Zorman 2010/b, 5).

Courts are thus assessing whether a priest works for the Church and whether the Church could be jointly responsible for deeds which its employee has performed at his workplace. Some other countries recognise the Church's joint liability. Some dioceses thus had to pay substantial damages to the victims. Irish dioceses have paid more than a billion euros of damages to 12,000 victims (Slatinek 2012, 140).

Slovenian journalists are thus asking what the Church is afraid of. Does it fear that it will have to recognise its joint responsibility for actions of its priests, or does it fear the amount of damages? Though it is true that there are paedophiles among priests, it is also true that the smear campaign against the Church in Slovenia is intense and that illegitimate pursuit of money is involved in most cases (Zorman 2010/b, 5).

2. Joint and several liability of defendants

The claims for damages for victims of sexual abuse committed by priests or pastoral workers are in Slovenia frequently filed against the perpetrators and the legal persons within the Church (parishes, dioceses, archdioceses) in which the priest or the pastoral worker worked when the damage was caused (Damage claims 2007-2012). Such decisions are frequently based on the premise that the defendants, both the perpetrator and the legal person within the Church, are bound by joint and several liability for the damaging event, while the joint and several liability of legal persons is interpreted on the basis of the following arguments:

a) Due to organisational association

Courts interpret the joint and several liability of defendants on the basis of the fact that they are interconnected parts of the same organisation (Damage claims 2007-2012). Since priests do their job in a certain parish, a diocese or an archdiocese, the pertaining legal persons in the Church are bound by joint and several liability for criminal offences of clerics. By the act of employing the priest, the local bishop established the organisational connection between the cleric and the legal person.

The Canon Law rejects entirely the joint and several liability of defendants due to organisational association. The organisational association of defendants or, in court lingo, "administrative territorial division", does not mean that the defendants in case of a damaging event act as a unity and thus assume joint and several liability. The fact is that defendants are independent legal persons, so that in case of a damaging event each defendant assumes his/its own responsibility. Their legal liability is clearly defined, any joint and several liability established in this way is consequently erroneous (Košir and Naglič 2010, 346-347).

b) Due to legal succession

Furthermore, courts interpret the joint and several liability of defendants on the basis of legal succession (Damage claims 2007-2012). Courts conclude that in case a bishop partitions his diocese into several parishes or in case boundaries between dioceses are altered, damaging acts never expire, not even in case a parish dissolves or in case a new diocese is formed. Courts maintain that in such cases joint and several liability is assumed by a new parish or a new diocese due to the legal succession.

The Canon Law does not recognise such interpretation of legal succession. When dividing a diocese into new dioceses or when dividing a parish into new parishes, it is not possible to conclude that now the new legal persons are bound by joint and several liability for the damaging acts which happened at former territories that have been legally incorporated into a new legal person due to the formation of a new parish or diocese (Saje 2007, 501-505). Let us say, merely as an example, that a parish where a damaging act occurred has been attached to a different diocese. One cannot say that this diocese is now on the basis of legal succession bound by joint and several liability for damaging acts which happened in the parish which has been attached to it. Similarly, in case of dividing business entities and founding a new one the Slovenian civil law says that "the draft division should define the legal relationships in a way which enables their individualisation and demarcation" (Prelič 2007, 661).

c) Due to employment relationship

Joint and several liability is interpreted by courts also on the basis of the employment relationship supposedly existing between the priest as a perpetrator of a damaging act and the legal person within the Church (a parish, a diocese, an archdiocese), in which the priest performs his work. According to the Slovenian civil legislation (Article 170 of the Obligations Act), courts conclude that a legal person (a parish, a diocese, an archdiocese) assumes joint and several liability for the damage which has been caused to a third party by a worker (priest or pastoral worker) during his work or in connection with his work. For establishing joint and several liability it is important that a worker (a priest or a pastoral worker) worked for a legal person at the time when the damaging act occurred.

The Canon Law does not agree with such interpretation of joint and several liability since in case of the Church, unlike in case of commercial companies, one cannot talk of "workers and employers". There is no relationship between a legal person within the Church (a parish, a diocese, an archdiocese) and the perpetrator of a damaging act (a priest or a pastoral worker) which is equal to employment relationship, the analogy is thus inadmissible (Košir and Naglič 2010, 344).

A parish, a diocese or an archdiocese (as legal persons within the Church) could assume joint and several liability according to the Slovenian civil legislation (Article 170 of the Obligations Act) only in case a priest (as a worker) works according to directions and under supervision of a parish priest or a bishop (as an employer). When an employer gives instructions to a worker and supervises him, a worker is not independent in his work and is merely an extension of his employer (345). In such case a legal person can be bound by joint and several liability for a damaging act of its worker.

According to the Canon Law, it is not possible to conclude that a priest works according to the instructions and under the supervision of a parish priest or a bishop. It is true, however, that a bishop gives a church job to a priest (or a pastoral worker). It is also true that a bishop transfers or removes a priest from a church job. Despite this, a priest is not a "worker" as defined by the Slovenian civil legislation (Article 622 of the Obligations Act). A priest does perform his work at the territory of a certain parish, a diocese or an archdiocese, yet he is completely independent in his work. The Church's Law Code describes a priest's rights, duties and tasks which he is obliged to perform. No legal person (a parish, a diocese, an archdiocese) in the Church carries out special supervision of priests' work and does not pay them. The relationship between a priest and the legal person in the Church has a biblical – theological dimension and cannot be equated with a working relationship in commercial companies. Consequently, joint and several liability of a legal person in the Church on the basis of a working relationship is ruled out.

Another aspect which is frequently pointed out by courts when interpreting the joint and several liability of legal persons in the Church for damaging acts of its priests is the fact that a priest as a worker works for the benefit of a legal person as his employer. In this context the legal person, if it benefits from its worker, assumes the joint and several liability for the damage caused by its worker in line of his work or in connection with his work (Damage claims 2007-2012).

The Canon Law rules out the possibility that a priest works for the benefit of a parish, a diocese or an archdiocese. Priests teach children faith and prepare them for the Communion and receiving of the Holly Confirmation. They perform their work completely independent and at the same time in the interest of Church, this means in the interest of believers. The Church does not derive some direct benefit from catechesis, as is the case with a worker who measures his gain by the income from his employees' work. Consequently, in case of a priest's work in a parish or in a diocese any analogy with a commercial company and with a relationship which is comparable with employment relationship is ruled out. Legal persons in the Church are organisational formations which completely differ from those in economy. The Canon Law does not use the term worker when referring to a priest, it uses the word shepherd, which indicates a position completely different from that of workers in a company. A priest's work benefits all members of the Church, that is all believers. Priests are as consecrated believers those who work on behalf of all and for all.

3. Liability for damages is assumed exclusively by the perpetrator of a damaging act

After we ruled out the joint and several liability of legal persons for criminal offences of clerics committed against minors, we need to again emphasise that the Slovenian law of damages is based on subjective liability of the person who caused damage (Article 170 of the Obligations Act). A legal person is bound by joint and several liability only when in a concrete case one can speak of the "worker – employer" relationship.

The Canon Law also says that only a person who is heavily responsible for external violation of law or order and who committed a criminal offence intentionally or due to negligence is punished (can. 1321 §1). More rigorously is punished a person who obstinately persists in a bad intention (can. 1326 §1,1). The Canon Law does not know collective liability, it only indicates it in cases when it can be legally established that several persons took part in a criminal offence. Even if a group of people participate in a criminal offence, the subjective guilt of each individual is always assessed. The perpetrator of a criminal offence is punished in order to remedy the corruption, establish justice and improve the perpetrator (can. 1341). The justice of which speaks the Canon Law in cases of sexual abuses committed against minors by priests or other pastoral workers can be established also by paying appropriate damages. For this reason the guidelines of the Episcopal Conference of Slovenia and the Congregation for the Doctrine of the Faith address also the issue of damages (SŠK 2006, 67; KVN 2001, 788). The perpetrator of a criminal offence is required to fully assume the liability for damages concerning the damaging act he committed.

Although the Canon Law profession says that the position of priests and monks in the Church contains some elements of the employment relationship as understood by the civil legislation of the Republic of Slovenia, priests and monks are in regard to the performance of their tasks completely autonomous. They carry out their basic task – proclaiming the God's Gospel – through the strength of the holly order sacrament, they appear and work in front of believers in the person of Jesus Christ (can. 1009 §3). The congregation thus in regard to clerics emphasises that we cannot allow the status of a cleric to be reduced to the level of an ordinary profession which could be in any way compared with profane jobs. It is also not allowed to pretend that an "employer – employee" relationship exists between a bishop and a priest (KK 1982, 643). Priests have a mission in the Church, not merely a job. An archbishop or a bishop is primarily a father, a brother and a friend of priests, only after that he is a superior to whom they owe respect and obedience (can. 212 §1). Priests are primarily a bishop's co-workers and advisors, only after that his subordinated servants (can. 384). Therefore, there are completely different bonds which exist between priests and a parish priest or a parish or a bishop and a diocese. Similarities with commercial companies are almost nonexistent, thus any possibility of establishing the liability for damages of legal persons for criminal offences of individual priests or other pastoral workers is unlikely (Košir and Naglič 2010, 350).

Through the said analysis of how the Canon Law understands the notion priest and the relationship of natural persons to legal persons (a parish, a diocese, an archdiocese) in the Church we can conclude that any endeavours by Slovenian courts trying to charge the Church's legal persons with the liability for damages in cases of damaging acts committed by clerics are unjust. The Canon Law strictly advocates the view that a perpetrator assumes the entire liability for every criminal offence. Yet since the modern secularised society is frequently not familiar with the Canon Law, it can be understood why in case of sexual abuse of minors by priests solutions are sought in the analogy with the civil legislation. And since damage claims do not seek a way to improve a perpetrator and make him appropriately repair the damage, but frequently only try to get money, the Church's fear of (unjust) damage claims is often warranted.

Sources and Bibliography

Juhant, Janez. 2012. Klerik med strahovi časa in vero, ki osvobaja. *Bogoslovni vestnik* 72 (3): 383-396.

Kazenski zakonik (KZ). 2008. *Uradni list RS,* n. 55.

Klemenčič, Stanislav. 2011. Javni protest proti sodni razsodbi v primeru župnika s Polenšaka. *Dnevnik,* 7th December, 18.

Kongregacija za klerike (KK). 1982. Declaratio de quibusdam associationibus vel coadunationibus quae omnibus clericis prohibentur. *AAS* 74: 642-644.

Kongregacija za verski nauk (KVN). 2001. Epistula a Congregatione pro Doctrina Fidei missa ad totius Catholicae Ecclesiae Episcopos aliosque Ordinarios et Hierarchas interesse habentes: de delictis gravioribus eidem Congregationi pro Doctrina Fidei reservatis. *AAS* 93: 785-788.

Kongregacija za verski nauk (KVN). 2011. Lettera circolare per aiutare le Conferenze episcopali nel preparare linee guida per il trattamento dei casi di abuso sessuale nei confronti di minori da parte di chierici. *Apollinaris* 84: 19-24.

Košir, Borut in Naglič, Andrej. 2010. Odgovornost katoliške Cerkve za dejanja duhovnikov. *Bogoslovni vestnik* 70 (3), 341-350.

Obligacijski zakonik (OZ). 2007. *Uradni list RS*, št. 97.

Odškodninske tožbe. 2007-2012. Arhiv Metropolitanskega cerkvenega sodišča v Mariboru.

Perlič, Saša. 2007. *Veliki komentar Zakona o gospodarskih družbah (ZGD-1)*. Ljubljana: GV Založba.

Saje, Andrej. 2007. Spolne zlorabe v Cerkvi in vprašanje odškodninske odgovornosti. *Bogoslovni vestnik* 67 (4), 491-505.

Slatinek, Stanislav. 2010. *Kazniva dejanja in kazni. Sankcije v Cerkvi*. Maribor: Slomškova založba.

Slatinek. Stanislav. 2012. Strah pred odškodninskimi tožbami. In: Juhant, J., Strahovnik, V., Žalec, B. (eds). *Kako iz kulture strahu? Tesnoba in upanje današnjega človeka,* Znanstvena knjižnica 33. Ljubljana: Teološka fakulteta.

Slovenska škofovska konferenca (SŠK). 2006. Smernice za ravnanje v primeru spolnega zlorabljanja mladoletnih oseb s strani duhovnikov ali drugih pastoralnih delavcev. *Sporočila* 4: 64-67.

Sperry, Len. 2008. *Spolnost, duhovništvo in Cerkev*. Celje: Celjska Mohorjeva družba.

Zakon o obligacijskih razmerjih (ZOR). 1978. *Uradni list SFRJ*, n. 29.

Zorman, Elizabeta. 2010/a. Pred sodiščem o odgovornosti Cerkve. *7 dni*, 20th January, 22.

Zorman, Elizabeta. 2010/b. Za bodoče žrtve. *Večer*, 29th October, 5.

THE MEANING OF RELIGION

FEAR, COURAGE AND HOPE: A HERMENEUTIC OF LOVE IN A CULTURE OF SUSPICION

Corneliu Constantineanu, Bucharest

Introduction

It is with a certain sense of pain when we affirm that one of the common characteristics of our cultures today is fear. Whether we speak about authentic or unreal fears, about the larger political fears or about various personal fears which come as consequences of the first, the culture of fear is a dominant feature of our society (see particularly Robin, 2004; Glassner, 2009; Furedi, 2006; Shlapentokh, 2006). To be sure, fear is experienced and expressed differently by different cultures but living in a global and globalized world we are also exposed to similar fears of terrorism, international conflicts, financial and economic crises, crimes and disease, global warming, unemployment, poverty, etc. The sense of fear in our culture has increased exponentially with the 9/11 events in New York capturing the entire societies under its grip. Moreover, it was this great tragedy also that illustrated a close and somewhat troubled connection between violence, fear, and (a certain kind of) religion. No wonder that religion has been regarded by many as a factor that contributes to rather than disperses fear. And, unfortunately, in many instances religion has been used to exacerbate the conflict situations in various corners of the world and was exploited towards violent political ends – as the religious motivated terrorist attacks illustrate. As a result, many people today think that we should simply dismiss religion all together from the social fabric.

Despite the ambiguity of religion in the public space, however, research studies show that religion represents an influential factor in society, a strong motivation for individual conduct, indeed as an "absolute necessity for democracy" (Von Schönborn, 2000, 87). Others have studied the relationship between religion, human rights and democracy and discovered that religion is a vital dimension of any democracy, as it offers the highest framework of reference and values, and gives content and coherence to the structure of human communities and cultures (Witte and van der Vyver, 1996). In the words of sociologist Peter Berger, religion represents "the sacred canopy," "the symbolic universe" within which people live and which helps integrate the various aspects of life, thus providing a comprehensive understanding of reality and the meaning of life (Berger, 2000; Berger, 1969). The religious factor cannot thus be ignored or dismissed since it plays a major role in the fabric of human society.

The argument I would like to propose in this paper is that there are important resources within the various religious traditions that could contribute significantly to an authentic living. More specifically, based on a Pauline passage from the Epistle to the Philippians, I would like to argue that in the predominant culture of fear the answer is not suspicion but love! The climate of fear and anxiety in our society requires that we discover concrete ways to deal with fear, ways that will enhance our life together despite our differences.

Fear, anxiety and the hermeneutics of suspicion

There are various and serious consequences of fear. People lose their sense of balance and control, overreact and are ready to do anything to regain a sense of security – including surrendering their power to those who will offer such security. The great danger is that the less personal power we exercise the less input we have for our own decisions. Similarly, fear limits people decision-making process, blinds people to solutions. Another consequence of fear in our culture is that we become very confrontational/oppositional to all those who are different, who are not like us – and this at a personal, national and international level. Ultimately, fear leads to suspicion and isolation.

Many people would agree today, without much difficulty, that one essential element in the complex architecture of the postmodern condition, is suspicion. Indeed, suspicion not simply as a singular phenomenon describing an individual attitude of mistrust and doubt, but suspicion as a phenomenon that permeates everything in society, creating a prevalent culture of suspicion. Suspicion is usually defined as an act of suspecting something, especially something wrong, on little evidence or without proof, a state of uncertainty, doubt. It seems that everything today starts from, or is dictated by, a basic point agreed by all, i.e. a hermeneutic of suspicion. Anthony C. Thiselton is thus right to remind us of the fact that:

> "Both, the human language and mind are not transparent and straightforward. This is the most important thing we learn from the three 'masters of suspicion': Freud, Marx, and Nietzsche (despite the temptation of Christian thinkers to dismiss their work as incompatible with the claims of Christian theology). But

their insistence that the human mind can deceive itself in variety of ways, often in the interests of individual or of social power, resonates with biblical and theological assertions about the deceitfulness, opaqueness, and duplicity of the human heart" (Thiselton, 1992, 14).

There is thus at least one aspect within our culture which 'demands' a hermeneutic of suspicion, namely the power of deception which makes everyone extremely circumspect to get anything for granted. You just cannot believe everything, the argument goes, you have first to be suspicious and encounter everything with a sense of distance, even irony. This will protect you from anyone who wants to take advantage of you. A further aspect that strengthens even more this hermeneutic of suspicion is the ready-made argument against *naiveté*. With the sophistication of the other that one encounters, we have to protect our innocence (of which we automatically presume) and so we cannot trust the other but rather are encouraged to suspect and distrust. And so we do. In all our encounters with the other, not excluding even the people we know, we ask many, many questions: What did s/he mean? Why did s/he put the problem in this way? Why did s/he look to me like that? What about his voice? S/he has really changed, hasn't s/he? And with very few exceptions (the number of which is still decreasing), the more we apply this hermeneutic of suspicion the more this becomes the normal way in which we relate to people around us.

I should stress it as very important, before I go any further, that we should take seriously the concerns of the hermeneutics of suspicion: deceitfulness, opaqueness, and duplicity of the human heart! There is also a strong biblical warning about the capacity of the human heart to deceive itself, as we read in Jeremiah: "The heart is deceitful above all things, and desperately corrupt; who can understand it?" (Jeremiah 17:9). But at the same time we should also ask whether these concerns can be taken with utmost seriousness by this kind of radical scepticism propagated today as the only way for life. A hermeneutic of suspicion with its disguise as the 'guardian' against any abuse of power and deception, trains us so well in suspecting and mistrusting everything and everyone that it makes almost impossible for us to trust, to learn, or to listen properly to the other. The guardian against deception has become itself a sophisticated self-deception of our time! It is understandable why for Bonhoeffer the attitude of mistrust and suspicion is "the revolt of inferiority" (Bonhoeffer, 1997, 345).

A radical alternative: a hermeneutic of love

The question one raises is whether there is not a better way forward, a way that will take seriously the concerns of the hermeneutic of suspicion but at the same time avoid its shortcomings. And as it happens, Apostle Paul does present us with a different, most excellent way – a hermeneutics of love! Writing to the Christians in Philippi, he responded to the questions of a community who was experiencing various dissensions, power struggles within an atmosphere of disunity and mistrust (Peterlin, 1995). In his response to the situation, Paul offers a hermeneutic for a new day, for a people who experienced the profound love of God. We find the text in Philippians 1:9-11:

> *And this is my prayer:that your love may grow more and more, in knowledge and understanding, so that you may be able to discern what is best and may be pure and blameless until the day of Christ filled with the fruit of righteousness that comes through Jesus Christ – to the glory and praise of God.*

In what follows I do not intend to offer an exegetical analysis of the text but rather make a few reflections on Paul's proposal for the hermeneutic of love. I begin by saying that this text about growing in love is a prayer which is a hint that Paul understood that love represents the very essence of Christianity, the one thing which distinguishes a Christian life. When one prays, he brings the most intimate, important, existential issues to the fore. For Paul love is paramount. We also observe that there is a certain kind of growing or progression in love, and so a common misunderstanding about love can be dismissed right away, namely that love is simply a feeling, an emotion, a sentiment.

The content of Paul's prayer reveals the nature of love he asks for. This is neither a naive love, nor one which 'closes the eyes' and it is so unable to see and discern things. On the contrary, he is praying that their love may grow in *knowledge* and *understanding*. True love knows, and understands. For indeed, what kind of love can there be if unable to know or understand? Can anyone imagine such a love towards one's spouse, or children, or friends – a love unable to know or understand? Love knows what, when, why she is doing and understands it. True love is not blind, despite the popular parlance to the opposite! But Paul proves again his greatness: the kind of knowledge and understanding he is referring to are not simple theoretical assets – the kind of mechanical or sterile knowledge, which eventually ends up constantly challenging the owner to pride and boast! He does not refer simply to knowledge as such, to facts, to the quantity of information one may possess, a knowledge detached from the context. On the contrary, Paul refers to knowledge in which the subject is engaged with, knowledge gained through personal involvement and attachment, through personal experience and engagement. I know something to be true not simply because I learned it, or because I heard about it, but also because it proved to be true in my everyday life. And this kind of knowledge is only possible through love.

Philosophers speak today about the difference between an intellectual, rationalistic epistemology on the one hand, and the affective, narrative, contemplative epistemology on the other hand. The later emphasizes the important role of experience, of the 'heart', the importance of the story, of narrative (Smith, 2010, 43). Such an epistemology of love, a contemplative way of knowing, has particular features which make it appealing (see Zajonc, 2006): *respect,* which means that the integrity of the other is respected in the inquiry, the other is free to speak the truth without our projection or correction; *gentleness,* enables us not to distort the object of our attention; *intimacy*, allows the inquirer to become intimate with that to which it attends and does not simply objectify nature; *participation*, which makes contemplative inquiry experientially cantered in the other, not in ourselves; *vulnerability*, the capacity to be comfortable with ambiguity and uncertainty, with not knowing everything; *transformation*, i.e. internalizing the object of our inquiry and assuming the shape, dynamic and meaning of the contemplative object which leads to a transformation in accord with object studied; *formation*, which is being shaped in a particular way, developed through the contemplative practice; *insight,* as the last stage in contemplative knowing, is a kind of knowledge born out of direct and intimate participation which is a kind of seeing, of direct perception or apprehension of the object investigated.

True love, we have seen, enhances proper knowledge and understanding. Apostle Paul goes even further and stresses that the purpose of growing in love, in knowledge and understanding, is that "you may be able to discern what is best" (v.10) It is at this point that a prevalent hermeneutic of suspicion is named, unmasked and engaged in a radical way. It is not suspicion that may protect one from naïveté, from 'taking it all for granted'! On the contrary, it is love who protects, who enables one to better understand and discern. The big lie of suspicion is exposed and made powerless. The way of love is the most excellent way because it best enables us to understand, accept and affirm the other. New Testament scholar, N.T. Wright captures well this dimension of the hermeneutic of love:

> "In love, at least in the idea of agape as we find it in some parts of the New Testament, the lover affirms the reality and the otherness of the beloved. Love does not seek to collapse the beloved into terms of itself; and, even though it

> may speak of losing itself in the beloved, such a loss always turns out to be a true finding. In the familiar paradox, one becomes fully oneself when losing oneself to another. In the fact of love, in short, both parties are simultaneously affirmed" (Wright, 1992, 64).

In a culture of fear and anxiety, the response is not suspicion and mistrust but love. As we have seen, the hermeneutic of love does not take things for granted. It cannot do so because it is inspired by the love of God and leads to proper knowledge, understanding and discernment.

Conclusion: Love, Courage, and Hope

By way of conclusion I would like to draw two brief implications from my reflection. What I have tried to suggest by the hermeneutic of love is not that we ignore the reality of fear and suspicion. It is neither about the fact that we do not feel fear! What I have tried to suggest is that we may chose to respond with love to the prevalent culture of fear. To do that, of course, one needs a strong sense of courage – the courage to love! And courage, Scott Bader-Saye reminds us, is "the capacity to do what is right and good in the face of fear. We become courageous when we learn to live for something that is more important than our own safety" (Bader Saye, 2007, 67). Aleksandr Soljenitsyn observed already in 1978 that one of the dominant characteristics of the western world is a decline of courage, a loss of the civic courage which transfers from the elites and the leadership to the common people thus creating an entire society with a lack of courage (Soljenitsyn, 1978). It is particularly the responsibility of leaders to act with integrity and offer ideas and even solution to the complex issues surrounding our societies. And to be sure, they should not ignore the tough questions regarding fear, but they have the obligation to develop and maintain a culture of courage and integrity. It is not easy to say and do the right thing. It takes real courage to do what is right and act with integrity. It is my hope that the hermeneutic of love may claim back a culture of courage.

Several chapters in the book present the idea that, to some degree, fear and anxiety are illusory, being based on an imaginary reality. And yet people chose to fear and be anxious. I think we can make a similar argument about hope: it is also, to some extent, illusory, being based on a word or a promise about a reality that is yet to come. And people chose to hope. From a Christian perspective, however, the imagined reality to which hope points is not an illusion and it is not self-deception either. On the contrary, the promise is sure because it is based on the Word of God, on the promise of God – who is love and who demonstrated this love by becoming one of us. Only true love can lead to hope. And "this hope does not disappoint us because the love of God was poured in our hearts, in Christ, through the Spirit" (Romans 5:5). It is exactly the experience of the love of God that motivates us to love in our own turn. In a predominant culture of fear and anxiety, I believe we need to embody true love which takes courage to know and understand the other. The culture of fear and despair can only be overcome by the culture of love, courage and hope.

Bibliography

Bader-Saye, Scott. 2007. *Following Jesus in a Culture of Fear*. Grand Rapids: Brazos Press.

Berger, Peter (ed.). 2000. *The Desecularisation of the World*. Grand Rapids: Eerdmans.

Berger, Peter L. 1969. *The Sacred Canopy: Elements of Sociological Theory of Religion*. New York: Doubleday.

Bonhoeffer, Dietrich. 1997. *Letters and Papers from Prison*. Edited by Eberhard Bethge. New York: Touchstone.

Furedi, F. 2006. *Culture of fear revisited: Risk-taking and the morality of low expectations*, 4th ed. New York: Continuum.

Glassner, Barry. 2009. *Culture of Fear: Why Americans Fear Wrong Things*. New York: Basic Books.

Peterlin, Davorin. 1995. *Paul's Letter to the Philippians in the Light of Disunity in the Church*. Leiden: Brill.

Soljenitsyn, Aleksandr. 1978. A world split apart. A discourse given at Harvard University, 8 June 1978. Available at http://elkorg-projects.blogspot.co.uk/2008/08/aleksandr-soljenin, accessed on 02/07/2012.

Robin, Corey. 2004. *Fear. The History of a Political Idea*. Oxford: Oxford University Press.

Shlapentokh, V. 2006. *Fear in contemporary society: Its negative and positive effects*. New York: Palgrave Macmillan.

Smith, James K.S. 2010. *Thinking in Tongues. Pentecostal Contributions to Christian Philosophy*. Grad Rapids: Eerdmans.

Thiselton, Anthony C. 1992. *New Horizons in Hermeneutics. The Theory and Practice of Transforming Biblical Reading*. Grand Rapids: Zoodervan.

Von Schönborn, Christoph. 2000. *Oamenii, Biserica, Tara. Crestinismul ca provocare sociala*. Bucuresti: Anastasia.

Witte, John Jr. and Johan D. van der Vyver (eds.). 1996. *Religious Human Rights in Global Perspective*.The Hague and London: Martinus Nijoff.

Wright, N.T. 1992. *The New Testament and the People of God*. London: SPCK.
Zajonc, Arthur. 2006. Love and Knowledge: Recovering the Heart of Learning through Contemplation. In *Teachers College Record*, 108.9, pp. 1742-1759.

THE FEAR OF THE LORD: SPIRITUALITY AS MEDICATION FOR OUR CONTEMPORARY FEARS

Daniel G. Oprean, Osijek

Introduction

Fear is a perennial existential companion in human history, therefore it was always a subject of analysis of thinkers from many disciplines. There are distinctions made between fear, anxiety and depression, naming fear as oriented towards something known, anxiety as being afraid to look at a negative emotion inside of us. This emotion could be anger, guilt, lust, envy, greed, resentment and ..."rather than face the emotion, a person buries it, denies it, ignores it, and refuses to let it to the surface and be seen."[1] Another category is that of rational and irrational fears,[2] or holy fear, self-preserving fear and slavish fear.[3] There are fears coming from relationships, there are also financial fears connected with the money problems, as well as fears of being rejected or being loved, fears of being alone, the fears of love.[4] There are fears that we acknowledge and there are unacknowledged fears that are "pervading dread of life."[5] And this state of affair is not a novelty. The contemporary fears are perennial realities in human societies, therefore even the way we categorize our fears could be new or different, but the fears are not.

The aim of this paper is to explore three of the fears that the Bible speaks of, namely the fear of people, the fear of tomorrow, and the fear of death. Moreover, the paper will argue the fact that an adequate understanding of God's character

1 Frank Minirth, Paul Meier, Don Hawkins, *Worry-Free Living* (Nashville: Thomas Nelson Publishers, 1989), 27.
2 Cecil Osborne, *Release from Fear and Anxiety* (Waco: Texas, Word Books Publishers, 1978), 25.
3 Carol Kent, *Tame you Fears & Transform them into Confidence & Action* (Colorado: NavPress Publishing Group, 1993), 13.
4 Ira J. Tanner, *Loneliness: The Fear of Love* (New York: Harper & Row, 1973), 2.
5 Lloyd John Ogilvie, *The Bush is Still Burning: The Christ who Makes Things Happen in our Deepest Need* (Waco: Texas, Word Books Publishers, 1980), 38-40.

provides a good platform for healthy spirituality that could constitute a proper medication for the three types of fear.

Methodologically, the exploration will start with the fear of people and with its proper spiritual medication that is the understanding of God's sovereign Lordship over the entire reality in Christ. The exploration will continue with the fear of tomorrow and its proper spiritual medication that is the understanding of God's providential care, and with the fear of death and its proper spiritual medication that is the understanding of God's gift of life. The exploration will end with the analysis of the three cardinal virtues of faith, hope and love as expression of the fear of God.

Fear of People and God's Sovereignity

The first fear to be analyzed from the biblical perspective is the *fear of people*, considered in the Bible as being a trap. In the book of Proverbs in the Old Testament it is said that "fear of man will prove to be a snare, but whoever trusts in the Lord is kept safe." (Proverbs 29: 25). Similarly, the New Testament records the teaching of Christ himself about this fear. In an address to His disciples about the conditions of their future mission in the hostile world where they will face adversities and interrogatories, Christ encourages them not to worry "about what to say or how to say it. At that time will be given what to say, for it will not be you speaking but the Spirit of your Father speaking through you" (Matthew 10: 19-20). Moreover, Christ encourages his disciples to "be on guard against men" but not to be "afraid of them" (Matthew 10: 17). Moreover, Christ says that "there is nothing concealed that will not be disclosed, or hidden that will not be made known … Do not be afraid of those who kill the body but cannot kill the soul. Rather be afraid of the One who can destroy both soul and body in hell (Matthew 10: 26, 28). According with the gospel of John, Christ explains to his disciples where should be the foundation for their trust in Him despite their troubles: "In this world you will have trouble. But take heart! I have overcome the world" (John 16: 33).[6]

6 Lesslie Newbigin, *The Light Has Come: An Exposition of the Fourth Gospel* (Michigan: Grand Rapids, William B. Eerdmans Publishing Company, 1982), 222.

In the light of Christ's message to his disciples to fear people would be a denial of His declared Lordship over the entire reality. This truth is of paramount importance also for Pauline proclamation of the Gospel, as Paul said: "For God put everything under the Son's feet (1 Corinthians 15: 27) … and the Son has the power to bring everything under his control" (Philippians 3: 21).[7] Therefore, a profound understanding of God's Lordship through Christ in the Spirit, over the entire reality, could produce the conviction that even in the midst of adversities of life and people, Christ has the control as He said: "All authority in heaven and on earth has been given to me … And surely I am with you always, to the very end of the age" (Matthew 28: 20).

Fear of Tomorrow and God's Providential Care

The second fear to be analyzed from the biblical perspective is the *fear of tomorrow.* It is again Christ himself that speaks of this fear in the context of His exposition of the providential care of God in the created order:

> "Therefore I tell you, do not worry about your life, what you will eat and drink, or about your body, what you will wear … Look at the birds of the air; they do not sow or reap or store away in barns, and yet your heavenly Father feeds them. Are you not much more valuable than them? ... See how the lilies of the field grow. They do not labor or spin. Yet I tell you that even Solomon in all his splendor was dressed like one of these … Therefore do not worry about tomorrow, for tomorrow will worry about itself" (Matthew 6: 25-26, 28-29, 34).

In the light of Christ's message to fear tomorrow would be a denial of God's providential care, as God is worthy to be trusted, as it is expressed in the experience of believers[8] from the ancient times. The Psalmist David reflects the providential care in hard times in his experience when says: "Cast your cares on the Lord and he will sustain you; he will never let the righteous fall" (Psalm 55: 22). This text is echoed in Apostle Peter's letter of encouragement addressed to churches facing persecutions and hard times: "Cast your anxiety on him because he cares for you"

7 Alec Motyer, The Message of Philippians: Christ Our Joy (Leicester: Inter-Varsity Press, 1984), 197.

8 John R.W. Stott, *The Message of the Sermon on the Mount: Christian Counter-Culture* (Leicester: Inter-Varsity Press, 1978), 163.

(1 Peter 5: 7). And the reason for the trust that is common to David and Peter is that the Heavenly Father is proved to be in the history of His people as the One that never gets tired to carry his beloved, from birth to old age:

> "Listen to me O House of Jacob … you whom I have upheld since you were conceived and have carried since your birth. Even to your old age and gray hairs I am, I am he who will sustain you, I have made you and I will carry you; I will sustain and I will rescue you" (Isaiah 46: 3-4).

Moreover the reason for the faithful providence of God[9] is in Luther's saying: "The love of God does not find, but creates, that which is pleasing to it."[10] That means that His love for us is not conditioned by our performances, and "God does not abandon the object in disgust until it changes its character. Instead, God seeks to recreate it to become lovable again."[11] Reflecting to this truth Paul says: "if we are faithless he will remain faithful for he cannot disown himself" (2 Timothy 2: 13). Therefore, a profound understanding of God's providential care in Christ through the Spirit, as expression of His faithfulness even in the context of our unfaithfulness is a medication for the fear of future or of tomorrow.

Fear of Death and God's Gift of Life

The third fear to be analyzed from the biblical perspective is the *fear of death.* In the message of the New Testament we have the proclamation of Christ's victory over death. We are told that the profound identification of Christ with our humanity, through His death, destroyed "him who holds the power of death – that is the devil – and free those who all their lives were held in slavery by their fear of death" (Hebrews 2: 14-15).[12]

Moreover, Paul speaks about the promise of life that is in Christ Jesus (1 Timothy 1:1), in harmony with the Johannine affirmation about Christ that "in Him

9 Philip Hacking, *Discovering Isaiah* (Leicester: Crossway Books, 2001), 126.

10 Martin Luther, *Luther's Works* (St. Louis: Mo Concordia, 1957), 31: 57.

11 Miroslav Volf, *Captive to the Word of God: Engaging the Scriptures for Contemporary Theological Reflection* (Michigan: Grand Rapids, William B. Eerdmans Publishing Company, 2010), 141.

12 Raymond Brown, *The Message of Hebrew: Christ above All* (Leicester: Inter-Varsity Press, 1982), 66.

was life, and that life was the light of men (John 1: 4) as He came in order that we may have "life and have it to the full" (John 10: 10). In addition, Paul says that Christ is our life in Colossians 3: 3-4 when says that "When Christ, who is our life, appears, then we also will appear with him in glory." In the light of these truths the fear of death would be a denial of the life given by God, through Christ in the Spirit. Therefore, a profound understanding of God's gift of life in Christ through the Spirit of life, as expression of the fact that "death has been swallowed up in Christ's victory" (1 Corinthians 15: 54) is the spiritual medication for our fear of death.

The Cardinal Virtues of Faith, Hope and Love as Expression of the Fear of God

For the realities of God's Lordship, providential care and gift of life through Christ in the Spirit to replace the fear of people, fear of tomorrow and the fear of death, it is necessary for the faith that a believer confesses to become fear of God. That means to let the „Fear not!" that God proclaimed in His promises that are ‚Yes' in Christ" (2 Corinthians 1: 20), to be the reality of „meeting your fears with faith." [13]

> Faith is the gift of God's grace,[14] and has the role of strengthening the reason, considering the fact that the start of every sin is a departure of the reason from the truth. This is the reason why faith is to become a life style, being an intellectual-volitional synthesis, an act that is a solution to the other intellectual-volitional act that is the fall into sin.[15] Consequently, "faith becomes *fear of God,*[16] and Staniloae says that there are two types of the fear of God. The first one is the fear of the slaves, fear of His punishment, and the second one is the fear of love, the fear to be without His kindness. The fear of God thus explained is the opposite of the fear of the world." The virtue of the authentic fear of God, in accordance with the Heideggerian classification[17] as he distinguishes between the fear "of something from the world (*Furcht*) and the fear of the universal

13 H. Norman Wright, *Afraid No More: Gaining the Faith you need to Live Fully and Confidently* (Wheaton, Ilinois: Tyndale House Publishers, 1989), 161.

14 Ibid 96.

15 Ibid 97.

16 Ibid 100.

17 Ibid 101.

emptiness of the world (*Angst*), so the virtue of the authentic fear of God is the rediscovery of the primordial, spiritual fear that was in the beginning simultaneously fear of separation from God into an empty way of existence and "fear united with the trust in God."[18]Therefore the fear of God should be the fear to sin through union with the world,[19] a revelation of a higher authority than that of the world (the imminent danger), namely God,[20] and the consciousness of the future danger, that of an "eternal existence that is unauthentic and unfulfilled," as the result of the last just judgment of God.[21]

Thirdly, the fear of God leads to *the virtue of repentance* for the past sins and self control for the future sins.[22] This repentance should be a permanent repentance,[23] with a continuous confession of sins,[24]and the patient overcoming of present sorrows,[25] a repentance that is to be directed to our vices and sins as well as to "our virtues always unfulfilled."[26] Yet there is a danger to be avoided, that of confusing repentance with discouraging uncontentment that is full with doubt. Rather, repentance is an acknowledgment of the actual limits, not the declaration of the final limits. In fact, discouragement is the opposite of repentance, as repentance should be always superior to every moral achievement and as such "a hand of God' that raises us and keeps us in an authentic relation with Him."[27]

The final result is that our contemporary fears (of people, of tomorrow and of death), are transformed by the spirituality of an authentic fear of God. This fear of God is the fruit of faith transformed in trust. This trust in its turn is rooted in the profound conviction of God's loving authority, providential care and gift of life in Christ through the Spirit. And as such, spirituality is the proper medication on the coordinates of continuous repentance and perseverance in the meaningful communion with God the Father, Son and the Spirit. Or in the words of Christ:

18 Ibid 101-102.
19 Ibid 102.
20 Ibid 102-103.
21 Ibid 103.
22 Ibid 104.
23 Ibid 105.
24 Ibid 105-106.
25 Ibid 106.
26 Ibid 107.
27 Ibid 108.

"If anyone loves me, he will obey my teaching. My Father will love him, and we will come to him and make our home with him" (John 14: 23). We can see that faith in God is inseparable from love of God and hope in God.[28] This triad of the cardinal virtues for the Christian Spirituality is the result of the authentic fear of God, as faith becomes trusting love, love that roots hope. This is reflected in the connection that John sees between the absence of fear in the presence of love: "There is no fear in love. But perfect love drives out fear …" (1 John 4: 18). Here could be added also the saying of Paul: "And God has poured out his love into our hearts by the Holy Spirit, and this produces the hope that does not disappoint" (Romans 5: 5).

Conclusions

We argued in this paper that spirituality could be a proper medication for the fear of people, fear of tomorrow and fear of death. Spirituality, as defined by the expression fear of God, is rooted first in an authentic knowledge of God, in his sovereignty, providential care and life-giving grace. Secondly, spirituality as defined by the expression fear of God, is expressed in the cardinal virtues of faith, hope and love, and is maintained in the inseparable synthesis of them in the continuum of firm belief, obedient trust, and continuous repentance.

Bibliography

Brown, R. 1982. *The Message of Hebrew: Christ above All.* Leicester: Inter-Varsity Press.

Hacking, P. 2001. *Discovering Isaiah.* Leicester: Crossway Books.

Kent, C. 1993. *Tame you Fears & Transform them into Confidence & Action.* Colorado: NavPress Publishing Group.

Luther, M. 1957. *Luther's Works.* St. Louis: Mo Concordia.

Minirth, F. Meier, P. Hawkins D. 1989. *Worry-Free Living.* Nashville: Thomas Nelson Publishers.

28 Jurgen Moltmann, *Theology of Hope: On the Ground and the Implications of a Christian Eschatology* (London: SCM Press Ltd, 1967). He speaks of "believing hope," 19. Also, Moltmann, *The Church in the Power of the Spirit: A Contribution to Messianic Ecclesiology* (London: SCM Press Ltd, 1977). Here he speaks of "remembered hope," 246, and of "living hope," 278.

Moltmann, J. 1967. *Theology of Hope: On the Ground and the Implications of a Christian Eschatology*. London: SCM Press Ltd.

__________. 1977. T*he Church in the Power of the Spirit: A Contribution to Messianic Ecclesiology*. London: SCM Press Ltd.

Motyer, A. 1984. *The Message of Philippians: Christ Our Joy*. Leicester: Inter-Varsity Press.

Newbigin, L. 1982. *The Light Has Come: An Exposition of the Fourth Gospel.* Michigan: Grand Rapids, William B. Eerdmans Publishing Company.

Ogilvie, L. J. 1980. *The Bush is Still Burning: The Christ who Makes Things Happen in our Deepest Need.* Waco: Texas, Word Books Publishers.

Osborne, C. 1978. *Release from Fear and Anxiety*. Waco: Texas, Word Books Publishers.

Stott, J. R.W. 1978.*The Message of the Sermon on the Mount: Christian Counter-Culture*. Leicester: Inter-Varsity Press.

Tanner, I. J. 1973. *Loneliness: The Fear of Love*. New York: Harper & Row.

Volf, M. 2010. *Captive to the Word of God: Engaging the Scriptures for Contemporary Theological Reflection*. Michigan: Grand Rapids, William B. Eerdmans Publishing Company.

Wright, H. N. 1989. *Afraid No More: Gaining the Faith You Need to Live Fully and Confidently*. Wheaton, Ilinois: Tyndale House Publishers.

FAITH TRIUMPHS OVER FEAR

Jože Mari Osredkar, Ljubljana

Introduction

In this paper we will talk about the "culture of fear". Fear, "a feeling caused by the nearness or possibility of danger or evil" (Oxford A. L. Dictionary) as defined by the Oxford Dictionary of current English, has become a part of our everyday way of life, culture in the broad sense of the word. We fear the moral, economic or financial crisis… But even when there are not all these crises, we are full of fear too. Within man confronts fear of the future, fear of old age and ultimately death; he dreads what may lie beyond this life: is there an afterlife? Aware of the presence of evil, man is apprehensive of adversarial people who block his quest for what is good. Foes may put up insurmountable obstacles that void any attempt for his self-realization in God. Thus in many life-instances, we found ourselves riveted by various fears. But, it will be asserted and affirmed that faith arms a man to triumph over this fear. In this paper we will show, how faith in the Gospels leads man to be victorious over his fear; we will explain in detail what it exactly means to prevail over that fear. However, first of all, let us elaborate on the function of fear.

Fear is fundamental to humans

Even though fear can be most unpleasant, life without this physical, psychological, and spiritual dread would be impossible. In fact, fear within us helps to maintain life. Psychologists commonly share this same opinion; and we are in strong agreement with them. Fear is much like a sensor in our security system, which informs us that an uninvited guest has intruded into our house, our personal and private space. It brings our consciousness to a level that informs us that something is awry. When confronted with phenomena that could endanger our lives, albeit material or spiritual in nature, fear of this presence warns us that we are threatened; tells us to be cautions; sharpens our senses; and focuses our attention. Fear brings us into a state of tension and excitement, adrenalin rises in us, thus enabling us to make appropriate decisions: defend ourselves, take flight, albeit, engage in appropriate actions. In the broadest sense of the word, fear can be seen as a protective mechanism of our material and spiritual lives (Starčević Vukajlović 2012).

In the Bible, most often in the Old Testament, we discover multiple texts that speak about human fear. Especially, we read about the admonishment "to fear our God": we must be afraid of Him. Biblicist Marijan Peklaj wrote, based on "Psalm 34" in the "Book of Proverbs", that religious fear is "something good and necessary". In the Jewish prayer "Shema", the imperative "Love the Lord your God" (Dt 6,5) is replaced by "Be afraid of the Lord your God". Love becomes the synonym of fear; fear of God is then something positive (Peklaj 2012, 413-414). Fearing God or loving God is giving Him the honor due to Him.

Our point of departure here is the affirmation that fear is useful because of its function to maintain the life of human beings: it focuses our attention on what is dangerous for us and, concurrently, on the will of our God. Fear pushes us to react by defending ourselves, by opposing in some manner the intrusions into our lives. However, in most cases we are not able to defend ourselves or we do not know how to defend us. We often lack the most efficient means to thwart the invader or threat. In these cases, especially in cases of illness, suffering and death, man despairs.

Bodily and psychological sufferings are such opponents to our well-being. And all humans are afraid of suffering. What can we do to extricate ourselves from this disposition? Different religious doctrines afford us a variety of answers (Eliade 1996). This paper will focus on the solutions that Christianity offers us. While Christ doesn't speak systematically about fear in the New Testament scriptures, fear is prevalent in the Gospels, wher suffering is the central theme.

What does it mean to prevail over fear?

The overarching message of the Gospel writers is to have confidence in God, who triumphs over all fears (Peklaj 2012). But what does it mean "to triumph over fear"? At first glance, the Son of God removes fear, when Jesus assures His Followers: "Don't worry about your life" (Lk 12, 22)! and "While you are in the world, you will have to suffer. But cheer up! I have defeated the world" (Jn 16, 33)! But on the other hand, He does not remove fear. The disciples themselves had often been forewarned about the inevitability of fear. In fact, they often expressed their fears or demonstrated them in their actions as followers of their Jesus. And finally the prevalence of fear in the New Testament is again noted within Christ. The scriptures report that even Jesus Himself trembled in the face of suffering and death during his agony in the Garden and as he passed the last hours of His earthly life on the Cross.

In a special way, maybe the answer to the question of what it means to overcome fear can be found in the Gospels of John and Luke. At the Last Supper, Jesus said to the disciples: "I give you peace, the kind of peace that only I can give. It isn't like the peace that this world can give. So don't be worried or afraid" (Jn 14,27). Also Luke reports the words of Jesus: "Look at the crows! They don't plant or harvest and they don't have storehouses or barns. But God takes care of them. You are much more important than any birds" (Lc 12, 24). With such expressions like "Not to worry" and "Cheer up" certainly He does not eliminate the presence of fear or forbearance of pain and suffering. With the words "Not to worry", Christ wants to inspire faith and hope in his apostles, who are in a state of fear. Christ says that fear tracks down and preoccupies the Gentiles. Believers on the contrary are fully aware that the Heavenly Father knows what His people need and accommodates them, as He cares for the wild flowers (cf. Lc 12, 27). Keeping the words of Jesus close to their hearts, Christians are more prone to keep internal peace while in the state of fear. Christ therefore encourages the disciples not to be overexcited while engulfed in their ever pervasive fear. The claim of being in a state of fear is no cause for internal unrest, because of the fact of God's Incarnation He lives among His people and protects His creation. The real question becomes then: how a man keeps so much hope in a state of fear, that is, how he remains calm in the face of the multiple dangers that threaten intrusion into his being.

The Gospel instructions for developing trust

How do we stay calm when facing our fears? The Gospel's answer is simple: fearing suffering and death, a man can remain calm while he accepts suffering and death in faith that suffering and death are followed by eternal life.

In the Gospel of Matthew, Jesus says firmly, that being his disciple means to accept suffering that life brings to man: "And unless you are willing to take up your cross and come with me, you are not fit to be my disciples" (Mt 10, 38) and in continuation "If any of you want to be my followers, you must forget about yourself. You must take up your cross and follow me. If you want to save your life, you will destroy it. But if you give up your life for me, you will find it" (Mt 16, 24). The cross, symbol of Christ's confronting his fears, is the key to our own forbearance of the inevitabilyity of suffering.

Only in the context of suffering does it become clear what it means to "save or lose life" and "to find life"! By extension, in the case of "avoiding our suffering", superficially speaking, it means to save our life, but in reality it means "to lose our life"! Not to accept pain because of fear means the loss of life. Why would this be the case? For in the case when we do not accept pain, it still will be necessary to suffer. Here no internal calm resides. A believer deepens his trust (faith) in

God's Salvation by willingly accepting suffering and death, which, in essence, are inevitable. Christ tells his disciples to renounce their lives (to renounce the desire for avoiding suffering), and thereby accept the suffering that is their due. Thus did He, and set an example when He said "yes" to His torture and accepted death that would lie ahead (cf. Mt 26, 39-40).

Christ's instructions on how to react to the state of fear can be further substantiated with references from the Gospel of Matthew. Here Jesus speaks about violence: "You know that you have been taught, 'An eye for an eye and a tooth for a tooth'. But I tell you not to try to get even with a person who has done something to you. When someone slaps your right cheek, turn and let that person slap your other cheek. If someone sues you for your shirt, give up your coat as well" (Mt 5, 38). For many critics of Christian doctrine, however, Jesus' request for unconditional forgiveness leads to the position that Christianity in its design is doomed to collapse. The Gospel doctrine is developed here such that a believer who wants to be faithful to the instructions of his Master must accept the suffering. But here we do not speak about masochism. One can defend himself from the evil and malicious person who intrudes on his person and violates his space, if he is able do so. But in the case where he cannot defend himself from ensuing suffering and eventual death, Jesus says to accept our lot with profound trust in God's help. Furthermore, a Christian can stay calm even within his persona when he commits a sin, because Christ does not abandon him and will speak to the Father for him: "My children, I am writing this so that you won't sin. But if you do sin, Jesus Christ always does the right thing, and he will speak to the Father for us. Christ is the sacrifice that takes away our sins and the sins of all the world's people" (1 Jn 2,1-2). The Gospel victory over fear is thus based on trust in God, which is possible by the adoption of "God's will"! Herewith the ethical rule which allows for survival lies. In the context of this ethical rule must be understood Christ's instruction about "the adoption of the cross".

In faith there is no fear

We can find the ethics of internal peace in the works of St. Francis of Assisi, who calls it "a perfect joy". St. Francis tells how he came to the door of his monastery one cold winter night, but the doorman did not open the door for him. Unshaken, St. Francis is not upset; he maintains internal peace. From this narrative, he develops the doctrine that "perfect joy and perfect virtue and salvation are found there where a man remains patient and not troubled" ("Writings of Saint Francis and Saint Claire", p. 174). It is essential, therefore, that man knows how to accept also the inconveniences of God's will. However, God will assist us on our way; and everything will end well. Faith in God, who is "with us," helps humans to endure life while being engulfed in the state of fear. The Gospel teaches Christians that God watches over man and protects him. Therefore, the Christian can be happy and peaceful in his interior even while confronting his fear of suffering and troubles. For he knows well that "God is always at work for the good of everyone who loves him" (Rom 8, 28).

Ethics of internal peace we find also in our contemporaries like Blessed Pope John Paul II. On May 1st 2011, Pope Benedict XVI beatified the Servant of God John Paul II. On this occasion, the Holy Father in his homily made reference to the famous words of Pope John Paul II spoken during his first solemn Mass in St. Peter's Square: "Do not be afraid! Open, open wide the doors to Christ!" John Paul II had triumphed over Fear by his strong faith. For 26 years he ruled over a church that could have moved in several directions. He was not afraid of German liberals like Hans Küng or ultra conservative archbishops like the Frenchman Marcel Lefebvre who opposed any liberalizing changes issuing from the Vatican II Council and the opening up of the Holy Catholic Church espoused by Pope John XXIII. He saw no confrontation in treading where few had gone before. He demonstrated no dread in offering a welcoming hand to representatives of non-Christian religions. John Paul II believed in ecumenical and inter-religious dialog. He reached out to Jews, asking for forgiveness, to Orthodox Christians looking for unity, and to Muslims with the hand of peace, while refusing to compromise on what he and his Church believed. His impact on interfaith relations and international affairs was immense and may well be his lasting legacy.

Blessed John Paul II's achievements and travels can only be judged as remarkable. We revere him as a prophetic voice that challenged and stood firm against a tide of secularism that was threatening to forgo traditional ethics in the Western world and destine them to oblivion. In the time of his pontificate, the Catholic Church was losing millions of practicing Catholics in Western Europe, and the Christian Faith was and continues to be in retreat against the forces of postmodernism. But John Paul II stood firm, though he seemed not to have an answer that persuaded Europeans to return to the Church. He stood firmly against the world and the ravages of postmodernity and the hedonism of Western culture even while he was facing his own mortality, as his final physical suffering slowed down but did not prevail over his contact with people and travels to far reaches of the earth.

Herein lies the reason to focus in this paper on the complex nature of "fear" in light of the mantra of John-Paul II: "Do not be afraid!" We acknowledge and show examples of the all so present reality of fear that tracks us down attempting to dishearten us. We can say to everybody: "have faith and you will not be afraid," because we evoked the realities of the evasive fear lying within us at all times and the personal work and struggles we engage in to "not be afraid." Philosopher Janez Juhant supports this same reasoning for he points out that the believer overcomes fear by trusting in God (Juhant 2012). The greater the trust, the calmer the believer will be. We might also mention Martin Luther who shares this sentiment, maintaining that "faith is a firm trust in God" ("Protestant Catechism"). "The Catechism of the Catholic Church", referencing Timothy 1, 18-19, says that Faith must be imbued with hope ("Catechism of Catholic Church" 162). In this context, we can say that faith overcomes fear. Pope Benedict XVI talks about a man as being of hope. However, the former, human hope, to which he resorted in the past and with which he had subsequently been disappointed, pales before the godly kind. He then concludes that the "only real hope is God, which is the first source of hope in its ultimate goal" (Benedict XVI, 2008). Christ preaches the Good News, the Gospel, requiring a change of thinking and trust. The Gospel lesson does not only reside in theoretical thinking. Salvation is accessible by internal conversion that is based on trust in God. The goal of trust is fullness of life and heaven.

Conclusion

Thus we should feel comfortable in our discomfort knowing that "fear" is inevitable. Being fearful, being afraid, and being anxious are integral to our life of faith. The Old Testament emphasizes a need to fear The Almighty. We have fallen down, bearing the sins of our forefathers because of original sin. The Old Testament scripture talks of plagues, destruction, and waywardness of humankind. In spite of the state of damnation in the Old Testament, from which humankind attempted in vain to extricate itself, the prophets tell of restarting the better times once lost. We can be calm, because we have our guide in the person of Jesus Christ, the Savior leads us to a new Promise Land. Man sinned and our double, the God Man, will die for these sins. We with all sorts of faults must hope, believe, and have faith in the Redeemer, the Appointed One.

The belief in Redemption is a fundamental article of our faith, the central focus being that God came to us because of the Father's love and wish that we rejoin Him. Love in the New Testament replaces the fear of the Old. Yes, this is a meta-level or overarching belief that must supplant our very human feelings of isolation, depression, unhappiness, and loneliness. This is the essence of our belief, faith, trust, sense of triumph. The New Testament scriptures remind us of this divine wish to be reunited; we will share the divine joy by being one with God.

Persistent or unresolved fear is the pulling away from a firm belief in God's love and any hope for eternal unity. We must assure our neighbors and ourselves that doubt, fear, fogginess, and obscurity test our faith. Christ was tempted or tested on numerous occasions by Satan, the World, and his own humanity. He is heard asking, "why Me," but He gave into the inevitability of his destiny and thus fulfilled his mission for Himself and frees and supports us even to this day.

Through the Catechism, Liturgy of the Word, Encounters, and Writings, the Church today mounts efforts to rebroadcast the Promise of the Commitment that Faith well worked out, well developed, tried, tested, and reinforced will restore us as true Children of God. Too often the World distracts us, our sentient being betrays us, and our knowledge of the options available for achieving this triumph fail us.

In this paper it has been shown that our inevitable fear succumbs to well-tempered faith. Hope and promise of a new life, albeit, eternal life, will be ours only if we live the Gospel now, if we succeed in supporting others to recognize that we all live or have lived a life of fear at many levels of our complex being. An affirming belief in God, seconded by the words of scripture, will activate our faith. Our final reward for a full life well lived, well focused, will be a triumph over fear.

References

Benedikt XVI. 2008. *Rešeni v upanju*. Cerkveni dokument 118. Ljubljana: Družina.

Eliade, Mircea. 1996. *Zgodovina religioznih verovanj*. Vol. 2, *Od Gotame Buddhe do zmagoslavja krščanstva*. Ljubljana: DZS.

Juhant, Janez. 2012. Klerik med strahovi časa in vero, ki osvobaja. *Bogoslovni vestnik* 2012/3: 383-395.

Katekizem katoliške Cerkve. 1993. Ljubljana: Slovenska škofovska konferenca.

Oxford Advanced Learner's Dictionary of Current English. 1974. Oxford: Oxford University Press.

Peklaj, Marijan. 2012. Ljubezen premaga strah. *Bogoslovni vestnik* 2012/3: 411-417.

Protestantski katekizem. 1995. Ljubljana.

Starčević Vukajlović, Marijana. 2012. Strah. //http://www.akropola.org/clanki/clanek.aspx?lit=130 (accessed October 29th 2012).

Sveto pismo Stare in Nove zaveze. Slovenski standardni prevod. 1997. Ljubljana: Svetopisemska družba Slovenije.

Spisi sv.Frančiška Asiškega in sv. Klare (Writings of Saint Francis and Saint Claire). 1982. Celje: Mohorjeva družba.

THE ALTERNATIVE OFFER OF RELIGIONS TO THE PRESENT LOGIC OF GLOBALIZATION AND FEAR OF THE FUTURE

Erika Prijatelj, Ljubljana

Introduction

In spite of self-confident predictions of social sciences at the end of the 19th and the beginning of the 20th century that religions would decline and that secularization of the world was inevitable, the consideration of globalization and the understanding of the present situation are closely connected to the appearance of religion.[1] In the beginning of the so-called "century of climate", the "age of fear and horror" (Smith 2008, 3), the relationship between globalization and religion and the tension between them recaptured the attention of many journalists and scientists after 11 September, 2001. Many started researching the connections between religion and violence, especially the role of Islamic extremists and fundamentalism as manifestations of globalized power, acting under the flag of antiglobalization. However, reflection on globalization and religion is by no means limited to certain forms of Islamic extremism; Christianity has also become globalized in a new way. It is not a "Western" religion any longer. The gravitational centre of global Christianity has started shifting towards the Southern hemisphere.

1. Interreligious and ecumenical dialogue

1.1 Religious diversity and interreligious conflict

Religious diversity has been present throughout history. Today, however, we are aware of the need for discussion and search for solutions to the interreligious

1 Occasionally we encounter the expression *return of religion*. It has to be pointed out, however, that this is a misleading expression that is mostly used in secular academic circles. In fact, religion has never departed. More about the pattern of the model of return can be found in Derrida 1998.

conflict. The global impact of local and regional disputes – if not caused by different religious beliefs, then at least justified and supported by religious values – has more than ever given rise to the issue of identity and effect of religions and their ability to represent either war or peace, separation or alliance. "On the one hand, globalization has brought us closer to each other than ever, it has intertwined our lives on national and international levels in a complex and complicated way. On the other hand, the new tribalism – regression towards old ways and towards rebellious loyalty – has separated us even further. In one way or another, religion is part of such processes. It can lead us to peace, and it can just as vigorously lead us to war. Politicians have power, but religions have something even more powerful – they have influence. Politicians move chess pieces, but religion changes lives. Peace may be concluded at the conference table, but unless it develops in everyday feeling and thinking, it does not last – perhaps it never even begins" (Sacks 2002, 7).

The challenge that Christianity is facing is its participation in the confrontation with the new tribalism. Its response will be subject to its understanding of faith, hope and love, as well as with the incorporation of these religious values into either a benevolent or an aggressive response to those outside the Christian community. Moreover, the main values of the Christian faith and the influence of Churches in conflict situations will be expressed in line with the attitude that Christianity will take towards other religions by accepting other religious truths outside the Church. All world religions share the experience of the transcendent and the experience of the Spirit that reveals the Truth. The acknowledgement of the universal experience of grace is the starting point for acceptance of the revelation of religious truth also in other religions, which is not an easy challenge. Today, theologies of religions have to be promoted which will support interreligious dialogue and understanding.

1.2 Necessity of interreligious dialogue

Religion and interreligious dialogue are extremely important for today's globalized world. They are based on trust, which is crucial for the future in the increasingly complex, anxious and intertwined society. A. Gittens (Gittens 2002, 152) emphasizes that we have to see the relationship between complexity and risk, as well as the need to trust people and structures, and to engage accordingly in the process of reflection and reconsideration of such structures and social practices in order to handle the risk correctly. When facing unfair economic systems, weakened family life, corrupt politics, pessimism, doubts about the future, the trust in God acquires a different and new power, while religions and believers get an indispensable place in the society. Genuine faith transforms, motivates and contributes radically to health, human development and prosperity of the society. It is of crucial importance that believers form their identity inwards, and at the same time open outwards for dialogue, where on the level of values, their first discussion partners can be believers belonging to other religious communities.

1.3 Christian efforts for peace, ecumenism

In the recent period, Christianity has intensified its efforts against war as well as efforts for peace. In this connection, it has reconsidered the term "just war" and strengthened non-violence as an ethical response to war. The efforts for justice and peace are adopted by Christianity as the standard and supplementary paradigm. (Thompson 2010, 133). Ecumenical efforts have become very meaningful in the last decades. Amidst accelerated development of globalization and secularisation, modern theology has become plural, confessional and ecumenical at the same time. Ecumenism is increasingly becoming the theology of 21st century and the key to the renovation of the Church, where Christians form their jointly – and not competitively – defined answers that will benefit modern man. This does not mean that theology is fading into abstract and non-confessional neutrality, but it means first the immersion into concrete tradition of the Church, so that theology remains genuinely confessional and at the same time open to dialogue with others.

Among the burning issues that Christian Churches are facing today are bioethical issues calling for respect and protection of human life, European merging processes that require that Churches discover and develop new forms of solidarity and understanding of religiosity as an important social factor in which Christianity should find its proper place. The NELCEE[2] association, acting in the framework of the World Council of Churches, has for the last few years been promoting the development of an ecumenical approach in upbringing and education in the territory of Eastern and Central Europe.

2 Network for Ecumenical Learning in Central and Eastern Europe.

2. Social teaching of the Catholic Church in a globalized world

2.1 Human dignity – the basis of the social teaching of the Catholic Church

When confronted with the culture of death, Pope John Paul II, in his circular *Evangelium vitae* (Janez Pavel II 1995), encouraged people to form a culture of life, and consequently to respect the sacredness of each and every human life, clearly rejecting abortion, euthanasia and death penalty. Pope Benedict XVI's circular *Caritas in veritate* (Benedict XVI 2009) emphasizes again that human life is sacred at each stage and in each situation. The respect for life is linked to integral development (§28), while respect for life and human dignity, that is human ecology, is linked to respect for the Earth, that is to say to environmental ecology (§51).

Although neither the social teaching of the Catholic Church nor Church itself is perfect, the Church with its considerations and endeavours for justice and peace has an important role in the modern globalized world. It primarily encourages the formation of a community or congregation, and provides an alternative to individualism and self-centeredness, which are so typical of modern man. In the eyes of the Church, the sacredness of life expresses itself in various forms of solidarity, support of human rights, fight for the poor, the exploited and the marginal, openness towards immigrants, striving for the right to work, protection of the creation, integral education etc. The Catholic social teaching sees the dignity of an individual as well as the needs of the society, thus avoiding individualism as well as collectivism, and is consequently critical towards capitalism as well as towards socialism. This equilibrium gives the Catholic teaching of the Church "realism and pragmatism, which is why the broader society accepts it and contributes to its efficiency" (Gaillardetz 2005, 90).

The social teaching of the Church is based on a natural law, which permits it to address all the people of good will. It is also based on the Bible, which facilitates ecumenical dialogue among Christian Churches. Representatives of various Christian Churches jointly research biblical foundations to teach peace and justice and form their arguments based on reason. In connection with other Christian Churches, the Catholic Church enters into a dialogue with the whole world society in a special way (Thompson 2010, 168).

2.2 Contribution of Catholic movements to the image of the world

Various Catholic movements do their best to change the image of individual continents and of the world. The motives for such engagement are not economic or technical; the motive is the recognition of the need for "the soul of existence" and the awareness of present and future responsibility for humanity. Until recently, the West has lived well, very well even, but primarily on account of those whose life was poorer. The suffering Christ inspires his disciples not to look at the world through the eyes of the market and of political power, but from the viewpoint of the victims of history. The Western society of today has the face of its victims, and that face is real. Pope John Paul II emphasized that the social teaching of the Church will gain credibility faster through witnesses of faith than through its inner logic and consistency. That is exactly what stimulates the Church to prioritize the poor (Janez Pavel II 1999, 57).

2.3 Catholic movements in various parts of the world

Looking at various Catholic movements, charity organizations, efforts for increased justice and solidarity, we are surprised and encouraged by their variety. It is not possible to introduce all of them here, but some are worth mentioning. In North America, where consumerism and individualism prevail, the Catholic social teaching first addressed immigrants from less individualist environments, who have a stronger community ethos. The so-called peace movements play an important part (e.g. Catholic Worker Movement, Pax Christi U.S.A.), in various Human Development campaigns financed by the national episcopal conference, and in various groups organized in order to build the society (Wood 2002, 14). Canadian bishops went even further than the bishops in the USA. They called the economic changes social evil and demanded radical social changes (Coleman 2010, 211).

In Asia, Christianity was considered a foreign religion, or the colonizers' religion, for a long time. As Christians are a minority in Asia, they are aware how important it is that the social teaching of the Catholic Church echoes in other religious and cultural societies. The key element of understanding of the Asian perspective is *harmony*, which in a special way constitutes the intellectual, affective, religious, artistic soul of the people and institutions, as pointed out by bishops already in 1984 in the framework of the Bishop's Institute for Interreligious Affairs on the

Theology of Dialogue BIRA[3]. The search for harmony connects Catholics, other Christians and followers of various religions in pastoral and social efforts. In a reciprocal relationship with other believers, Asian Catholics understand harmony as equilibrium, benevolence, wisdom, compassion, respect for dharma[4], plurality, reciprocity and each other's space. The general stance in Asia is: Wait and see. Bishops encourage activity and their message is that in order to achieve a true dialogue with the people and the authority, the conflict is frequently unavoidable (Brazal 2010).

In the field of the Catholic social teaching, *Australia* is known in practice by the *Australian Catholic Social Justice Council, The Catholic Commission for Justice and Peace, Caritas Australia, Commissions for Australian Catholic Women,* the research and projects related to the Catholics' care for the Planet Earth, etc. Activities are organized on a parish, diocesan, national, and more and more frequently on an international level. Catholic universities and theological institutes are very helpful, as are the efforts of various monastic communities, orders, the Jesuits in particular (e.g. the website Faith Doing Justice, the magazines Eureka Street, Australian Catholics), of Christian Brethren (e.g. Edmund Rice International for Social Justice, ERISJ) and Sisters of Mercy (e.g. Mercy Commitment). Catholics actively participate in various movements, e.g. Young Christian Workers, Australian Catholic Movement for Intellectual and Cultural Affairs, etc.

During a special assembly in 1996, African bishops made the commitment that the Catholic Church would establish a better dialogue on the continent and fight even more resolutely against social, cultural and economic uncertainty (Shorter 1996, 11). There were demands for personal transformation, for transformation of the Church, as well as for interpersonal and institutional solidarity. This is one of the main goals of AFCAST[5], which under the leadership of Jesuits is working towards educating good citizens by means of workshops, seminars and publications. In Africa, catholic social teaching focuses on the idea that we all belong

3 Bishop's Institute for Interreligious Affairs on the Theology of Dialogue.

4 The word dharma is a polymorphic and important term in Indian religions and philosophies. It can mean: natural or legal law, custom, duty, law, justice; substance, essence, feature, truth, reality; virtue, religion, education, doctrine; phenomenon, fact of consciousness, and even atom.

5 African Social Teaching. Regional Forum for East and South Africa.

to one family, as we are all created in God's image. Solidarity is understood as a moral virtue and a moral duty.

In Europe, Catholics participate in at least five different forms of movements. These are: classical international Catholic movements (Christian Workers' Movement, Catholic Farmers' Leagues, Caritas International, Justice and Peace Commissions, Catholic Organizations of Employers, etc.), movements in orders (Jesuit Refugee Service, Dominican Volunteers, Vincentian Family, etc.), spiritual movements (Economy of Communication, Movimento Populare in Comunione et Liberazione, several social initiatives of the Sant'Egidio community, etc.), radical Christian movements (Christians for Socialism, ATD Quart Monde[6], Movement of Missionary Commitment in Flanders, etc.), secular social movements (Doctors Without Borders, Greenpeace, Amnesty International, etc.). All these movements play an important role in the broader society, especially in relation to the poor. They also prove that to be Christian does not only mean a certain way of thinking and believing, but that that it also implies transformative presence inspired by the word of God, it means to be open for the signs of time, including acceptance of the fact that Europe is no longer the centre of the world.

All the above represents how the Church serves the world today, and proves that even today man is indeed the path of the Church. It is interesting how in the process of globalisation the focus of the teaching of the Catholic Church has shifted from the universal to the local, from principles to implementation, and from documents to people (Massaro 2008, 175).

Conclusion

We are approaching a time that will mark and define the history of future centuries. Although each historic period is unique in its own way, the present is a specific combination of huge changes in religion and among religions, as well as in science, technology, industry, free market and elsewhere. It is the simultaneousness and globalism of all these developments that distinguish the present situation from all other periods of history.

6 Although the initiator of the movement was the Catholic priest Joseph Wresinski, this is not a Catholic movement in itself.

The secularism of the modern civilization cannot provide an answer to the basic challenges of the modern world, characterized by general misery, increasing uncertainty and fear of the future. On the contrary, with its motto "take care of yourself", the world of today legalizes greed more than ever, which has a devastating effect on interpersonal relations and on the environment. Cultural imagination is slipping through the fingers of modernism (Falk 2001, 43-59). 840 million people – equalling the total population of Europe, USA, Canada and Japan – go to bed hungry every night. Social inequality and disproportion, which is not only a global phenomenon, but is also reflected on interpersonal, local, regional and national levels, has gradually dissolved the ancient values, such as taking care of one's fellow people, helping people in need, which used to be practised by all religions.

What can religion offer as an alternative to the present logic of globalization in the culture of fear? The answer is: values and virtues that give life a meaning, principles and ideals, personal and mutual responsibility. In opposition to the competitive and – sooner or later – hopeless struggle for success and wealth, which has captured individuals and corporations, religion brings hope and the "vision of life" (Henning 2009, 193) based on a different order and values. By its respect for the sacredness of life, religion creates the foundation of a significantly more compassionate, fair and emphatic approach to man, and consequently paves the path to dialogue, forgiveness, reconciliation, long-term relationship building, life in a community. Today, religions are becoming increasingly aware of the fact that it is not enough to be tolerant. Tolerance may cause indifference; therefore religions encourage us to be open for others and to express mutual support and solidarity.

Religious and interreligious activities may encourage and strengthen various social forces to join in their efforts to establish an ethical, peaceful and spiritually sensitive global society.[7] It seems that globalization of tomorrow is very uncertain and will not be achieved at the same pace in various parts of the world. In the future, therefore, religion with its manner of facing globalization and humanization

7 At the International Meeting for Peace and the 10th anniversary of the terrorist attack of USA (11 Sept. 2011), approximately 300 religious leaders gathered in Munich, together with several high ranking politicians. The meeting, 25th in a row, was first organized in 1986 in Assisi, on the initiative of the then Pope John Paul II. Since that time, it has been organized at a different place every year.

of globalization will play an important, probably even crucial, role in the survival of humanity and in the development of quality personal and social life of us all.

References

Benedict XVI. 2009. *Ljubezen v resnici.* Ljubljana: Družina.

Brazal, A. M. 2010. A Mediation for Catholic Social Teaching (East Asian Discourses on Harmony).In: D. McDonald (ed.), *Catholic Global Teaching in Global Perspective,* p. 118-146. New York: Orbis Books.

Coleman, John A. and William F. Ryan (eds.). 1999. *Globalization and Catholic Social Thought.* New York: Orbis Books.

Derrida, Jacques. 1998. Faith and Knowledge: The Two Sources of Religion at the Limits of Reason Alone. In: Jacques Derrida and Gianni Vattimo(eds.). *Religion*, 1-77. Paolo Alto: Stanford University Press.

Falk, Richard. 2001. The Religious Foundations of Humane Governance. In: Patricia M. Mische and Melissa Merkling (eds.). *Toward a Global Civilization? The Contribution of Religions,* 43-59. New York: Peter Lang.

Gaillardetz, Richard R. 2005. The Ecclesiological Foundations of Modern Catholic Social Teaching. In: Himes, Kenneth R. et al. (eds.). *Modern Catholic Social Teaching: Commentaries and Interpretation*, 110-134. Washington: Georgetown University Press.

Gittens, Anthony. 2002. *A Presence that Disturb.* Chicago: Liguori Publications.

Henning, Brian. 2009. From Despot to Steward – The Greening of Catholic Social Teaching. In: David Matzko McCarthy, ed. *The Heart of Catholic Social Teaching – Its Origins and Contemporary Significance.* 193-218. Dayton: Brazos Press.

Janez Pavel II. 1995. *Evangelij življenja.* Ljubljana: Družina.

Janez Pavel II. 1999. Centesimus annus. Ljubljana: Družina.

Massaro, Thomas. 2008. *Living Justice – Catholic Social Teaching in Action.* Lanham: The Classroom Edition.

Sacks, Jonathan. 2002. *The Dignity of Difference: How to Avoid the Clash of Civilizations*, London: Continuum.

Shorter, Alyvard. 1996. *Christianity and the African Imagination: After the African Syno: Resources for Inculturation.* Nairobi: Paulines Publications Africa.

Smith, James K. 2008. *After Modernity? Secularity, Globalization, and the Reenchantment of the World.* Waco: Baylor University Press.

Thompson, J. Milburn. 2010. *Catholic Social Thought.* New York: Orbis Books.

Wood, Richard. 2002. *Faith in Action.* Chicago: Chicago University Press.

ABSTRACTS

Tomáš Halík
Fear and Faith

It is necessary to distinguish three phenomena clearly: fear, anxiety and awe ("Timor Domini"). The concept of awe is a religious phenomenon – to feel dizzy in front of a great and encompassing being, the Sacred. Since the beginning of the Enlightenment and through the process of secularization, this awe has been disappearing from our culture together with the emphasis on the individual's sovereignty (and emancipation from religion). This disappearing, however, opens space for fear and anxiety. The biblical image of God has been increasingly replaced by "trivial god," a machine to satisfy human needs. This trivial goodnature and easy going god was often complemented with fear of hell in the popular religious culture. The tragedies of 20th century, nevertheless, challenged both – the goodness of this trivial god and the fear of hell. Today, the radical evil is present in horrors of political conflicts; fear has become part of virtual reality in media. Christianity knows only one therapy – perfect love that overcomes fear.

Key words: *fear, anxiety, awe of God, faith, love.*

Jože Trontelj
Fear as a Human Companion Throuhg the Ages

Today we can only guess how the life of our ancestors several tens of thousands of years ago looked. It seems likely that they suffered from copious justified as well as baseless fears and anxiety. Their life was presumably full of stress and serious dangers, and survival, even to the next day, was uncertain.

Today, many millennia later, survival of the human race seems guaranteed, at least in the short term, and many threats have completely disappeared. Fear and anxiety have increasingly become a subjective, private experience. Parents are concerned for the well-being and future of their children. Many of us are concerned about our health or threats to our welfare.

Yet another kind of fear is produced by the misuse of political, economic, social and even emotional power. This has been an instrument of control over weaker human beings since time immemorial, and continues to be so. It permeates all

levels of human relations, ranging from that between two closely-knit people to nations and even the global society. One can only guess how widespread it is, for example, behind the walls of family homes.
When, at the time of terminal illness, we approach the end of our life, we experience a new kind of fear and anxiety. It appears new because our prevailing western culture has not taught us how to face imminent death and how to accept our final farewell and departure. Modern men and women are used to feeling fearful and anxious, but they avoid thoughts about death and postpone preparations for their own end. A possible, but inappropriate, response to anticipated suffering during a terminal illness is resorting to euthanasia and physician-assisted suicide. In fact, suffering can be adequately relieved by palliative medicine. The important personal and societal role of dying can be restored by respectful and sensitive responses to the real needs of the patient and his family. Modern medical knowledge can and should be used to a much greater extent than it is at present.
The society we wish to build for a better future should be free of unnecessary fears, both those caused by foreseeable natural events, where risks are manageable, and those caused by our fellow human beings wilfully misusing their influence and power. It is not clear how successful we will be in such endeavours. However, any step in this direction will be valuable, since it can relieve some of our significant human suffering.

Key words: *fear, anxiety, human suffering, misuse of power, control of weaker human beings.*

Janez Juhant
The Post Totalitarian Fear

A highly characteristic sign of maintaining (sustaining) totalitarian regimes is fear. This is very much related to the mechanisms of obedience and to a specific view of man. Throughout their history, Slovenes were trained in obedience by the Church and by the authoritative Austro-Hungarian state, and the communists made use of these mechanisms and deepened the dependence of Slovenes on them. Is there a connection between the fear of God and the fear of worldly authorities, in particular fear in totalitarian regimes? Fear has an existential dimension, while it saves the life of man it has to be regulated by establishing healthy interpersonal relations. The authoritative and especially totalitarian regimes did not stimulate these healthy personal relations, but they reinforced dependence and fear as a mechanism to enslave their citizens. The consequences still persist in the post-communist era. Measures of education and of political decision towards democratic civil solidarity should be implemented.

Key words: *fear, person, Slovenes, interpersonal relations, authoritarianism, totalitarianism, communism.*

Stanko Gerjolj
Fear and Education in Ideological Post Totalitarian Society

Educational work after the fall of ideological totalitarianism is a complex and dramatic process as it relates to the processing of multigenerational history and also lasts for generations. One typical characteristic of ideological totalitarianism is that it creates an environment that prevents direct communication. The ideological totalitarian society is full of taboos and unwritten "rules" that cannot be interpreted, and the whole system deliberately encourages fear both from free and independent thinking and even more from expressing own thoughts. Idols become some kind of a "golden calf" which is fanatically worshiped like gods, even though many people know that we are misguided in the way. Two-pronged strategy of education, which was formed under communism so strongly that it became the habit and turned into something "normal", even after the fall of totalitarianism creates problems, because it created in communication "a vacuum" between people, which is difficult to fill with the naturalness and spontaneity and with confidence and sincerity. In this context, the younger generations are invited to sensible understanding and to strengthening the ability to forgiveness, which will encourage the elderly to opening and discovering of honest communication.

Key words: *education, totalitarianism, fear, communicational vacuum, honesty.*

Bojan Žalec
Fear and Love as a Basis of Ethical Life: From St. Thomas Aquinas to Albert Schweitzer

The author argues for the thesis that the basis of ethical life is not only love, but also fear, because love is impossible without fear. Love is a necessary condition of ethical life because love is necessary for overcoming of fear. Such overcoming is needed for our being able of sacrifice of ourselves which is in turn necessary for real ethical life. Yet not any kind of love and any kind of fear provides such a basis, only special kinds of them. For this reason the paper presents various kinds of fear and explains the important distinctions and relations between them. It deals also with a (comparative) analysis of some other relevant concepts as anxiety, love, respect and reverence for life. It interprets some important principles and commands (biblical command "Honor everyone!"). The most important constituents of the frame of the reference of discussion are the Bible and the work of St. Thomas Aquinas and Albert Schweitzer.

Key words: *fear, respect, reverence for life, love, fear of God, filial fear, fear of suffering, sacrifice, ethical life.*

Anton Jamnik
Do not be Afraid: Community as the Power to Accept Fragility and Mortality in Seeking the Courage of Being

Man has been created to form relationships, and not to lead a lonely and selfish existence, the morality of which is in submitting to universal laws and rules of the herd. Love and care of the Other overcome the distance which originates in monadological individualism, pragmatism and self-interest. The distance is replaced by closeness, personal relations and decentralism of the subject, born out of the subject's free decision to exist for others which leads to new joys of existence.
Hope impels us to what is beyond our sight. It is in a sense blind, our reaching out for more than we can imagine. Courage is clear-sighted. We bravely dare to open our eyes and see how vulnerable we are and how much we are likely to get hurt on our way to happiness. Unless one dares to face one's fragility and mortality, then one will never be brave.

Key words: *hope, mortality, courage, fear, freedom, community, individualism, responsibility, postmodernism.*

Robert Petkovšek

Fear and Courage in Existental Analytic and in Radical Phenomenology

Questions of fear, anxiety and courage are in the foreground of existential analitic. They are analyzed in the context of the possibility of non-being, which appears at the core of the existence. Heidegger shows that existence is a drama played between being and non-being. In his answer, he insists that being can be properly understood only if considered as positivity, which doesn't need any reason to be. Being is "to be" in itself. Radical phenomenology as developed by Michel Henry makes a step forward by pointing out that being is not able to prevail over non-being by itself, but in as much as it is given sense by the newborn life. Life, which is an absolute auto-affirmation, gives sense to the future and new being.

Key words: *positivity of being, life, fear, courage, existential analytic, radical phenomenology.*

Branko Klun

The Age of Technology and the Question of Fear

The modern age has been characterised by overwhelming progress in technology, which is not only an instrument at our disposal, but a way in which humans relate to the world. Since man is not only externally surrounded by technology, but also internally determined by the way of thinking that it creates, the fear of technology does not primarily refer to the external threats of the technological progress (Jonas), but rather to the challenge that it represents for understanding ourselves and our humanity (Heidegger).

Key words: *technology, fear, Jonas, Heidegger, responsibility.*

Vojko Strahovnik
Beyond the Culture of Fear: Fear and Responsibility

A culture of fear can be defined as a state of society in which it appears that fear pervades and encompasses all aspects of our lives and where the "fear perspective" is the dominant perspective through which we perceive the world around us. Proper understanding of the concept and/or the phenomenon of the "culture of fear" is thus the starting point of investigations in the paper as well as the question what is the nature of fear that we are talking about in this regard. In the second part the paper discusses the diminished responsibility as one of the most widespread external manifestations or symptoms of such a culture of fear. In the concluding part the discussion centres on causes for such a culture of fear and suggests a possible way out of it towards a culture of trust and hope.

Key words: *culture of fear, risk, responsibility, trust, hope.*

Zvezdan Pirtošek
The Enemy Within: Brain Circuits of Fear

"The enemy is fear. We think it is hate; but, it is fear." (Gandhi)
Fear is a full-body experience. While the brain initiates, controls and coordinates the process, the entire body gets activated to create the fear response. In the brain, all stimuli enter the central brain sensory structure, the thalamus, which cannot categorize a stimulus as dangerous or not dangerous and will therefore activate two circuits for further stimulus processing: (1) a short lower 'quick and dirty' circuit to the 'fear centre' amygdale, taking no chance and initiating the fear response 'just in case'; and (2) a long higher circuit to sensory cortices, slower but more precise and cautious in interpretation of events. Both circuits eventually reach the hypothalamus, the ancient survival centre which triggers the fight-orflight response. Circuitries of fear in the brain are established by two mechanisms: one is innate, created by evolution, the other by conditioning. With the emergence of the prefrontal lobe, the modern man tends constantly to anticipate disasters that are never – or unlikely - going to happen, or events that will or may happen in a distant future. Such anxieties shape our culture and our everyday life, with some ancient fears being reshaped (e.g. the fear of death) and new ones being born (e.g. fears of losing one's uniquely human essence).

Key words: *brain, fear, anxiety, amygdale, prefrontal lobe.*

Veronika Szánto

Precaution and Fear-Mongering in Bioethics

Modern bioethics is critical reflection on the technological developments achieved in the life sciences and applied in a range of fields from medicine through cybernetics to food industry. Modern bioethics as a discipline has been called to existence by fears induced by biotechnology. In this paper I investigate how bioethics deals with this fear and how it should deal with it. I distinguish between alleviation, acknowledgement and utilization of fear. I argue that whilst reasonable precaution is pre-requisite for sound bioethical discussion and practice, fear itself cannot be an argument against biotechnological procedures even if influential bioethical thinkers have been argued for the wisdom of repugnance and horror.

Key words: *bioethics, cloning, genetics, Leon Kass, precaution.*

Tadej Strehovec

Bioethics: Neutralizing the Power of Fear

Man in the postmodern society is often the victim of various forms of fear, which are related to terrorism, atomic energy, cloning, euthanasia, genetically modified organisms, climate change, epidemics, etc. One of the main goals of bioethics is to establish cross-disciplinary dialogue, which anticipates different kinds of ethical dilemmas and related fears and offers a methodology how different kinds of ideologies and ethical theories confront themselves. The media and politics are the most important place where bioethics neutralizes the power of fear through the interdisciplinary dialogue.

Key words: *bioethics, Christian ethics, ethics of fear, media, dialogue.*

Krešimir Šimić

Fear in 16th Century Croatian Religious Literature

The Russian literary theoretician Mikhail Bakhtin thinks that a carnivalisation of literary culture took place in the Renaissance. Moreover, Bakhtin thinks that the carnival element swept away many obstacles and adopted a particular world view. However, he notes, carnival laughter is deeply ambivalent. Generically, it is linked to the oldest forms of ritual laughter, but all forms of ritual laughter are linked to death and rebirth. Using the methodological principles of New Historicism compiled in the journal *Annales d'historie économique et sociale,* Jean Delumeau has established that it was precisely during the Renaissance, usually characterised by freedom of conscience, that the emotions of fear and guilt were dominant. In his work *La Peur en Occident (XIV–XVIII siècles)*, a reconstruction of emotional life in the West between the 14th and 18th centuries, Delumeau established that, at a particular moment in history, a pessisimistic view of the world, the outbreak of the plague, the Turkish incursions, religious schism and the Hundred Years War collided, leading to new, exacerbated fears regarding the end of the world, the coming of the Antichrist, and the activities of witches, wizards and heretics. He analyses figures of fear, mostly eschatological, in 16th century Croatian religious poetry. However, other reasons for the significant appearance of eschatological figures of fear, along with those identified by Delumeau, may be attributed to theology, particularly the theology of fear of Thomas Aquinas (*Summa theologica* I-II, 41-45).

Key words: *Renaissance, Croatian religious poetry, images of fear, Mihail Bakhtin, theology of fear.*

Béla Mester

Fear and Pride as Fundamental Elements of the Anthropology of Early Modern Political Philosophy

The motto of *Leviathan* on its frontispiece describes Hobbes's metaphor of earthly power with a Scriptural quotation: "Non est *potestas* Super Terram quae comparetur ei". Regarding the whole text of Job 41: 33–34; we should realise that the power of *Leviathan* is based on its *fearlessness*, and on the *pridefulness* of all the other beings, as the cause of their *fearfulness*. "Non est *potestas* super terram, quae comparetur ei, qui factus est ut *nullum timeret*. Omne sublime videt: ipse est *rex super universos filios superbiae*." (KJB: "Upon earth there is not his like, who is made *without fear*. He beholdeth all high things; he is *a king over all the children of pride*".) In my lecture I will analyse some features of theological background of early modern opinions, especially Hobbes's ones, about the *fearfulness* and *pridefulness* of *human nature*, and their consequences to our faculties for making *political communities*.

Key words: *Calvin, fear, Hobbes, human nature, pride.*

Gábor Kovacs

Fear, Politics, Power – Civilization as the Education of Power

The role of fear has traditionally been a classical subject of political thought. It was Saint Augustine who put forward this problem in his political theology. At the rise of modernity it was Thomas Hobbes who based his political theory on the notion of fear. Fear, in his theory, instigates human beings to conclude a social contract to put to end the fearsome situation of bellum omnium contra omnes. Existentialism, in the 20th century, described the fear of death as the main characteristic of human personality. Guglielmo Ferrero, the Italian philosopher, and István Bibó (1911–1979), the Hungarian political thinker, who was his disciple, described fear as the main motive of human beings in their conduct of life. Political institutions, in their views, are channels canalizing and humanizing fear. My paper intends to give an analysis concentrating upon the relation of fear, politics and civilization.

Key words: *fear, courage, power, politics civilization.*

Paul Chan, Ian Fitzgerald, Rafal Smoczyinski
Anti Polish Migrant Moral Panics and Trade Unions in the UK

With the 2004 enlargement of the EU the United Kingdom witnessed an unprecedented inflow of economic migrants from Poland. Because of the growing number of migrants, in some parts of indigenous British society there has also developed a complex set of anxious societal reactions triggered by this challenge and some public institutions involved with housing, labour policy and social cohesion have experienced significant pressure. On the other hand, for a large number of Polish workers the early migration meant suffering quite horrendous conditions both in the workplace and in the community. This included unpaid wages, poor working conditions, poor housing and indeed destitution, as well as reported slave and forced labour. The following article will conceptualize anti-migrant societal reactions as moral panics. Further, it will explore the crucial role of British trade unions which campaigned on behalf of migrants and were committed to give them a voice.

Key words: *Polish migrants, United Kingdom, societal reactions, trade unions, moral panic.*

Mateja Pevec Rozman
Culture of Fear and the Meaning of Authority; What are We Afraid of?

Contemporary times are sown with the seed of fear on different fields of human life. We are facing with the fear of survival because of the economic crisis, political and social instability, environmental pollution etc. Fear permeates on all spheres of human being and paralyzes our ability for leaving flourishing life. On the other hand fear is emotion that plays an important and also positive role at the question of human survival.

Fear of want of knowledge, fear of nonsuccess, fear of being un-beloved, fear of rejection, loneliness, disrespect for human dignity and many more are fears that -in the final stage- they are all a reflection of the existential fear: fear of the death. *What we are afraid of* is topic of this research in which we'll also try to focus on role of authority and tradition. In the first part of this paper I shall talk about fear (Angst) in general. In the second part I shall argue that tradition and within it authority is one of the possible opportunities that could offer such a frame that helps an individual to get rid of existential fear or at least to mitigate it.

Key words: *fear, hope, existential fear, death, freedom, authority, tradition.*

Tamara Griesser-Pečar

Fear as an Instrument of Repression in Communist Regimes. "Udba" and "Stasi". A Comparision

Slovene secret police Udba (founded in 1944 under the name of Ozna - till March 1946) and Stasi, the official state security of German Democratic Republic (established in 1950 and based on Soviet predecessors) used scare tactics to submit people to communist regime. Both agencies were tools of the regime to keep it in power and spread terror all around the country. Beside the official employees there was a net of unofficial collaborators. From the very beginning on these agencies injected fear, uncertainty and suspicion. Free was only a person who agreed with everything the party prescribed, but even that had to be controlled to get sure that nothing was done or uttered which might be against the regime. Stasi is widely regarded as the most efficient secret police agency in the communist world. Ozna/ Udba was involved in mass slaughter, show trials, inhuman investigations. It also controlled concentration and labor camps. Similarities and differences are subject of the paper.

Key words: *totalitarian regime, secret police, scare tactics, unofficial collaborators, violation of human rights.*

Igor Bahovec

Some Sociological Aspects of Fear in Slovenia: Communist Repression and Contemporary Consequences

The Communist regime used force, restrictions of freedom, and other totalitarian instruments to engender high levels of fear in people. In this paper we analyse the relationship which Slovenes have to their past and to the post-war mass slaughters. The paper focuses on the following aspects: the extent to which people have fear of discussing the post-war slaughters ; what are the attitudes to that period and to communicating that part of history to the younger generations; what hinders a reduction of fears which would make it possible to be more relaxed in speaking of that era and to get rid of divisions. In our analysis we combine the results of our own quantative research (carried out in 2012) with data from other surveys.

Key words: *Fear, communist regime, post-war mass slaughters, memory, social power.*

Tomaž Erzar & Katarina Kompan Erzar
Fear and Inhibited Initiative

In the article we describe the two-fold nature of experience of fear in humans. On the one side the feeling of fear intensifies inner feelings of helplessness and being a victim, on the other side it may result in a feeling of deep connectedness and security in sincere relationships. Fear can be overcome when a person risks total risk exposure to the feelings of helplessness and shame, which accompany fear, further, when the source of fear is recognized and stopped, and finally when a person experiences a feeling of total security of the inner self. If, on the contrary, due to insecure attachment, chronic fearfulness and lack of appropriate nurturance, children growing up cannot face up to their fears and shame, their initiative in sincere relationships will be inhibited and long term patterns of avoidant behavior will be established.

Key words: *fear, initiative, image of self and others, culture of fear, shame, hatred.*

Jernej Letnar Černič
Culture of Fear in Slovenian Society

In the last century Slovenia survived several crimes against humanity of totalitarian regimes. Such totalitarian crimes have in the contemporary Slovenian society domesticated culture of fear. This article examines how the Slovenian society deals with culture of fear and crimes against humanity. It analyses four key components of the transitional justice: an objective assessment of historical facts, the liability of the perpetrators and victims' rights and education for the future, and an assessment of the Slovenian transitional justice. The article thereafter highlights the necessary measures to eliminate culture of fear in the Slovenian society.

Key words: *culture of fear, crimes against humanity, transational justice, victims' rights, education.*

Stanislav Slatinek
(Un)Justified Fear of Damage Claims

Slovenian courts assess whether the Church in Slovenia is responsible for the conduct of priests or not. In case of sexual abuse of minors by priests or pastoral workers, the victims decide for damage actions against the perpetrator and against the legal person in the Church (a parish, a diocese, an archdiocese). The law firms which represent victims of sexual abuse are frequently convinced that the Church is bound by joint and several liability for criminal offences committed by clerics. They interpret the joint and several liability of legal persons for damaging acts in three ways, namely a) on the basis organisational association, b) due to legal accession and c) due to employment relationship. Since damage claims do not seek a way to improve a perpetrator, but frequently only try to get money, the Church's fear of damage claims is often warranted.

Key words: *priest, damages, sexual abuse, damage action.*

Corneliu Constantineanu
Fear, Courage and Hope: A Hermeneutic of Love in a Culture of Suspicion

It is a truism to say that we live today in a prevalent culture of anxiety and fear which takes multiple faces. There is fear of environment, fear of crime, fear of losing the job, fear of the other, fear of terror, and the list could continue endlessly. The recent financial and economic crises, the horrible terrorist attacks in various parts of the world in the last decade are only the most visible and perceptible causes that exacerbate this attitude of fear around us. Fear grips human activity and society as a whole. Fear paralyses our ability to act and to find solutions. Religion has been regarded by many as a factor that contributed rather than dispersed the fear. The argument of this paper is that, contrary to common perception, there are recourses within the biblical texts which point to appropriate ways to deal with fear and suspicion. We argue that in a predominant culture of fear the answer is not suspicion but love! Not a naive love but one which takes courage to seek to understand, value and love the other and which lead to respect, greater understanding and human flourishing. We argue for a hermeneutic of love and hope in a culture of fear and despair.

Key words: *fear, suspicion, the other, courage, understanding, hermeneutic of love, hope.*

Daniel G. Oprean
The Fear of the Lord: Spirituality as Medication for our Contemporary Fears

Our contemporary world is characterized by an increased state of anxiety. The first type of fear that the people of the contemporary society share is *the fear of death*, a fear that have expression in many facets of human behavior. The second type of fear is the *fear of other people* that have important expressions also in today's society, and the third type of fear is the *fear of tomorrow*. All three types of fear that will be under scrutiny in this paper have a direct address in the Scripture. By exploring the message of the Bible in regard with the three types of fear we will try to argue that authentic spirituality, that produces an appropriate understanding of God, of human nature and of the world, could constitute the elements of what could be called spiritual medication for the contemporary fears.

Key words: *fear, society, world, spirituality, medication.*

Jože Mari Osredkar
Faith Triumphs over Fear

The Gospel encourages us to confront our fear of suffering and death with the directive to embrace suffering and death. Furthermore, Christ claims that "whoever finds his life will lose it, and whoever loses his life for Him, will find it" (Mt 10, 38-39). It is in the context of suffering that it becomes clear what is meant by "to solve or lose life" and "to find life"! A founder of Christianity clarifies that "avoiding suffering" equates superficially to "saving life" and in doing so "life is lost"! Christ tells his disciples, in essence, to renounce life (to renounce the desire to avoid suffering) and to accept the suffering. Christianity tells us, in effect, to accept inconvenience, failures, falls and pain. Herein a guide to overcoming our fear of failure lies.

Key words: *Gospel, fear, suffering, death, win.*

Erika Prijatelj

The Alternative Offer of Religions to the Present Logic of Globalization and Fear of the Future

In this new century, globalization and religion are strongly and fatefully intertwined. In our presentation a particular attention is given to the variety of faiths and the need to seek a solution to the interreligious conflict. In this context it focuses on interreligious dialogue, work on peace and justice and Christian ecumenical endeavours. The social teaching of the Catholic Church with the wealth of contributions from Catholic movements on all continents, changes the face of the globalized world, and demonstrates increasingly that these theories can be put into practice. The prophetic aspect of religion in overcoming fear is seen today in its contribution of hope and a view of life based on a different order and values from those of current economic logic.

Key words: g*lobalization, fear, interreligious dialogue, ecumenism, religious pluralism, social teaching of the Catholic Church, Catholic movements.*

THE AUTHORS

Msgr. Prof. Tomáš Halík
PhD, DD. Now he is a Professor of sociology of Charles University, Prague (Department of the Religious studies, Faculty of Art), pastor of the Academic Parish, and President of the Czech Christian Academy (since 1990).
E-mail: tomas.halik@gmail.com

Jože Trontelj
Prof., President of the Slovenian Academy of Sciences and Arts, Ljubljana, Slovenia
E-mail: joze.trontelj@kclj.si

Janez Juhant
Prof., PhDr Theol Mag., Faculty of Theology, University of Ljubljana, Slovenia
E-mail: janez.juhant@guest.arnes.si

Stanko Gerjolj
Prof., Faculty of Theology, University of Ljubljana, Slovenia
E-mail: stanko.gerjolj@teof.uni-lj.si

Bojan Žalec
Associate Prof. of Philosophy, Ph. D., Faculty of Theology, University of Ljubljana, Slovenia
E-mail: bojan.zalec@teof.uni-lj.si

Anton Jamnik
Th.D., Bishop, Associate Prof., Faculty of Theology, University of Ljubljana, Slovenia
E-mail: anton.jamnik@guest.arnes.si

Robert Petkovšek
Ph. D., Associate Professor of Philosophy, Faculty of Theology, University of Ljubljana
Mail: Faculty of Theology, Poljanska c. 4, SI–1000 Ljubljana
E-mail: robert.petkovsek@guest.arnes.si

Branko Klun
Associate Professor of Philosophy, Faculty of Theology, University of Ljubljana
E-mail: branko.klun@teof.uni-lj.si

Vojko Strahovnik
Ph. D., Faculty of Theology, University of Ljubljana
Assistant professor and the head of the chair for Legal Theory and Ethics & Public Policy at the Faculty of Government and European Studies in Kranj.
Mail: Poljanska 4, 1000 Ljubljana
E-mail: vojko.strahovnik@guest.arnes.si

Zvezdan Pirtošek
Prof., University Medical Centre, Ljubljana, Slovenia
E-mail: zvezdan.pirtosek@kclj.si

Veronika Szántó
Ph. D., President of the Hungarian Bioethics Association
Research fellow, Eötvös Loránd University, Budapest
E-mail: santov@gmail.com

Tadej Strehovec
Assistant Professor, Faculty of Theology, University of Ljubljana,
Mail: Tržaška 85, 1000 Ljubljana, Slovenia
E-mail: tadej.strehovec@teof.uni-lj.si

Krešimir Šimić
Assistant Prof., Faculty of Philosophy, Osijek, Croatia
E-mail: ksimic@ffos.hr

Béla Mester
Ph. D., Senior Research Fellow of the Institute of Philosophy, Research Centre for Humanities, Hungarian Academy of Sciences, Budapest, Hungary; share-time Associate Professor of the Department of Philosophy, College of Nyíregyháza, Hungary; vice-president of the Hungarian Philosophical Society
E-mail: mester.bela@btk.mta.hu

Gábor Kovács
Ph. D., Senior Research Fellow of the Institute of Philosophy, Research Centre for Humanities, Hungarian Academy of Sciences, Budapest, Hungary
E-mail: kovacsg@webmail.phil-inst.hu , gbrkvcs3@gmail.com

Paul Chan
Lecturer at the University of Manchester

Ian Fitzgerald
Senior lecturer at Northumbria University

Rafal Smoczynski
Assistant Professor, Institute of Philosophy and Sociology of the Polish Academy of Sciences, Poland
E-mail: rafalsmoczynski@yahoo.com

Mateja Pevec Rozman
Assistant Prof., Ph. D., University of Ljubljana, Faculty of Theology, Department of Philosophy
E-mail: mateja.pevec@guest.arnes.si, Mateja.PevecRozman@teof.uni-lj.si

Tamara Griesser-Pečar
Assistant Prof., Study centre for national reconciliation, Ljubljana, Slovenia
E-mail: tamara.griesser@inode.at

Igor Bahovec
Ph. D., Assistant Professor of Sociology of religion, University of Ljubljana, Faculty of Theology
E-mail: igor.bahovec@guest.arnes.si

Tomaž Erzar
Associate Professor, Doctorate Program in Marital and Family Therapy, Faculty of Theology, University of Ljubljana, Slovenia
E-mail: tomaz.erzar@guest.arnes.si

Katarina Kompan Erzar
Assistant Professor, Faculty of Theology, University of Ljubljana, Slovenia

Jernej Letnar Černič
Assistant Prof., Faculty of State and European Studies, Kranj, Slovenia
E-mail: jernej.letnar@googlemail.com

Stanislav Slatinek
Assistant Prof., Faculty of Theology, University of Ljubljana, Slovenia
E-mail: stanislav.slatinek@guest.arnes.si

Corneliu Constantineanu
Associate Prof., Pentecostal Theological Institute, Bucharest, Romania
E-mail: corneliu_c@yahoo.com

Daniel G. Oprean
Senior Lecturer in Theology
Evangelical Theological Seminary, Osijek, Croatia
E-mail: daniaoprean@gmail.com

Mari Jože Osredkar
Ph. D., Assistant Prof., Fundamental Theology and Religious Studies, Faculty of Theology, University of Ljubljana,
Mail: Poljanska 4, SI-1000 Ljubljana
Address for mail correspondence: Brezje 72, SI-4243 Brezje
E-mail address: mari.osredkar.ofm@siol.net

Erika Prijatelj
Assistant Prof., Faculty of Theology, University of Ljubljana, Slovenia
E-mail: erika.prijatelj@teof.uni-lj.si

Theologie Ost – West

Europäische Perspektiven

hrsg. von Prof. Dr. Janez Juhant (Universität Ljubljana) und Prof. Dr. Albert Franz (Universität Dresden)

Janez Juhant; Bojan Žalec (Eds.)
Humanity after Selfish Prometheus
Chances of Dialogue and Ethics in a Technicized World

Neither any technological development nor any institutional mechanisms (economical, legal, political etc.) can compensate the lack of ethical persons. Reaching sustainable development and life of quality is possible only on the basis of view which is not trapped, flat and reducing, on the basis of an effort, which ca – founded on temperance and humility (in relation to the nature, self, others and (O)other) - (co)create cooperation, higher order synthesis and synergy of the crafts that are the conditio sine qua non of survival, harmonious world and (decent) existence of a human (as a human) in it.

Bd. 15, 2011, 304 S., 19,90 €, br.,
ISBN 978-3-643-90075-3

Janez Juhant, Bojan Žalec (Eds.)
Reconciliation
The Way of Healing and Growth

The book considers reconciliation from various points of view: biblical foundations of reconciliation, philosophical aspects, Girardian and Bonhoefferian reflections on reconciliation, intellectual and (post)totalitarian history, psychotherapeutic approaches ... The authors consider reconciliation also in very concrete (historical) contexts (Hungary, Russia, Slovenia, Islam and Christianity). Despite some disagreements, their common message is clear: human history and present times are covered with blood, suffering (of innocent victims) and negative emotions. Hence the only acceptable way is cultivation of the culture of reconciliation. Read the book to find out how.

Bd. 16, 2012, 304 S., 19,90 €, br.,
ISBN 978-3-643-90202-3

LIT Verlag Berlin – Münster – Wien – Zürich – London

Auslieferung Deutschland / Österreich / Schweiz: siehe Impressumsseite